KNITTED
HISTORICAL FIGURES

**Other Search Press books
by Jan Messent**

Knitted Gardens
Have you any Wool?
Wool'n Magic
Knit a Fantasy Story

Needle Crafts series
Stitchery
Embroidery Design

Craft Library series
Knitted Gnomes and Fairies
Knit an Enchanted Castle
Knit the Christmas Story

KNITTED HISTORICAL FIGURES

JAN MESSENT

First published in Great Britain 1992
Search Press Limited,
Wellwood, North Farm Road,
Tunbridge Wells, Kent TN2 3DR

The author would like to thank the following yarn spinners for their
help in the making of this book: Twilleys, Güttermann, Coats, and
Madeira. Also, thanks to Yvonne Cutright for knitting several
underskirts.

If you have difficulty in obtaining any of the materials or equipment
mentioned in this book, then please write for further information to
the publishers: Search Press Ltd., Wellwood, North Farm Road,
Tunbridge Wells, Kent TN2 3DR

ISBN 0 85532 733 2 (hb)

ISBN 0 85532 747 2 (pb)

Composition by Genesis Typesetting, Laser Quay, Rochester, Kent
Printed in Singapore by
Huntsmen Offset Printing Pte Ltd

Contents

Introduction

The reasons for writing this book are simple but varied. First of all, I love making small, original models with lots of separate parts and details. Next, I am fascinated by historical costume, although my ignorance of the subject greatly exceeds my knowledge and my admiration for costume experts is boundless. Having acquired many books on the subject and borrowed even more, after months of research I am still discovering its complexities. Then again, I still lapse at regular intervals into the world of fantasy and exotic characters, either from the theatre or fairy-tales, as I believe I must have been pushed into adulthood before I was ready for it! Lastly, but by no means least, I love having some knitting which I can pick up and put down, especially projects made up of small pieces which fuse together and keep pace with my enthusiasm.

Mix all these devices and desires into one basket of yarn and out comes a pageant of historical characters, to enchant not only the creator but also the recipient. I can only hope that making these figures will give you as much pleasure as I have derived from creating them. I also hope that you will overlook with charity, any errors in the style of costume and terminology. This can be partly excused by my lack of expertise on the subject (I'm still working on this) and also to my attempts at a compromise between adapting the figures to knitting techniques yet making them look reasonably authentic. These two aims do not always coincide easily.

The figures are all based on a framework of wire covered by padding, wrappings of yarn and then a knitted skin. They should *not* be regarded as toys for young children, but rather as costume figures for the collector. They stand at exactly the same height as the popular jointed plastic dolls collected by children today, and have more or less the same dimensions, so it is possible that the costumes for these toys will also fit all the figures. The padded wire frames are quite straightforward to make, and should present no problems as long as the instructions are followed exactly. The stretchy nature of the knitted garments allows for a little portliness here and there!

Although the pattern instructions are complete in every detail, there is still tremendous scope for individual expression, depending on the yarns at your disposal and your personal interpretation of the costume and period. It would make me very happy to know that you were using these instructions simply as a basis for your own ideas, and I wish you many hours, days, or weeks of pleasure in creating your own individual characters.

Basic figures

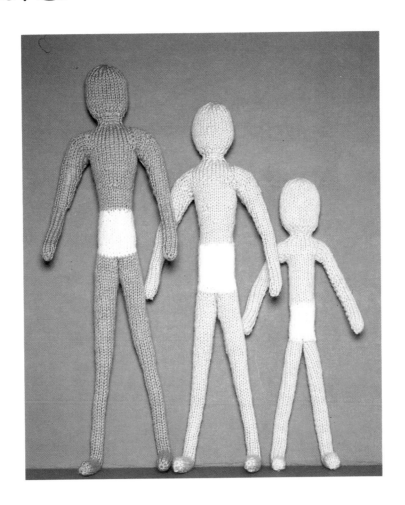

Simple wire shapes form the basis for all of the figures. These shapes are then padded and held in position by binding all the sections with yarn.

Materials for adult figures

Strong but bendable wire; for each adult figure you will need 195cm (77in).

Wire cutters and fine pliers.

Synthetic foam padding, 1cm (½in) thick, see below for amounts.

Pink or white smooth DK yarn for binding.

Sharp scissors and strong, long, sharp needle with large eye.

Ruler and tape-measure.

Measurements

Male stands 33cm (13in) tall, without hair.
Female stands 30cm (12in) tall, without hair.
Child stands 24cm (9½in) tall, without hair.

Padded wire body

1. This is in three sizes, to fit a man, woman and child. Each is made in the same way, only the measurements and amounts of padding are different. The most important point to remember when making these figures is that if the 'skins' are to fit correctly at the next stage, then the instructions for the framework must be *followed to the letter* and no additional padding must be applied. Exact amounts for this are specified for each size, so do keep to it for good results.

2. The second point of importance to note is that the figures *will* look very emaciated, even when covered with their knitted skins. This is essential, as knitted clothes are bulkier than woven ones. You therefore have to begin with a much thinner figure, to obtain a normally slender one wearing a full set of clothing. Some of the clothes are very gathered and elaborate, so this factor must be taken into consideration at the start.

3. Be meticulously exact in all your measurements when making the body, as proportions are important and the loss of 1cm (½in) can prevent the skin fitting exactly. Check the measurements at all stages and take time to amend them, if necessary. No padding is needed for a woman's hips or bust, as all costumes are designed to camouflage these areas.

4. Centimetre and inch changes in the instructions are indicated first in centimetres, and then in inches in brackets, as follows:
Man: woman: child in centimetres, then (man: woman: child in inches).

Padding

The method of cutting the strips from one rectangle is shown in diagram 1. These are the lengths needed, in centimetres and inches, just for reference.

Arms: one piece, 26.5 × 2.5cm (10½ × 1in).
Legs: 46 or 44 × 5cm (18 or 17¼ × 2in).
Body: 36 × 5cm (7¼ × 2in) folded in half.
Extra body: 15 × 5cm (6 × 2in).
Head: 18 × 5cm (7 × 2in), two pieces, both folded in half.
Leg bandages: two pieces, 56 × 2.5cm (22 × 1in).
Upper arms and shoulders: two pieces, 25 × 2.5cm (9¾ × 1in).
Upper body: 31 × 2.5cm (12¼ × 1in).
Note: keep all spare pieces for padding the face, the wig and some of the garments.

Making and padding the framework

For the child's figure, note that at the completion of the following step 18, no more padding is required. However, some yarn should be wrapped round to smooth out any bumps, to almost cover the padding and to *slightly* thicken the shoulders. The legs are pencil-width all the way up and the arms only slightly thinner than this. The body has no shaping but is approximately 1.5cm (¾in) wide from the top of the legs to the underarms.

At step 25, turn the feet up as for the adults, using the same measurements, and bend the arms slightly forwards in the same direction as the feet.

Finally, read the checklist in steps 27, 28 and 29.

1. Cut a length of wire measuring 142: 132: 102cm (56: 52: 40in) long. Fold this piece in half and straighten out the kinks, see diagram 2 for all sizes. Use pliers to turn up the cut ends no more than 1cm (¼in) and nip tightly. Nip the fold with the pliers.

2. Fold the doubled wire again but do not nip the top curve as this will be the head end. Check that all the ends are level.

3. From the top of the curve, measure downwards exactly 5: 3.5: 3.5cm (2: 1½: 1½in) to the neck, cross the wire over at this point and tie tightly with yarn. Leave the ends hanging. With pliers, gently ease the top loop open above the tie, to make an oval shape.

4. From the neck tie, measure downwards exactly 7.5: 7.5: 6cm (3: 3: 2½in). Tie the wires together tightly at this point and leave ends hanging. This marks the bottom of the body. Slightly open out the legs below this tie to prevent it slipping downwards. Do *not* turn the feet up.

5. For the arms, cut a length of wire 53: 50.5: 38cm (21: 20: 15in) and turn up the ends slightly as before. Fold this length in half and nip the curve tightly.

6. Measure exactly half-way on the arms and tie the yarn tightly round the wires. Leave the ends hanging.

7. Place this half-way marker at the neck tie on the body and use the hanging yarns to wrap criss-cross over the arms, neck and body to hold them

Basic figures
Diagram 1
Padding

plan of padding for adult figures

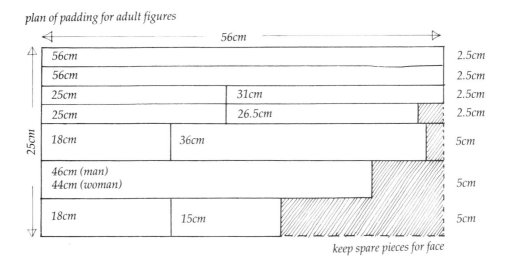

56cm

56cm		2.5cm
56cm		2.5cm
25cm	31cm	2.5cm
25cm	26.5cm	2.5cm
18cm	36cm	5cm
46cm (man) 44cm (woman)		5cm
18cm	15cm	5cm

25cm

keep spare pieces for face

plan of padding for child's figure

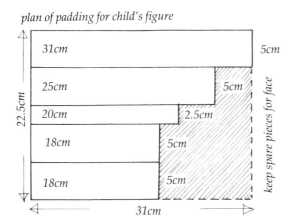

31cm		5cm
25cm		5cm
20cm	2.5cm	
18cm	5cm	
18cm	5cm	

22.5cm

31cm

keep spare pieces for face

Basic figures
Diagram 2
Wire frame

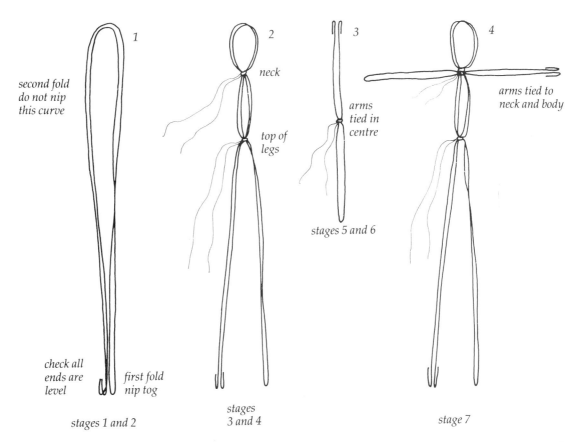

1

second fold do not nip this curve

check all ends are level *first fold nip tog*

stages 1 and 2

2

neck

top of legs

stages 3 and 4

3

arms tied in centre

stages 5 and 6

4

arms tied to neck and body

stage 7

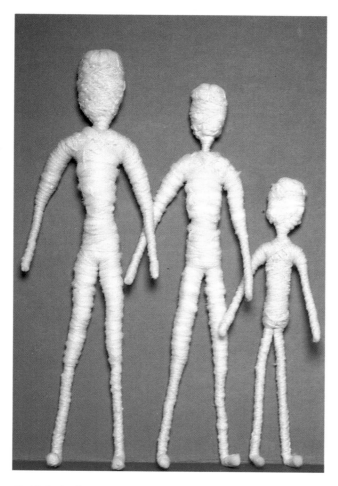

Padded wire figures.

together. Tie this tightly in a knot and check that both arms are straight and the same length. Gently twist the arms, legs and head round to face in the same direction.

8. Now begin the padding, to the individual measurements given above. For the arms, take the strip of padding and lay this along the entire length of the arms from one hand to the other. Fold over a tiny bit at the ends to cover the wire, squeeze the padding over the arm wire and use the pink DK yarn to bind it on, wrapping it round firmly, but not too tightly. Begin at one end and continue across to the other, binding at intervals of about 1cm (½in) to hold it in place.

   Cross over the neck and body as you pass, then return, but this time wrapping more heavily and tightly over the hands and forearms. In this way, make three or four journeys from one end to the other eventually making the arms about as thick as a pencil, but still not completely covering the padding. The shoulders will be padded later.

9. Thread the wrapping yarn into a strong pointed needle and stitch it into the padding to secure the end. The arms should now have a smooth, rather thin line with no bulges of padding. Check that the arms have not moved up into the head area.

10. For the legs, take one strip of padding and find the exact centre point. Tie this point very tightly to the tie at the lower end of the body, using the hanging ends. The ends of this strip will just reach to the ends of the feet.

11. Enclose the leg wires in the padding and, beginning at one foot, bind with the DK yarn up one leg and down the other, until evenly covered. Keep the two legs quite separate at the top. Keep the ends of the feet well covered, and continue to bind until the legs are just a little thicker than the arms.

12. Now take the body padding and fold this in half. Find the centre of the doubled piece and snip out a tiny hole. Ease this over the head to sit on the shoulders.

13. Squeeze the padding on to the body and begin binding with the DK yarn under the arms, moving downwards and criss-crossing round the tops of the legs and upwards again. Cross the yarn over the shoulders and upper arms but don't pull it too tightly, and repeat the yarn-wrapping until the body is about 2cm (¾in) wide.

14. For the child's figure only, omit step 14 and go on to 15.

   Take the extra body padding and, keeping it single, repeat the process as above. This piece will not reach the legs but is meant to thicken the top of the body, shoulders and upper arms. Blend the lower edge of the padding into the body and gently bind the shoulders.

15. To pad the head, fold one piece in half, fold the doubled piece over the top of the head to come just short of the neck.

16. Squeeze it in tightly at the bottom of the head and begin binding with the DK yarn, working from the neck upwards towards the top, criss-crossing over and down again. Wrap tightly round the wire at the base of the neck, noting that there is no padding here, and shape the head with the wrapping. To keep this in place, stitch into the top of the head taking the needle over the top from front to back through the loop of wire.

17. Repeat steps 15 and 16 with the second piece of padding, which is the same size, placed in the opposite direction, from side to side. For extra firmness and smoothness, stitch many times into the head padding. This helps to stabilize the head wrapping. The neck area must only be wrapped with yarn and must measure a clear 1.5cm (½in) long. Do not allow the body and arms to slip upwards into this space.

18. Measure 3: 2.5: 1.5cm (1¼: 1: ¾in) from each side of the neck across the shoulders and at these points bend the arms downwards slightly. The male figure bends at a sharper angle here, while the female and child are slightly more rounded. At this point, the instructions for the child's figure stop.

19. To pad the upper legs and hips, long bandages of

padding are used to wrap round the figure and these are kept in place by binding with the DK yarn. Using one of the leg bandages, and beginning at a point *just above* midway on one leg, bandage quite tightly round one leg and overlapping as you move upwards so that it becomes thicker towards the top. Finish just below the waistline and sew this in place, as before, into the padding. Concentrate the padding on the legs rather than the body.

20. Bandage the second leg in the same way. Keep both legs quite separate at the top, otherwise the body will lengthen, the legs shorten, and the skin will not fit correctly. Sew both securely in place below the waistline.

21. Now bind with yarn as before to define the legs into smooth and tapered shapes. They will still be very thin but don't add more padding.

22. Take the padding bandages for the upper arms and shoulders and using one strip for each arm, begin bandaging tightly from just above the middle of the arm, on to the shoulder, overlapping as before and ending at the front of the body. Stitch in place and bandage the other arm and shoulder in the same way.

23. Twist the arms slightly forwards and bind closely with yarn to almost cover the padding. Use the needle to darn the ends in securely, then squeeze gently into shape. The lower arms will still be only about as thick as a pencil.

24. If necessary, bind the neck with yarn, but this should still only be 1.5cm (½in) long and no thicker than the lower arm.

25. For the feet, use the pliers to bend these sharply forwards at right angles exactly 2.5cm (1in), and strengthen with more yarn if necessary. They should be the same thickness as the rest of the lower leg. Check that the figure stands quite level.

26. For the upper body, take the last strip of bandaging and wrap this closely round the body, underneath the arms and end *just above* the waistline. Sew it to the body and bind gently in place with more yarn.

Checklist

27. Check that all the binding is secured and that none of it will slip off. All limbs should be smooth, with no lumps or bumps anywhere. Bind with more yarn, if necessary, to get a smoother line, but don't add any thickness in so doing.

28. Check that the neck of the figure is still there!

29. Check that the arms are bent slightly forwards, so that you know which is the front and the back of the figure. One side may be better than the other, but the position of the feet will decide this. You must be able to distinguish between the front and the back when you cover the frame with the knitted skin, so take care!

Knitting yarns

The yarn and colours chosen to work the figures in this book, also the complexity of patterns and the care with which the garments are assembled, will make the difference between a home-made toy and a handmade model.

Throughout this book, only yarns finer than double knitting qualities have been used, as the scale of the figures calls for knitted stitches of a reasonably fine texture. Ideally, fine lace and 2plys, crochet cottons and similar threads would be preferable, but not only are these hard to find in a range of suitable colours, but they would probably make knitting a chore for many people.

When making clothes for these figures, the important point to consider is the size of the stitches and the density of the fabric. Many costumes are well nigh impossible to portray accurately, because knitted fabric will not drape in the same way as softly-woven cottons, velvets or silks. The texture is also different, and the behaviour of small detailed pieces is sometimes quite a problem, so these costumes must be a compromise between practicality and authenticity.

Most of the instructions call for 4 ply yarns, occasionally 3 ply, and some of the accessories require a fine crochet cotton. Much use is made of metallic yarns of the same thickness as 3 and 4 plys, and these are available in many colours in 25gm (1oz) balls; one ball will last for several figures. Fine glitter thread is also often mixed in with ordinary yarn to give added sparkle, for instance, in Madame de Pompadour's dress. This is the type of thread bought on bobbins for machine embroidery, and it is so fine that it does not add any thickness to the yarn being used.

Four ply random-dyed, multicoloured and speckled and flecked yarns are especially useful for these costumes, as they suggest woven patterns and embroidery. Be aware, though, of the effect of the changing colours when knitting only a few stitches in a random-dyed yarn. The colours often tend to stack up in 'blocks' in a way which is quite different from when many stitches are in use. Look out for fine sock wool, which usually has a speckled effect and is excellent for a rough homespun look. Only small amounts of any yarn are needed, rarely more than 50gm (2oz) of one colour, so home dyeing is a real possibility.

Body yarn colours are not always easy to find so those used in this book have all been dyed in tea. In this way, many different flesh-tones were achieved, varying from very pale to sunburnt, and even the two ancient Egyptians were coloured in this way. For this purpose always buy pure machine-washable wool in white, or creamy white. Wind the balls into hanks and tie in four places to avoid tangling. To dye one hank, have a 1.5 litre (2 pint) jug or basin holding two tablespoons of loose tea of a reasonably strong variety to make a good dark brown brew. Pour on boiling water nearly to the top, stir and leave to stand until it has cooled. Meanwhile, place the wool in clean warm water and allow it to become thoroughly saturated. Strain the tea twice, remove the wool from the water, squeeze it gently and place it in the tea. 'Dunking time' is anything from one second to two minutes, depending on the depth of colour required, so don't walk away and leave it! As the brew weakens, the dunking time will be longer, but there is no need to boil it. Remove the hank, squeeze it gently and rinse. Colour fastness is not critical, as the yarn will not be washed at any time. Press the hank gently in a dry towel and hang it up to dry naturally, before rewinding. To dye as much as 400gm (14½oz) of 4 ply yarn, use 100gm (3½oz) of tea, or approximately 7 tablespoons, to 3.5 litres (6 pints) of boiling water.

Colours used for hair are more or less open to choice, though there *are* occasions where this must be restricted as, for example, with the ancient Egyptians, or the white powdered wig of the 18th century courtier. Flecked yarns are most useful for variations in hair colours and subtle use of glitter threads add a sheen.

Clothes colours are also your own choice, although care should be taken over the colours most commonly worn for a particular garment of a certain period. Not all colours were popular at all times and there were many rules, social, religious and political, concerning their use. Puritans of the seventeenth century, for instance, always wore sombre colours with little or no decoration, and the colours worn by Victorians were restricted by social class, marital status, and occasion. Read as much as possible about the fashions of the period and choose your colours accordingly.

Special yarns, some looking like fur, leather or velvet are available in 3 and 4 ply thicknesses and these can be used to good effect, especially for borders. However, these have not been included in the instructions, as it was important to stipulate yarns which are more readily available to everyone.

Amounts of yarn given at the beginning of each set of instructions are only approximate but, to be on the safe side, do not obtain less than the stated amount. Extra yarn will allow for any mistakes and can be used to make accessories, such as hats, scarves, shawls and borders. Where 'oddments' are mentioned, these are so small as to weigh only about 10gm (½oz) or less. In fact, it may just be a few metres (yards) in length and when wound, would look about the size of a golf ball.

Knitted skin

Although instructions are given here for a pink, or flesh-coloured skin, other versions are possible which not only economize on your precious hand-dyed yarns, but also provide a set of in-built underwear! For example, instead of changing from white underpants to flesh-colour at the waistline, you can continue with the white yarn up to the neck, or to the end of row 24,

a p row. Nearly all the men's clothes have closed necklines and this part will be covered, but this cannot be said of all the women's clothes.

Before you begin, decide whether to have a sleeveless vest and have the arm entirely in flesh-colour, or whether to have full-length, elbow length, or wrist length sleeves. Just change from white to flesh-colour wherever you choose, making a note of the row number, and be sure to make the other arm the same.

When picking up stitches from the bottom edge of the body to continue downwards for the legs, the same extension of the white underpants can also be made here. The pattern changes to flesh-colour after only two rows, but you can actually change anywhere you wish for longer underpants, or even make a completely white leg, to represent stockings, as this part may eventually be covered by clothing.

Check on the costume before you begin to see which areas of flesh-colour show and make your economies accordingly, thus saving more flesh-colour for another figure. Without wishing to confuse the issue too much, the last white row worked before the changeover to flesh-colour can be in rev ss, to give a more definite edge to the neckline, sleeves or pants.

MATERIALS
For the knitted cover for the male and female figures, use 4 ply in a skin-colour: 50gm (2oz) will make 2 adults and one child so allow 25gm (1oz) per figure for safety, unless extending white underwear.
Oddment of white 4 ply needed for underpants.
Sizes 2, and 2¼mm needles.

BODY AND HEAD
Begin at base of body with underpants. Using white yarn and leaving a tail of about 50cm (20in), cast on 27 sts and work in ss for 14 rows.
Break off white yarn and join in skin-colour.
Row 15: (k2 tog, k3) 4 times, k2 tog, k5.
Work 7 more rows ss on these 22 sts.
Row 23: (inc, k4) 4 times, inc, k1.
Work 5 more rows on these 27 sts.
Row 29: (k4, inc), 5 times, k2.
Work 7 more rows on these 32 sts, as far as the underarms.
Row 37: k6, cast off 4 sts, k12 (counting the st on RH needle), cast off 4 sts and k to end of row.
On the first set of 6 sts, work 7 more rows ss, then cut yarn.
Rejoin yarn to centre sts and work 7 more rows. Cut yarn.
Rejoin yarn to last 6 sts and work 7 more rows, do not cut yarn.
Now k across all 24 sts, weaving loose ends in on back.
Next row: p24.
Shape neck as folls:
Row 1 of neck and head section: (k2 tog) 12 times.
Row 2: p12.

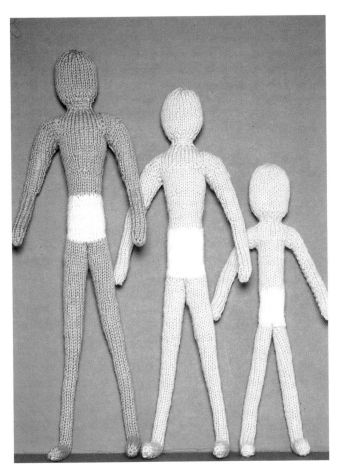

Knitted skin for male, female and child figures.

Row 3: (k2 tog, k3) twice, k2 tog.
Row 4: p9.
**Row 5: inc once into every st. 18 sts.
Row 6: p18.
Row 7: (inc, k1) 9 times. 27 sts.
Work 15 more rows, then check to see whether, with the addition of the last 3 rows, this headpiece will be long enough for your model. If not, work a few extra rows at this point.
Row 21: (k2 tog, k1) 9 times.
Row 22: p18.
Row 23: (k2 tog) 9 times and gather these sts on to a wool needle.**

LEGS

These are made by using the long cast on tail at the beginning of the body to pick up sts to knit downwards to the feet. This makes a smoother line than sewn edges but you can make them separately on 18 sts if you prefer.
Right leg: with the RS of the body facing you, use the white cast on tail to pick up 13 sts from the cast on edge as far as the centre.
Row 2: cast on 3 sts, p16 then cut white yarn.
Row 3: join in skin-colour and cast on 2 sts, k18.
****Work 7 more rows in ss.
Row 11: k2 tog, k to last 2 sts, k2 tog.

Work 11 more rows.
Row 23: (k2 tog, k5) twice, k2 tog. 13 sts.
Work 11 more rows.
Row 35: as row 11.
Now continue without shaping on these 11 sts, working 41 more rows for the female figure and 47 rows for the male. Gather the last row up on to a wool needle for the end of the foot**
Left leg: with the RS of the body facing you, join in the white yarn and pick up 13 sts from the LHS of the cast on edge.
Row 2: cast on 2 sts, p15. Cut white yarn.
Row 3: join in skin-colour, cast on 3 sts, k18.
Now work from ** to ** as for the right leg.

ARMS (make 2 the same)

Cast on 20 sts and shape the shoulder as folls:
k to the last 2 sts; turn and p to the last 2 sts; turn and k to the last 4 sts; turn and p to the last 4 sts, turn.
Cont in this way, leaving an *extra* 2 sts each time at the end of every part-row until there are 8 unworked sts at the end of both needles, with 4 sts in the centre.
Next row: (RS) k12.
Next row: p20.
Now continue to shape the arm as folls:
Row 1: k2 tog, k16, k2 tog.
Purl all alt rows.
Row 3: (k2 tog, k6) twice, k2 tog.
Row 5: k2 tog, k5, k2 tog, k4, k2 tog. 12 sts.
Work 3 rows in ss.
Row 9: k2 tog, k8, k2 tog, 10 sts.
Cont in ss for 34 more rows then gather the sts on to a wool needle for the end of the hand.

EARS

For hair-styles which reveal the ears, make these as folls on size 2mm needles.
Cast on 3 sts and work 4 rows in ss.
Row 5: k1, k2 tog, pass first st over 2nd and fasten off.

MATERIALS

For child figure
20gms (¾oz) 4 ply yarn, plus an oddment of white 4 ply.
Size 2¼mm needles.

BODY AND HEAD

Begin at lower edge of body with white yarn and cast on 18 sts. Work 12 rows in ss, change to skin-colour and cont straight for 18 more rows.
Row 31: k4, cast off one st, k8, cast off one st, k4.
Work on these 3 groups of sts separately for 5 rows each, then work across all 16 sts for 2 more rows.
Shape neck
Row 1: k2 tog, k1, (k2 tog) 5 times, k1, k2 tog. 9 sts.
Rows 2 and 4: purl.
Row 3: knit.
Now work from ** to ** as given for adult figure.

LEGS (make 2 the same)
Cast on 9 sts and work 48 rows in ss.
Gather the last sts on to a wool needle for the end of the toe.

ARMS (make 2 the same)
Cast on 12 sts and work 2 rows in ss.
Rows 3 and 5: k2 tog, k to last 2 sts, k2 tog.
Rows 4 and 6: purl.
Cont on these 8 sts for 38 more rows then gather the last sts on to a wool needle for the end of the hand.

SHORT UNDERPANTS FOR ALL FIGURES
For those times when it may be useful for the figure to wear separate pants, other than those built into the skin cover, this simple piece can be lengthened, or frilled in any way you wish.
Use 4 ply white yarn and size 2¾mm needles. Cast on 26 sts and work in ss for about 5cm (2in). Cast off.
Sew up the sides and place the centre seam at the back. To divide the legs, stitch the two bottom edges tog in the exact centre with 3 or 4 sts. No fastenings are needed.

Making up the skin

All stitching, except b, is done from the RS.

a. Insert arms through armholes into body piece.
b. With RS tog, sew up approx 4cm (1½in) of the feet. Turn to RS and slip the feet into the skin cover, leaving the thread loose.
c. Pull the head and neck skin into position and pin edges tog. Do not sew up at this stage.
d. Pull top of white pants tog at back waist and pin. Pull top of legs at the cast on edges through to back and pin. Sew white pants centre back from waist downwards, then catch in base of pants or top of leg tog between legs.
e. Pin back opening tog, then sew from waist up, on to neck and one-third of the way up the head. Leave the rest open with the thread hanging.
f. Pin leg skins tog, manoeuvring the seam into the centre of the back leg as you pin. Sew tog from either end, then gently manipulate the skin into position and straighten where necessary.
g. Attach the arm coverings as follows; use the gathering tail to sew up about 2.5cm (1in) at the hand end and slip the hand into this. Leave the rest of the thread hanging. (See Note below).
h. Pull the shoulder skin up to the top and use the cast on tail to sew the two side edges tog and make a few sts down the arm. Leave the rest open for the moment and pin the shoulder edges to the body.
i. Sew all round the arm and body join.
j. Turn the figure upside-down and complete the arm seam. Turn the seam to the inside of the arm and complete the other arm in the same way.
Note: if you find that the wire at the end of the hand has become exposed during handling, place a tiny wad

of padding inside the skin before inserting the hand. Then sew up.

k. Before closing the back of the head, model the face as follows; pull down the top part of the head covering and insert a small piece of padding into the chin area. Use the point of a knitting needle to arrange this piece, then pull up the cover.
l. Insert a small, long piece on the forehead in the same way but don't let it bulge out, then sew up the back of the head.
m. Using the same yarn as the skin, and a long sharp needle, make a knot at the end of the thread, insert the needle from the back of the head and bring the point out at one eye position. Use the same thread to indent two eyes half-way down the head, set well apart, see diagram 3. Pull the thread in gently to do this and squeeze the chin in slightly too. At this point you will see that the back of the head has flattened somewhat, but don't worry, as the knitted hair is always padded at the back and this will eventually give the head its correct shape.

To embroider the features

On this small scale, a double length of sewing cotton, or stranded embroidery cotton, makes a more precise line than the knitting yarn, see diagram 3. Use a fairly long sharp, small-eyed needle and make your stitches as small as possible. First, indent the eyes as shown in the diagram, then begin the embroidery.

a. For the eyes, use double grey or mid-brown thread, stitch the eye shape using tiny backstitches or stem stitch. The distance between the two almond-shaped eyes should be no less than the width of one eye from corner to corner, see diagram.
b. Choose the eye-colour in sewing cotton, used double, and fill in the centre of the eye as shown, with the sts vertical and the needle horizontal. The sts here must touch the outer rim of the eye but not exceed it.
c. Embroider the black pupil with sts going across the top of the eye-colour. Only about 3 sts will be needed but make them touch the top rim of the eye, as shown. Tiny dots of white may also be added at each side to highlight the pupil, if required.
d. Embroider the brows using the same colour as the hair. Use any outline stitch and make two or three rows if necessary, beginning at the extreme LH side and working towards the centre, then from the centre of the other brow to the outer edge. Keep them well apart and no nearer each other than the eyes. Men's brows will be somewhat thicker and lower than women's.
e. For the nose, take a long and very sharp needle and thread this with the *skin-covering* yarn. Make a knot in the end and bring the needle through from the back of the head to the corner of one eye. Pass the needle *across* the face between each eye-corner under the bridge of the nose into the point where

Basic figures
Diagram 3
Embroidering the face

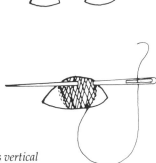

*indent eyes
about half-way
down head*

actual size

*outline eyes as near
to this shape as
possible with width
of one eye between*

*keep the needle horizontal and sts vertical
to embroider the iris
make sts touch rims at top and bottom
aim for a cup shape rather than a complete circle*

*embroider black pupil over top of the iris
across-wise
3 or 4 sts should be enough
do not allow iris colour to show above pupil
make it touch top rim as shown*

*brows are thicker in the centre
men's are thicker and often more
uneven than women's*

centre

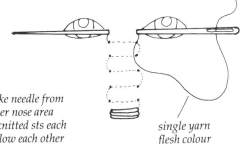

*to make nose take needle from
side to side under nose area
take in same 2 knitted sts each
time in rows below each other
pull gently and pinch nose forwards
finish base with a few satin sts*

*single yarn
flesh colour*

the yarn emerges and into the corner of the other eye. Pull gently. Now take more stitches across and through the nose from side to side, pulling the nose slightly forwards each time. At the base, take the needle to the back of the head again and come straight back through to the front at the base of the nostrils. Go back in again and pull the bottom of the nose inwards.

To build up the tip of the nose, make a few satin sts across on the surface, allowing them to build up. Use your thumb-nails to ease the sts into position and keep the nose in line while you do this.

f. For the mouth, not illustrated, first establish the width of the mouth in one line from corner to corner with a single stem stitch line, then build up lip thickness at the top and bottom of the lips above and below, with a series of stem stitches. Each line of sts can be made from the same corner by taking the needle back to the left to begin a new row. Use pink double sewing cotton rather than bright red, especially for men.

Abbreviations

alt	alternate(ly)	psso	pass the slipped stitch over to decrease
beg	begin(ning)	rem	remain(ing)
cm	centimetre(s)	rep	repeat
cont	continue	rev ss	reverse stocking stitch
dec	decrease	RS	right side of fabric
DK	double knitting yarn	RHS	right-hand side
foll	follows(ing)	sl 1	slip one stitch on to the right-hand needle without knitting it
gm	gram(s)		
g st	garter stitch, knit every row	st	stitch(es)
inc	increase, by knitting into the front and back of the same stitch	ss	stocking stitch (US stockingette st)
in	inch(es)	tbl	through back of loops
k	knit	tog	together
k-wise	knit-wise, with the yarn at the back	WS	wrong side of fabric
		yb	yarn back
k2 tog	knit 2 stitches together to decrease	yo	yarn over top of needle to back
LHS	left-hand side	yrn	yarn round needle, used to make an extra stitch between 2 purl stitches and also at the beginning of a row before a k2 tog. On RH needle, take yarn from front over top of needle and bring back to front again ready to purl
mm	millimetres		
ms	moss stitch		
oz	ounce(s)		
p	purl		
p-wise	purl-wise, with the yarn in front		
p2 tog	purl 2 stitches together to decrease	yfwd	yarn forward to front of work

Omissions

The instructions are written for the knitter of average ability, including the expert, of course, who is able to adapt, if need be, and improvise. With this in mind, and also to save much repetition, such commonplace instructions as 'darn in all ends on WS; fasten off; turn to RS; fit on to figure', etc., have been omitted, except where you may not do this automatically. It is taken as read that knitters will work this out for themselves and act accordingly.

Ancient world

The term, 'Ancient Egypt', spans many hundreds of years, beginning even before the establishment of the Old Kingdom in c.2778BC, to beyond the end of the New Kingdom, c.200BC. Although costumes obviously developed during this lengthy time span, the interesting thing is that the changes are not nearly as great as one might expect. The length of garments, together with head-dress and drapery styles seem to have been where the main changes occurred but fine linen, cotton, and later silk, were still the favoured fabrics.

Because of the intense heat in Egypt, clothing was particularly scanty, with fine pleating much in favour. Members of the noble families wore heavily jewelled collars of gold, belts and sashes, open sandals, and adorned themselves with gold jewellery. Stylized patterns were prominent and the lotus and scarab-beetle are details which are familiar to us today, from the many surviving wall-paintings which portray everyday religious and royal life.

Dyes were regularly used and henna in particular, was much in vogue as a cosmetic. Wigs were worn and came in many colours from bright red to black.

The following two noble figures represented here in knitting, reflect a composite style derived from several sources, which are reasonably typical of those costumes worn at the height of Egyptian sophistication. The predominant colour seems to have been white, although many other colours were also worn as decoration, but not black. Red was also unpopular for clothing. Decoration along the borders shows a rich assortment of colours, including gold and silver threads.

Some of the fashions adopted were as extreme as those we find today; bald, polished heads were regarded as beautiful, and dancing girls wore cones of perfumed wax on top of their hair, so that the warmth would gradually melt it and release the perfume. Priests wore whole leopard skins and the variety of crowns worn by the royal family reflects the periods of Egypt's history, as well as the geographical areas. However, these are basically simple to construct.

Although noblewomen preferred to be seen as pale skinned by annointing themselves with lotions, these figures have been given a more realistic dark skin. However, all shades are correct except the very fair skin associated with blonde Nordic types.

Egyptian man

The nobleman is identified by his huge collar, which extends over the shoulders and is studded with precious lapis-lazuli of a deep rich blue, and turquoise. Gold 4 ply is used in two different tones for the abundant covering of jewellery on the figure.

His gown consists of a sleeveless vest top, reaching no further than the underarms and two skirts, one long in double rib, bordered by a gold band, and the other short and semi-circular in single rib to suggest narrow pleats. This is topped by a hip-sash and a long narrow apron of gold and jewels, a sign of nobility. He wears a gold and turquoise band on his head, gold wrist-bands and gold-strapped sandals. His underpants are knitted in with his skin.

Materials

Hair: an oddment of black, charcoal-grey or deep purple 4 ply, and some additional padding.
Headband: approximately 5m (5½yd) each of gold metallic yarn and turquoise 4 ply. Matching sewing cotton and needle.
Collar: oddments of gold metallic yarn, as above, and turquoise 4 ply.
Gown and overskirt: 50gm (2oz) white or cream 4 ply and an oddment of gold metallic yarn for the border.

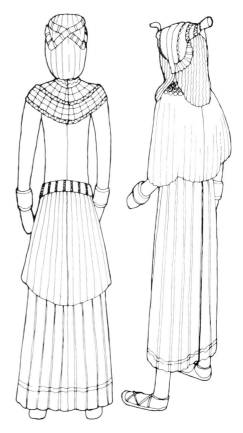

This shows the back of the costumes. Note the centre back seams of the skirt, cape, collar and the position of the head-dresses and belt.

18

Sash: oddments of gold metallic yarn and turquoise 4 ply. Any beads and sequins of the same colours, to cover half of the sash.

Bracelets and sandals: oddments of gold metallic yarn.

Needles: sizes 2, 2¼, 2¾, 3, 3¼ and 4mm.

Note: make the basic skin as usual, see pages 12–14, and add ears to the figure. Embroider the face with dark features, see pages 14–15.

Hair or wig

In paintings, wigs often appear to be black but were, however, available in a variety of colours. The one seen here was knitted in a deep wine-red, almost brown, but any dark colour can be used. It has been substantially padded at the back to give extra fullness. Use a loose cast on for the first edge to make gathering easier.

With dark yarn and size 2¼mm needles, cast on 28 sts loosely and work in single rib for 2 rows. Shape the back.

Rows 3 and 4: rib to last 4 sts, turn.

Rows 5 and 6: rib to last 8 sts, turn.

Row 7: rib to end of row.

Row 8: rib 28 sts.

Rep rows 3 to 8 once more.

Rows 15 and 16: cast off 3 sts at beg of rows, rib to end. Work 6 rows in rib.

Rows 23 to 27: as rows 3 to 7.

Rows 28 and 29: cast on 4 sts, rib to end of row. 30 sts.

Rows 30 and 31: inc in first and last sts. 34 sts.

Rows 32 and 33: cast on 5 sts, rib to end. 44 sts.

Row 34: rib 3, (k2 tog, rib 2) 9 times, k2 tog, rib 3. 34 sts.

Row 35: keeping new rib patt intact, rib 24, turn.

Row 36: rib 14, turn.

Rows 37 and 38: rib to end of rows.

Row 39: (p2 tog) 17 times.

Row 40: (k2 tog) 4 times, k1, (k2 tog) 4 times.

Gather the last 9 sts on to a needle and draw up securely for the top of the wig.

To fit the wig to the head:

a. sew up the centre of the fringe and pin this well down on to the forehead, see diagram 1.

b. Pull the two lower corners forwards on to the neck and fit the shaped areas round the ears. Pin in place.

c. Begin sewing from the lower corner upwards round the ear, leaving these exposed and embroidering a few satin stitches in front of the ears for the side pieces. Continue up on to the fringe and down the other side in the same way. Leave the back edge unstitched for the moment. Insert the padding at the back of the head.

The Egyptian man is richly embellished with studded collar, golden bracelets and sandals, headband and decorative hip-sash.

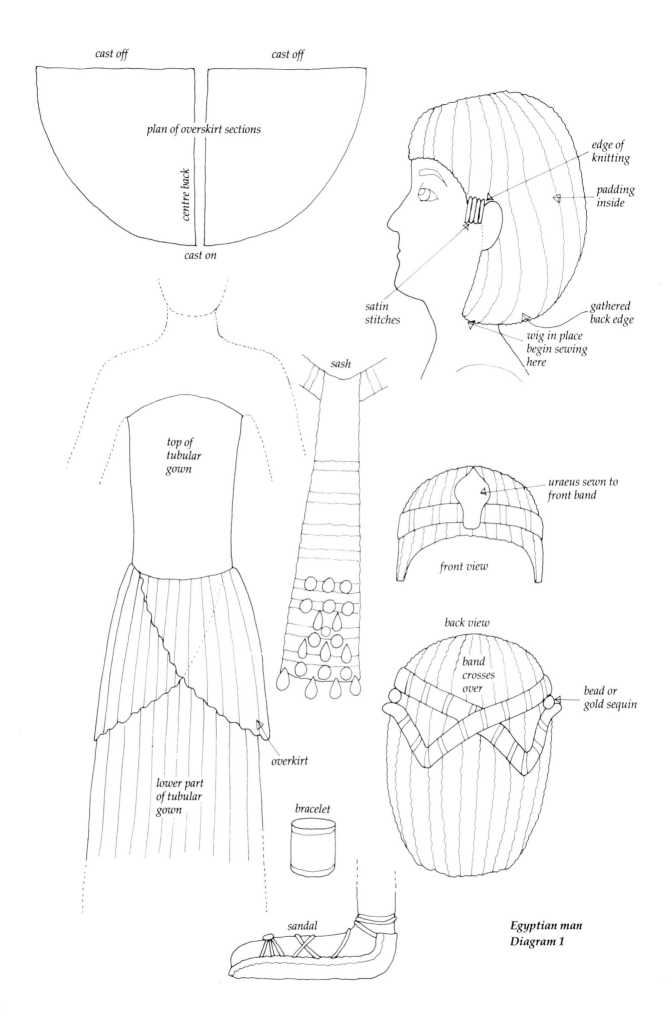

cast off   cast off

plan of overskirt sections

centre back

cast on

edge of knitting

padding inside

satin stitches

gathered back edge

wig in place begin sewing here

sash

top of tubular gown

uraeus sewn to front band

front view

back view

band crosses over

bead or gold sequin

overkirt

lower part of tubular gown

bracelet

sandal

Egyptian man
Diagram 1

20

d. With the same yarn, run a gathering thread along the lower edge at the back of the wig and leave the thread hanging. Adjust the padding and fasten off the thread.

Headband

With gold thread and size 2mm needles, cast on 2 sts and knit for about 2cm (¾in). Change to turquoise and knit alt rows of 2 turquoise and 6 gold, twisting the 2 colours tog at beg of 3rd and 5th gold rows. Cont until band measures 25cm (10in) when unstretched. Work about 4 more rows of gold to match the beg, then cast off.

a. Arrange the band round the top of the wig to cross over at the back, bringing the ends up again to form a sharp 'V'. The ends represent the cobra's head, (the uraeus), which has a golden orb balanced on it. For this purpose, use a large golden bead.
b. To sew the band on to the head, use a small sharp needle and double sewing cotton. For the uraeus, cast on 2 sts in gold and k 6 rows, then inc into both sts to make 4. Knit 2 rows then k2 tog twice and cast off. Darn this end in and use the other one to sew this to the front band as shown, bending it into an 'S' shape.

Collar

With metallic gold yarn and size 2mm needles, cast on 22 sts and knit 2 rows.
Row 3: (inc, k4) 4 times, inc, k1.
Row 4: p27.
Row 5: change to turquoise, (inc, k2) 9 times.
Row 6: p36.
Row 7: change to size 3mm needles, (k1, p1) to end of row.
Row 8: (p1, k1) to end of row to form ms.
Row 9: change to gold, (k3, inc) 9 times.
Row 10: k45.
Row 11: change to turquoise, knit.
Row 12: (k1, p1) to end of row.
Row 13: change to size 4mm needles, (k1, p1) to end of row.
Row 14: change to gold, purl.
Cast off
Place the collar round the neck of the figure, sew up the two edges and place at centre back.

Gown

This is simply a full-length tubular piece, ribbed at the lower edge and smooth stocking stitch above. The change over from ribbing to stocking stitch is covered by a semi-circular overskirt, which is made in two pieces, sewn down the back and crossing over slightly in front, see diagram 1.
With white yarn and size 3¼mm needles, cast on 78 sts and work in double rib for 2 rows.

Now join in the gold yarn and rib 2 rows, then 26 more rows in white.
Row 27 (counted above the gold band): (k2, p2 tog) 19 times, k2. 59 sts.
Row 28: (p2, k1) 19 times, p2.
Row 29: (k2, p1) 19 times, k2.
Rep the last 2 rows 6 more times.
Row 43: (k2 tog, p1) to the last 2 sts, k2 tog. 40 sts.
Row 44: purl.
Cont in ss until this piece measures 23cm (9in) (i.e., as far as the underarms), then cast off.

a. With the WS tog, sew up the 2 side edges and turn to RS. Slip the tube on to the figure, fitting the top well underneath the arms. Pin in place at back and front.

Overskirt

Note: increases take place on one edge only and the single rib pattern must be maintained throughout.
With white yarn and size 2¾mm needles, cast on 10 sts.
Rows 1, 2, 4, 6, 8, 10 and 12: work in single rib to end of row, incorporating new sts.
Row 3: cast on 3 sts and rib to end of row.
Row 5: cast on 4 sts and rib to end of row.
Row 7: as row 3.
Row 9: cast on 2 sts and rib to end of row.
Row 11: as row 3.
Row 13: inc, rib to end.
Row 14: rib to last st, inc. 27 sts.
Rows 15 and 16: rep rows 13 and 14. 29 sts.
Row 17: as row 13.
Row 18: rib.
Rep rows 13 and 18 until there are 36 sts.
Now cont without shaping for 8 more rows.
Cast off in rib and make another piece in the same way.
The cast off edges are the top of the overskirt and the 2 pieces should be sewn together along the side edges to form the centre back seam, see diagram 1.

a. Without gathering, set this piece around the hips over the top of the gown, overlapping the front points. Pin in place, then slip st the top edge in place on the gown.
b. Sew the top edge of the gown on to the body, bearing in mind that the collar must overlap at the front and back.
c. Pull the collar well down over the shoulders and the top edges of the gown, and slip st in place with gold thread.

Sash

With gold metallic yarn and size 2¼mm needles, cast on 4 sts and knit 4 rows.
Rows 5 and 6: join in turquoise and k4 sts.
Cont to work in g st with 2 rows gold, 2 rows turquoise

for 82 rows, (i.e., 20 turquoise bands). Finish off with 4 gold rows.

Cast off and darn turquoise ends in. This is the waist part.

Now make the front piece: with double gold yarn, cast on 12 sts and k 3 rows.

With single turquoise yarn, k 2 rows.

Rows 6, 7, 8 and 9: k in gold.

Rows 10 and 11: k in turquoise.

Row 12: in gold, k2 tog, k8, k2 tog.

Rows 13, 14 and 15: k10.

Row 16: in turquoise k2 tog, k6, k2 tog.

Row 17: k8.

Rows 18, 19, 20 and 21: in gold, k8.

Row 22: in turquoise k2 tog, k4, k2 tog.

Row 23: k6.

Cont straight on these 6 sts for 22 more rows, keeping patt of gold and turquoise as before. Finish with 4 rows of gold, then cast off.

a. For extra effect, beads can be attached to the front hanging piece before you fix it to the figure. Arrange these in any way you wish.

b. Place the sash low down on to the hips with a slight dip at the front where the two gold edges meet. Sew the edges together, then continue sewing the lower edge of the belt to the overskirt.

c. Pin the front piece in position with the narrow gold edge adjoining the gold 'buckle' of the waist-sash and sew these pieces together with gold yarn.

d. Catch down the lower corners of the sash on to the gown with one or two stitches.

Sandals

With gold metallic yarn and size 2¼mm needles, cast on 14 sts. Leave long ends of about 20cm (8in). Work 6 rows in g st.

Row 7: k2 tog, then cast off the rest of the sts, leaving another tail of the same length before cutting the yarn. Make another piece in the same way.

The two attached lengths of yarn are passed round the ankle and should then be threaded on to two needles and taken into the edges of the sole on each side, criss-crossing over the top of each foot. It is easier to do this if the sole of the sandal is first pinned to the under-side of the foot.

Darn ends in securely and trim after tying the ends on top of the foot.

Bracelets

Make one for each wrist.

With gold metallic yarn and size 2¼mm needles, cast on 14 sts and work 5 rows in ss. Cast off p-wise and sew up the 2 side edges to form a circle.

Egyptian lady

The Egyptian lady is probably a princess, as she wears a royal head-dress in the shape of a bird with the striking cobra at the front. This is worn over her sparkling purplish-black wig of long hair.

She also wears a huge jewelled collar, which is stitched down on top of the cape of creamy-white pleated linen worn over her shoulders. Her tunic is a simple affair of double ribbing, seamed down the back and joined to the lower edge of the cape. There are no sleeves.

Round her waist is a long, gold-edged sash and gold bracelets adorn her wrists. Her sandals are simple cross-overs, like those of her partner. Her pants are knitted in one with her skin.

Materials

Hair: an oddment of black, charcoal or deep purple 4 ply.

Head-dress: one ball, or part-ball of metallic 3 or 4 ply in pale gold, deep gold and green. Oddment of turquoise 4 ply.

Skirt and cape: 50gm (2oz) white or cream 4 ply, oddments of pale, medium and deep gold metallic, green metallic and turquoise 4 ply. For the collar, tiny gold and green beads.

Sash: oddments as above.

Bracelets: oddments of any metallic yarns and some skin-colour.

Sandals: oddments of metallic gold.

Needles: sizes 2¼, 2¾, 3, 4 and 6mm.

Note: embroider the face as shown on pages 14–15, before making her wig. Use black or dark brown for the eyes and eyebrows.

Hair

This is worked entirely in g st. With dark yarn of your choice, and size 2¾mm needles, cast on 22 sts and k 2 rows.

Row 3: cast off 16 sts and k to end.

Row 4: k6.

Row 5: cast on 16 sts and k to end.

Row 6: k20, inc, k1.

Row 7: k19, turn.

Row 8: k17, inc, k1.

Row 9: k24.

Row 10: k22, inc, k1. 25 sts.

Row 11: k21, turn.

Row 12: k21.

Cont in g st without increasing, working 2 complete rows then 2 part-rows, as rows 11 and 12, for 16 more rows, ending at the lower edge.

Row 29: k1, k2 tog, k to end.

Row 30: k24.

Row 31: k1, k2 tog, k to last 4 sts, turn.

Row 32: k19.

Row 33: as row 29.

Row 34: k22.
Row 35: as row 3.
Row 36: k6.
Row 37: as row 5.
Row 38: k22.
Row 39: k18, turn.
Row 40: k18.
Row 41: cast off 16 sts, k to end. 6 sts.
Row 42: k6.
Row 43: k4, turn.
Row 44: k4.
Rows 45 and 46: k6.
Rep the last 4 rows twice more, the cast off.

a. Sew the cast off, fringe edge to the cast on edge, to close the shape.
b. Gather the open section at the top of the crown and draw up securely. Sew to the head as shown, just above the eyebrows, see diagram 2.

Head-dress

With deep gold yarn and size 2¼mm needles, cast on 40 sts loosely and work 2 rows in single rib.
Row 3: p2 tog, k2 tog, p2 tog, (k1, p1) 14 times, p2 tog, k2 tog, p2 tog.
Row 4: cut gold and join in green metallic yarn.
p2 tog, (k2 tog) twice, (p1, k1) 11 times, (k2 tog) twice, p2 tog.
Row 5: (p2 tog) twice, (k1, p1) 10 times, (p2 tog) twice.
Row 6: cut green and join in turquoise, (k2 tog) twice, (k1, p1) 8 times, (k2 tog) twice.
Row 7: p2 tog, rib to last 2 sts, p2 tog. 18 sts.
Rows 8 to 10: cut turquoise yarn and join in pale gold, and k18 for next three rows.
Row 11: (k2 tog, k6) twice, k2 tog.
Row 12: p2 tog, p4, p2 tog, p5, p2 tog.
Row 13: (k2 tog, k3) twice, k2 tog.
Row 14: p2 tog, p5, p2 tog.
Row 15: k2 tog, k3 tog, k2 tog.
K on these 3 sts for 12 more rows, then p3 tog.
With turquoise yarn, pick up 28 sts from cast on edge about 1cm (½in) from the edges, see diagram 2.
Row 2: p28.
Row 3: (RS) p2 tog, p24, p2 tog.
Row 4: p2 tog, p22, p2 tog, leave turquoise yarn hanging.
Row 5: join in green metallic yarn, k2 tog, k2, k2 tog, k12, k2 tog, k2, k2 tog.

The lady of ancient Egypt wears a royal head-dress with a cobra at the front, a large jewelled collar, and a finely pleated dress of ribbing.

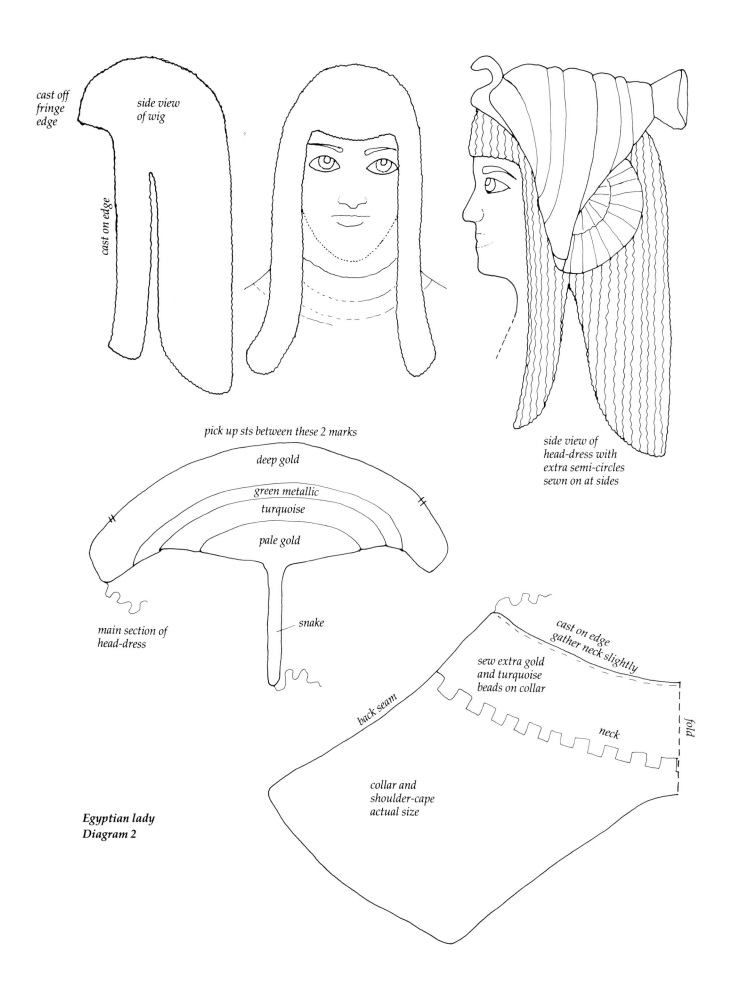

cast off
fringe
edge

side view
of wig

cast on edge

pick up sts between these 2 marks

deep gold

green metallic

turquoise

pale gold

main section of
head-dress

snake

side view of
head-dress with
extra semi-circles
sewn on at sides

cast on edge
gather neck slightly

sew extra gold
and turquoise
beads on collar

back seam

neck

fold

collar and
shoulder-cape
actual size

*Egyptian lady
Diagram 2*

Row 6: p2 tog, p16, p2 tog, cut yarn.
Row 7: with turquoise, k2 tog, k14, k2 tog.
Row 8: (WS) k2 tog, k12, k2 tog.
Row 9: k2 tog, k10, k2 tog.
Row 10: p2 tog, p8, p2 tog.
Row 11: p2 tog, p6, p2 tog.
Row 12: join in pale gold, p8.
Rows 13, 14, 15 and 16: work in single rib.
Row 17: (inc, p1) 4 times.
Cast off in pattern.

a. Stitch the 2 side edges of the gold 'tail' tog to form a tube. Fasten off, then make the side pieces as folls. Make 2 the same. With pale or deep gold yarn, cast on 14 sts loosely and work 2 rows in single rib.
   Row 3: (k2 tog, rib 4) twice, k2 tog, cut gold.
   Row 4: join in metallic green, (k2 tog) 5 times, k1.
   Row 5: p6.
   Row 6: (k2 tog) 3 times.
b. Gather the last 3 sts on to a wool needle and draw up tightly. Fan these two pieces out so that semi-circles are formed. These are sewn in place after the head-dress has been attached to the hair.

Skirt

With white or cream yarn and size 2¼mm needles, cast on 60 sts and work in double rib for 16 rows. Change to size 3mm needles and continue until the piece measures 17cm (6¾in).
Cut the white yarn and join in gold metallic yarn. Work 2 rows then change to turquoise and work 2 more rows. Cast off. Sew this piece up to form a tube.

Sash

With size 2¼mm needles and gold yarn, cast on 100 sts. Cut the gold and join in metallic green. Knit one row then cast off. Tie this round the top of the skirt as shown, a little way above the natural waistline.
Note: this model is wearing an alternative 'crochet' version, made as follows; using gold metallic yarn and a size 4.00mm hook, make a chain of 100. Work double crochet (American single crochet) for one row, then a row of white, then the last row in gold.

Shoulder-cape and collar

The collar and cape are knitted in one piece to reduce bulk on the shoulders. Begin with the collar.
With medium gold metallic yarn and size 2¾mm needles, cast on 30 sts and knit one row.
Row 2: (inc, k4) 6 times, then cut yarn.
Row 3: join in deep gold, p36.
Row 4: (inc, p5) 6 times.
Row 5: k42, cut yarn.
Row 6: join in pale gold, (inc, k6) 6 times.
Row 7: k48.
Row 8: join in turquoise and work in patt as folls, k3 gold, then (2 turquoise, 2 gold) to last st, 1 gold, cut gold.
Row 9: p1, (inc, p5) 7 times, inc, p4. 55 sts.

Row 10: join in white, (k2 turquoise, 2 white) to end of row, cut turquoise.
Row 11: join in gold, (p2 white, 2 gold) to end of row, cut gold.
Row 12: in white, knit.
Divide for cape as folls:
Next row: (k1, p1) 13 times, cast off 3 sts p-wise, (p1, k1) to last st, p1.
Work on these 2 sets of 26 sts separately. Keeping the side edges straight, noting that this is the back seam, decrease only on the centre edges by knitting, or purling 2 tog at the end of every RS row. Keep the single rib patt intact at the same time. Cont in this way until only 22 sts rem, then work one more row.
Now change to size 4mm needles and cont to dec as before until 20 sts rem. Work one more row.
Change to size 6mm needles and dec one st at the centre edge on each of the next 4 rows. 16 sts. Cast off.
Work the other side to match, dec at the end of every WS row.

a. Darn in all loose ends. Fold RS tog and sew up back seam as far as the gold collar.
b. Embellish the collar with tiny gold and turquoise beads and sequins. Use a fine beading needle and double sewing thread for this.
c. Run a gathering thread round the edge of the collar and fit it round the neck, sewing up the rest of the back seam at the same time.

Bracelets

Make one for each wrist. With metallic yarn and size 2¼mm needles, cast on 14 sts.
Work 5 rows g st, using metallic and skin-coloured yarn in stripes.
Cast off and sew up the 2 side edges to form a circle.

Sandals

Work as given for man's sandals, but cast on 12 sts.

Rabbi from Old Testament times

The word 'rabbi' means teacher, and in Old Testament times this name was given to men who were also scribes and lawyers, and expert in the interpretation of Jewish law in everyday life. A famous Pharisee, Gamaliel, was also a rabbi and a member of the Sanhedrin (i.e., the Great Council of the Jewish Church). He was active at the time of Christ and interceded on behalf of the Apostles against the Sadducees (Acts chapter 5, v. 34).

Our model is shown wearing the ordinary dress of older men. A full-length gown of cotton or linen is tied round the waist with a broad sash. Over this is worn a loose coat of striped fabric and the head is covered by a large tasselled shawl. The rabbi wears a small leather box, called a phylactery, strapped to his forehead in which is kept passages of scriptures written on a minute piece of parchment. On his feet he wears simple leather sandals.

Without his loose coat, the figure on the left shows the long plain gown with a broad sash sewn round the waist. His phylactery is fastened on to his forehead by a strap worn underneath the head-shawl. The latter is draped over the shoulders with the point in the centre of the back.

This model is a particularly simple one to make as the clothes are almost shapeless. The white loincloth is knitted in to his skin in the form of longish underpants and his short-sleeved vest is also knitted in to his skin.

Materials

Hair, moustache and beard: 10gm (½oz) white 4 ply yarn.
Gown: 25gm (1oz) neutral linen-coloured 4 ply.
Sash: oddments of coloured 3 or 4 ply.
Coat: 25gm (1oz) light brown 4 ply and other oddments of coloured yarns to make random stripes.
Shawl: 20gm (¾oz) white or cream 4 ply.
Sandals and phylactery: oddment of brown 4 ply.
Needles: sizes 2¼, 2¾ and 3¼mm.
Note: for the body, use a medium to dark skin-covering with built-in white vest and longish underpants, see notes on pages 12–14. No ears are needed. Embroider the face as shown, with thick white eyebrows to match the hair, unless you decide to make a dark-haired rabbi, but do not embroider a mouth.

Moustache and beard

With white yarn and size 2¼mm needles, cast on 7 sts.
Row 1: (k1, p1) 3 times, k1.
Row 2: (p1, k1) 3 times, p1.
Now inc one st at both ends of every row, keeping the patt of single rib correct, until there are 19 sts.
Row 9: (k1, p1) 3 times, k1, cast off 5 sts k-wise in the centre, then rib the last 7 sts.
Row 10: rib 7, turn, and cast on 5 sts, turn, and rib 7 to end of row. This makes a hole for the mouth.
Row 11: (k1, p1) 9 times, k1.
Row 12: inc in first st, k5, cast off 7 sts, k5, inc in last st. Work on these 2 sets of sts separately as folls:
Row 13: p7.
Row 14: k2 tog, k4, inc in last st.
Row 15: p5, p2 tog.
Row 16: k2 tog and cast off to end of row, cut yarn.
Row 17: rejoin yarn to other set of sts, p2 tog, p4, inc in last st.
Row 18: k5, k2 tog.
Row 19: p2 tog and cast off to end of row.

a. Sew the moustache and beard to the face as shown in diagram 3.

Hair

For a bald pate, with the same white yarn, cast on 28 sts, leaving a longish tail for sewing up. Work in single rib for 18 rows.
Row 19: k2 tog, rib 6, k2 tog, rib 8, k2 tog, rib 6, k2 tog. Cast off in rib, noting that this is the top edge.

a. Pin the hair to the head leaving a bald area on top. Make the lower edge fractionally higher than the point of the beard.
b. Stitch in position round the face and head, leaving the bottom edge free. Catch the two lower front points to the beard as shown.

A small leather box, or phylactery, would have been strapped to the forehead of the rabbi, containing passages of scripture on a minute piece of parchment.

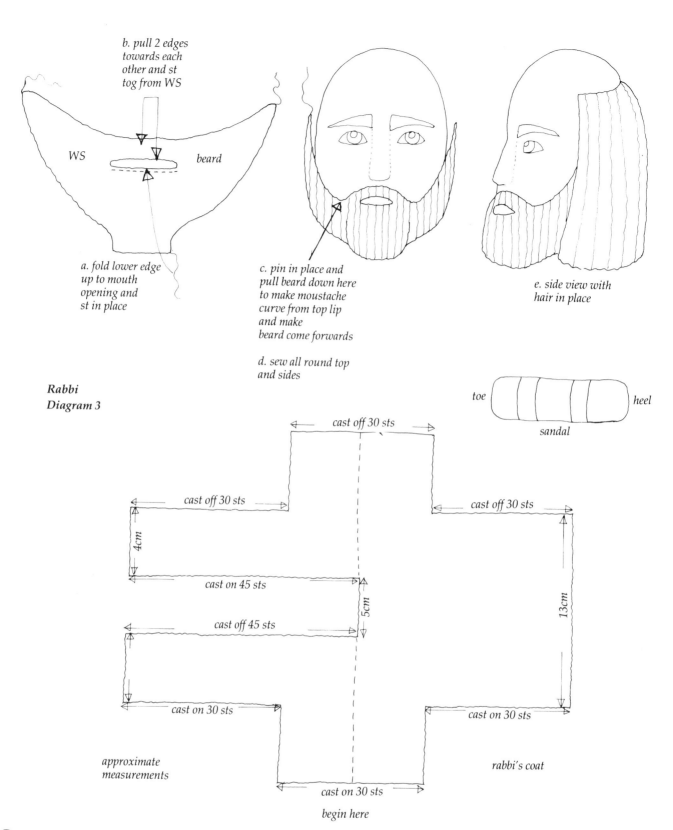

b. pull 2 edges towards each other and st tog from WS

WS

beard

a. fold lower edge up to mouth opening and st in place

c. pin in place and pull beard down here to make moustache curve from top lip and make beard come forwards

d. sew all round top and sides

e. side view with hair in place

Rabbi
Diagram 3

toe

heel

sandal

cast off 30 sts

cast off 30 sts

cast off 30 sts

4cm

cast on 45 sts

5cm

13cm

cast off 45 sts

cast on 30 sts

cast on 30 sts

approximate measurements

rabbi's coat

cast on 30 sts

begin here

Gown

With the neutral yarn and size 3¼mm needles, cast on 80 sts. Work in a k3, p1 rib for 70 rows.
Row 71: (k2 tog, k1, p1) 20 times.
Row 72: p60.
Row 73: (yfwd, k2 tog) 30 times.
Row 74: p60.
Work in ss without shaping for 10 more rows, then divide for armholes.

Row 85: k13, cast off 4 sts, k26, cast off 4 sts, k13.
Work on each set of sts separately in ss for 11 more rows.
Next row: k52 across all sts.
Next row: p52.
Next row: (yfwd, k2 tog) across all sts, then cast off.

Sleeves

Make 2 the same. Cast on 18 sts and knit 4 rows.
Row 5: p18.
Work 14 more rows in ss.
Row 20: inc in first st, p to last st, inc.
Work in ss for 3 more rows.
Row 24: as row 20.
Work in ss for 3 more rows.
Row 28: as row 20. 24 sts.
Work in ss for 5 more rows, then cast off.

a. This garment slips easily over the head without a back fastening. Sew the 2 side edges for the centre back seam.
b. Sew the sleeve seams to form tubes and set these into the armholes of the gown.
c. Make draw-string cords for the neck and waist, slip the gown on to the figure and gather the neck closely under the beard and hair. Tie at the back. The waist tie is optional, as this will be covered by the sash.

Sash

With oddments of coloured yarns and size 2¾mm needles, cast on 12 sts and work in ss with 2 g st selvedges on every row. Continue until the piece measures 15cm (6in), then cast off. Press gently.

a. Place this round the waistline of the figure and sew the two back edges together.

Coat

With light brown yarn and size 3¼mm needles, cast on 30 sts. Diagram 3 shows how this garment is made all in one piece, beginning at one sleeve edge. It is made entirely in g st, and every 2 rows of light brown are alternated with 2 rows of colour. Keep this colour pattern constant throughout all shapings.
Rows 1 and 2: light brown, knit.
Rows 3 and 4: colour, knit.
Rep these 4 rows 5 more times.
Row 25: cast on 30 sts, k to end of row.
Row 26: cast on 30 sts, k to end of row. 90 sts.
Cont to knit in stripes for 15 more rows.
Row 42: (WS) cast off 45 sts, k to end of row.
Cont on rem 45 sts for the back of the coat for another 23 rows.
Row 65: (WS) cast on 45 sts, k90.
Row 66: k90.
Cont on these 90 sts for 15 more rows.
Row 82: (WS) cast off 30 sts, k to end of row.
Row 83: cast off 30 sts, k to end of row. 30 sts.
Work 23 more rows, then cast off.

a. Fold across the shoulders, shown as dotted line on diagram 3.
b. From WS, sew side edges and underarms.
c. Turn to RS and pick up 48 sts from bottom edge only, using main colour. Knit 2 rows then cast off.

Shawl (triangular)

With white or cream yarn and size 3¼mm needles, cast on 3 sts.
Row 1: k3.
Row 2: k1, p1, k1.
Row 3: inc, k1, inc. 5 sts.
Row 4: k1, p3, k1.
Row 5: k1, (inc, k1) twice.
Row 6: k1, p5, k1.
Row 7: k1, inc, k to last 3 sts, inc, k2.
Row 8: k1, p to last st, k1.
Rep rows 7 and 8 until the piece measures 20cm (8in) along the side edges, (approx 63 sts), then cast off.

a. Pin the piece out flat and press gently.
b. To make the phylactery, use brown yarn and size 2¼mm needles. Cast on 50 sts and then cast them off again.
   Fold this cord in half and sew through both thicknesses on the 4th st from the fold to make a tiny bump. Place this in the centre of the forehead, making a few sts behind, and into the skin to hold it in place. Fix the 2 ends tog at the back of the head. Back st along the band and into the hair, then secure the ends.
c. Place the centre of the long edge of the shawl just behind the phylactery and pin in place. Arrange the folds of the shawl as shown, pin in place and then, if necessary, make one or two sts here and there to keep it in place on the head and shoulders.

Sandals

With brown yarn and size 2¼mm needles, cast on 12 sts to make the soles. Knit 6 rows, then cast off.
Make 4 straps as foll: cast on 10 sts then cast off again immediately. Sew these straps, 2 to each sole, as shown in diagram 3 and slip on to the foot. There are no heel fastenings.

Simple leather sandals were usual for the ancient rabbi.

High priest

The high priest in Jerusalem held a most important and respected position as the chief spokesman for God, with extensive authority not only in religious matters but also in civil law. He was the head of the Sanhedrin, the official Jewish court, and the character plays an important role in many stories of both the Old and New Testaments.

Aaron, elder brother of Moses, was the first high priest; Zadok was the high priest who annointed Solomon, (961–922BC), and Caiaphas was high priest from about AD18–36, and was responsible for handing over Jesus to Pilate at the trial.

The costume for these characters, although far apart in time, would be more or less the same, as the information on which the clothes are based was given by God to Moses and this has remained unchanged in every generation. An exact and detailed description of the consecration robes can be found in the Book of Exodus, chapter 28, vv.4–39, and in chapter 39, vv.1–31.

A certain amount of license has been taken in our version, which is understandable if you read the original, but in many respects it is reasonably accurate. The white undergown and blue robe, instead of being separate are in one piece, as this makes things much simpler. The 'embroidered' tunic is made from two oblongs without any shaping, sewn only at the shoulders. Use a 4 ply metallic gold yarn with a multicoloured random-dyed 3 ply yarn, although any alternative to this is acceptable. The pattern for this is a very simple slip stitch, which uses only one colour to a row. The breastplate is made separately, which is just a bit fiddly, but worth the effort, and then glued to card for rigidity. There are no shoes, as most references indicate that the high priest walked barefoot, but of course this was his uniform, not everyday wear. Underneath his gown, the high priest wears long trousers of white linen.

Materials

Hair and beard: 10gm (½oz) mixed dark brown and grey 4 ply used double. Padding.
Trousers: 25gm (1oz) white 4 ply.
Robe: 10gm (½oz) white 4 ply, 25gm (1oz) blue 4 ply, oddment of gold metallic 4 ply and 60 gold, 10 green and 10 red beads for decoration.
Short tunic: one 25gm (1oz) ball gold metallic 4 ply, as for robe, referred to in the pattern as A. 25gm (1oz) random-dyed or multicoloured oddments of 3 or 4 ply yarns mainly in reds, purples, violets and blues, referred to in the pattern as B.
Sash: oddments of white 4 ply, multicoloured 4 ply and gold metallic.
Breastplate: short lengths of bright jewel-coloured 3 or 4 ply in blue, violet, red, pink, yellow, orange, green and black, or any other bright colours available.

Front and back views of the official uniform, under which a pair of long white trousers is worn. The rigid breastplate ties round the waist under the sash.

Embroidery threads work well for this purpose as they can be stranded to the same thickness as the metallic gold and can also be bought in small quantities. Also needed, about 10gm (½oz) metallic gold 4 ply, as for robe, thin card for backing, and glue.
Turban: oddments of white 4 ply, blue 4 ply and gold metallic. Small piece of thin card, glue or staples. Padding. Tiny piece of gold card for decoration.
Shoulder ornaments: gold card, 2 pieces of onyx or similar buttons.
Needles: sizes 2¼, 2¾, 3, 3¼mm and size 2.50mm crochet hook.
Note: for the body, use a darkish skin covering. No ears are needed.
Embroider the face with dark brown and grey threads for the eyes, with dark rims and black pupils. For the eyebrows, use brown and grey thread together and embroider these in a straight line close to the eyes.

Beard

With a mixture of dark brown and grey yarn, used double, and size 2¾mm needles, cast on 3 sts and k 8 rows.
Row 9: inc, k2.
Rows 10, 12, 14, 16, 18 and 20: knit.

The high priest, as head of the official Jewish court, can be found in many stories in both the Old and New Testaments. His richly decorated short tunic has been worked in an array of coloured and metallic yarns.

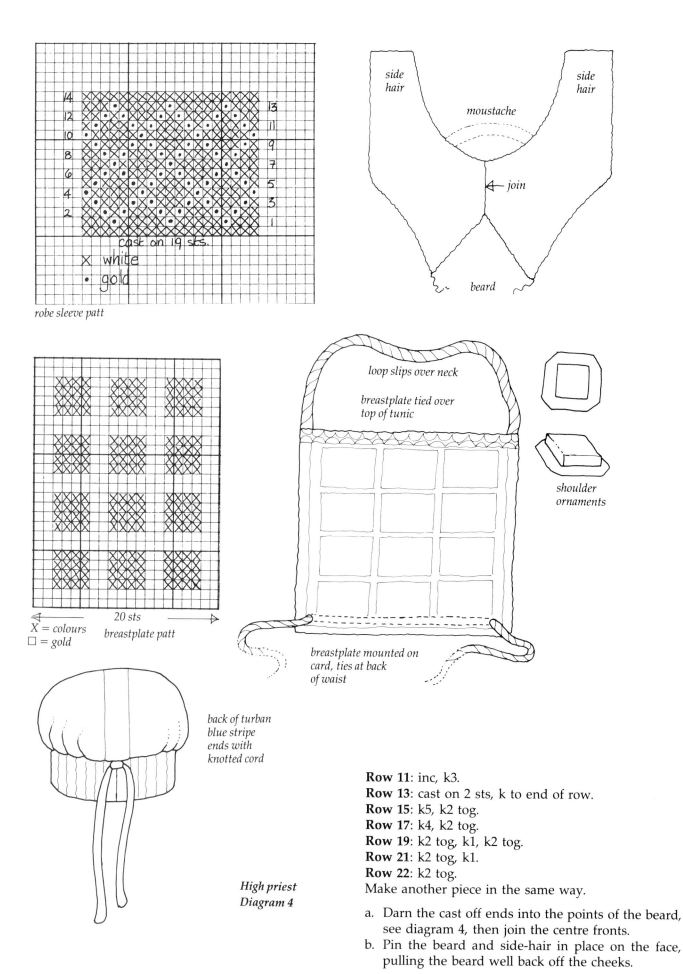

robe sleeve patt

cast on 19 sts.

14 13
12 11
10 9
8 7
6 5
4 3
2 1

X white
• gold

side hair

side hair

moustache

← join

beard

X = colours
☐ = gold

20 sts

breastplate patt

loop slips over neck

breastplate tied over
top of tunic

shoulder
ornaments

breastplate mounted on
card, ties at back
of waist

back of turban
blue stripe
ends with
knotted cord

*High priest
Diagram 4*

Row 11: inc, k3.
Row 13: cast on 2 sts, k to end of row.
Row 15: k5, k2 tog.
Row 17: k4, k2 tog.
Row 19: k2 tog, k1, k2 tog.
Row 21: k2 tog, k1.
Row 22: k2 tog.
Make another piece in the same way.

a. Darn the cast off ends into the points of the beard,
   see diagram 4, then join the centre fronts.
b. Pin the beard and side-hair in place on the face,
   pulling the beard well back off the cheeks.

32

c. Sew down each side and round the face, leaving the points of the beard free.
   For the moustache, use the crochet hook to make, a chain 2.5cm (1in) long.
d. Attach the moustache in an arch below the nose, leaving a space for the mouth.

Hair

With the same yarn and needles, cast on 10 sts and k 2 rows.
Row 3: purl.
Cont in ss for 10 more rows, then cast off.

a. With the cast on row at the bottom, pin this piece to the back of the head, first sewing down each side to the edges of the beard. Leave the top and the bottom open. The top of the head will be covered by the head-dress.
b. Run a gathering thread along the bottom edge and draw up gently to fit the nape of the neck closely.
c. Place padding into the pocket of hair to round out the shape. Do not stitch up.

Trousers

These are hidden underneath the robe.
With white yarn and size 3¼mm needles, cast on 16 sts for the left leg and work in ss for 14 rows, beginning at the waist.
At the beg of the next 2 rows, cast on 4 sts, then cont in ss for 52 more rows. Cast off and make the right leg in the same way.

a. With RS tog, pin centre back and centre front and sew all round.
b. Pin legs tog and sew both leg seams in one go.
c. Run a thread through the top edge and tie on to the figure.

Robe

With white yarn and size 3¼mm needles, cast on 70 sts.
Work 18 rows in ss then cut white yarn.
Join in blue yarn, weaving white end in on WS of next row.
Knit 2 rows, then work in ss for 60 rows.
Next row: (k1, k2 tog) 23 times, k1.
Cont on these 47 sts for 3 more rows.
Next row: (divide for armholes) k10, cast off 3 sts, k21, cast off 3 sts, k10.
Work on these 3 sets of sts separately with 11 rows of ss on each.

a. With RS tog, fold the shoulders tog and pin. Sew only half-way across each of the back shoulders, (i.e., 5 sts), leaving the neck open.
b. Press the white cast on edge of the robe to prevent curling but do not press the blue and white join.
c. Pin the back edges tog and sew up from the hem as far as the decrease row at the high waist.

Sleeves

Work in ss. Use white yarn and size 3mm needles and cast on 19 sts. Knit one row. On the next row, join in the gold yarn and begin the patt of 14 rows from the chart, see diagram 4. At the end of the 13th row, cut the gold yarn and weave the end in on the back of the 14th row.
Cut the white yarn and join in the blue.
Rows 15 and 16: knit.
Cont in ss for 4 rows, then inc one st at each end of the foll 2 knit rows.
Row 24: p23.
Row 25: inc in first st, k10, inc, k10, inc.
Row 26: p26.
Row 27: cast off 3 sts, k to end.
Row 28: cast off 3 sts, p to end.
Rows 30, 32 and 34: purl.
Rows 29, 31 and 33: k2 tog, k to last 2 sts, k2 tog.
Cast off and make another sleeve in the same way.

a. With RS tog, join sleeve seams and set into armholes of gown, matching centres to shoulder seams.
b. The hem of the gown is hung with bells and pomegranates – 'of violet and other materials, so that he may be heard as he moves about'. Our version is made up of gold beads in two sizes and in clusters to represent bells; green and gold beads together and red and gold beads together. Decide for yourself how you will do this with the materials you have available.
c. Slip gown on to the figure and sew up the back opening.

Short tunic

With size 3mm needles and gold metallic yarn, cast on 31 sts and k one row. The patt is made as folls, noting that the first and last 2 sts on every row are knitted.
A = gold and B = multicolour.
Row 1: A, knit.
Row 2: A, k2, p27, k2.
Row 3: B, k3, *sl 1, k3*, to last 4 sts, sl 1, k3.
Row 4: B, k2, p1, *sl 1, p3*, to last 4 sts, sl 1, p1, k2.
Row 5: as row 1.
Row 6: as row 2.
Row 7: B, k5, *sl 1, k3*, to last 2 sts, k2.
Row 8: B, k2, p3, *sl 1, p3*, to last 2 sts, k2.
These 8 rows form the patt. Rep them 7 more times, then rows 1 and 2 once more. Cast off.
Make another piece in the same way.

a. Press both pieces to exactly the same size.
b. Place with RS tog and cast off edges at top. Join shoulders from outer edges for 2.5cm (1in),leaving a gap of 5cm (2in) for the head to pass through.
c. Place tunic over head of figure and arrange beard to lie on top.

Sash

This measures approx 43cm (17in) and is worked in g st throughout, in a mixture of coloured oddments and gold on a white background. This is open to any design interpretation you wish, as three sources were all quite different. The 'official' description reads 'a sash of embroidered linen'.

With gold yarn and size 3mm needles, cast on 6 sts and k 6 rows.

Each end of the sash is worked as folls:

6 rows gold, 4 rows purple.

2 rows gold, 4 rows red.

2 rows gold, 2 rows white.

2 rows gold, 2 rows violet.

2 rows gold, 10 rows white.

After every 10 rows of white, work 2 rows of colour alternately with 2 rows of gold until about 38cm (15in) have been worked.

Then make the other end to match the beginning, in reverse order.

a. Fold the piece lengthways to enclose all ends and sew the edges tog along the entire length from the RS.

b. Tie this in a knot around the waist, quite low down.

Breastplate

Using size 2¼mm needles and gold metallic yarn with oddments of blue, violet, red, pink, yellow, orange, green and black, work this square piece from the chart over 20 sts and 26 rows, see diagram 4.

The first and last 2 sts are knitted on every row, and also the first two rows and the last two rows are in g st. This makes a more rigid border.

The easiest way to work these small blocks of colour is to cut off lengths of about 30cm (12in) and join three of these into row 3 at the appropriate places and weave them into the back of row 7. Join three more colours in on rows 9, 15 and 21, weaving ends in as they are finished with on the row above.

a. Trim all ends or darn them in.

b. Cut a piece of postcard measuring 6.5cm × 6.0cm (2½ × 2¼in), and round off the corners.

c. Cover one side lightly with glue and press the WS of the knitting on to this, pulling the knitting just beyond the edges of the card. Allow to dry thoroughly.

d. To fasten the top edges round the neck of the figure, use gold yarn to cast on 30 sts. Knit one row then cast off. Use the tails to sew this card to one corner of the breastplate, pass the cord round the neck and sew the other end to the other corner.

e. To fasten the lower edges to the waist, make a blue crochet or twisted cord about 30cm (12in) long and thread this through both bottom corners (i.e., through both card and knitting), passing it *behind* the lower front edge and out at each corner. Take

this cord under the sash at both sides and tie round the back, see diagram 4.

Turban head-dress

This consists of a disc of white knitting with a stripe of blue across the centre. This disc is then gathered round the edge and drawn up on to a circular band of card which is covered by a strip of gold knitting.

Begin with the white disc, using white yarn and size 2¼mm needles, cast on 20 sts and work in ss for 2 rows.

Row 3: inc in first and last sts.

Row 4: purl.

Rep rows 3 and 4 until there are 28 sts.

Rows 11, 12, 13, and 14: work in ss without shaping.

Row 15: join in blue yarn and work 4 rows of ss.

Row 19: cut blue yarn, pick up white and work 4 rows of ss.

Row 23: k2 tog, k to last 2 sts, k2 tog.

Row 24: purl.

Rep the last 2 rows until there are 20 sts.

Work 2 more rows without shaping, then cast off.

a. Use one of the tails to run a gathering thread round the extreme edge of this piece and draw it up slightly to make a dome. Do not fasten off yet.

b. Cut a piece of bendy card 1cm (½in) wide and long enough to go entirely round the head just above the eyebrows, leaving an extra bit for the overlap.

c. Curve this strip into a circle, check for a close fit, then glue or staple the ends together. This piece will be covered by knitting.

d. With gold yarn cast on 5 sts and make a strip of ms long enough to encircle the card. Sew the two short ends tog, cover the outside of the card with glue and slip the knitting over. Press firmly.

e. Complete the gathering of the turban to fit the gold base and fasten off. Place a flat piece of padding inside and glue the turban on to the top of the gold base, easing the white edge just inside with the points of scissors. Note that the blue band is placed from front to back, see diagram 4.

f. To fit this to the head, glue the inside of the head-dress and push well down on to the head to cover the open back and top.

g. Cut a tiny circle of gold card and glue this to the front of the head-dress as shown.

h. Make a blue cord measuring about 10cm (4in), fold in half and sew the fold to the back of the blue band on the turban so that the cords hang down the neck.

Shoulder decorations

To make the shoulder ornaments, pieces of real onyx were glued to small rounded squares of gold card, but if this is not available, consider using large flattened beads or buttons of a greenish-brown colour, see diagram 4. These can be glued or sewn to each shoulder.

Fifteenth and sixteenth centuries

Portraits of men and women of substance from this period are fortunately plentiful and these give us an excellent insight into the extravagant and sumptuous styles in costume and coiffure. Italy led the whole of Europe in this excess and although the country was still divided into warring states, dominated by wealthy and powerful families, the rivalry between them no doubt contributed considerably to the desire to be thought not only the best, but the wealthiest.

The same period shows the flowering of the Renaissance in England, with King Henry VIII and Queen Elizabeth I leading the way. The pomp and splendour of their courts became legendary and, without doubt, this era of history produced some of the most remarkable artists and craftsmen who ever lived.

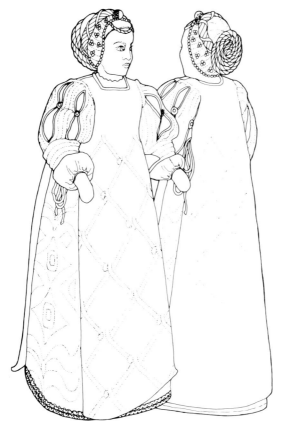

Front and back views show how the green diamond-patterned overgown reveals the green and white pattern of the chemise, the long sleeves of which also appear through the slashes and at the wrists. The overgown ties beneath the arms.

Italian Renaissance lady *c.*1450

The model's costume is taken from several portraits of the fifteenth century in Italy, at a time when portraiture became a sign of importance and wealth, social stability and power. Styles of dress are numerous, as the various city-states differed from each other in many respects, although not in the richness of their fabrics and the ingenuity of design.

This lady wears a white high-necked, long-sleeved, under-dress showing a rich brocade pattern at each side of the skirt between the front and back panels of the overgown. The skirt of the latter is knitted in a simple patterned stitch, using a combination of a multi coloured 3 ply yarn in pink and green, and a fine glitter thread. This yarn is also used on the patterned panels of the under-dress in combination with white. The front and back panels are divided, being tied together under the arms with cords. Each sleeve is made in four separate strips, edged with a 4 ply glitter yarn and built on to a garter stitch cuff. This allows the white sleeve of the under-dress to show through, and beads or sequins are used to catch together these strips at intervals.

Her extravagant costume includes a lace-edged underskirt, or petticoat, from the waist, shoes, and knee-length stockings with garters. She also wears separate, not knitted in, underpants. Her hair is an elaborate confection of braids and coils, tied up into a jewelled band topped with a large gold-clasped bead, see the illustration of the front and back of the figure. The head-dresses and hair-styles of this period are amazingly intricate and many alternatives can be found, some simpler, some more elaborate. However, Italian women did not favour the tall pointed head-dresses so popular in other parts of Europe at this time, nor the closed hoods of the early Tudors.

Materials

Hair: 10gm (½oz) blonde-coloured 4 ply.
Head-dress: 10gm (½oz) gold metallic 4 ply. Padding. One large jewel. About 50 tiny white seed-pearls.
Shoes and stockings: oddments of dress-colour, white 4 ply and metallic gold for garters and laces. Padding.
Petticoat: 20gm (¾oz) white 4 ply.
Chemise with patterned side panels: 25gm (1oz) white 4 ply. 10gm (½oz) contrast used tog with fine glitter thread. Oddment of gold metallic for border.
Open-sided overgown: use the same, or similar yarn as that used on patterned side panels of chemise, about 25gm (1oz), used with the same fine glitter thread for extra sparkle. Oddment of metallic gold for sleeve edgings. Small gold beads and sequins.
Needles: sizes 2, 2¼, 2¾, 3 and 3¼mm.

The rich overgown of the Italian Renaissance lady is worked in an open-diamond pattern, using 4 ply yarn mixed with glitter thread, metallic gold, beads and sequins.

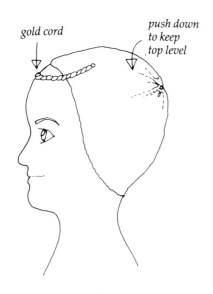

gold cord

push down to keep top level

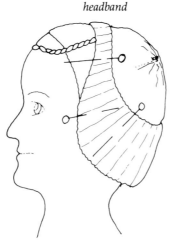

headband

pin gold band well down over ears and backwards on top of head

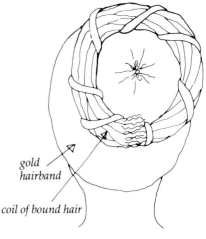

gold hairband

coil of bound hair

back view

Italian Renaissance lady
Diagram 1

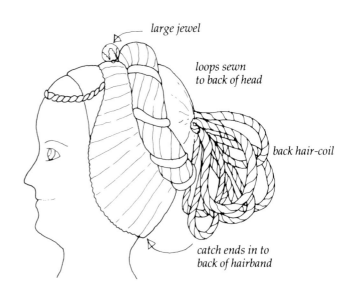

large jewel

loops sewn to back of head

back hair-coil

catch ends in to back of hairband

Note: embroider the face as for a blonde colouring, as blondes were highly regarded at this time. Eyes, greyish-blue, pale eyebrows, pale pink mouth.

Hair and head-dress

With hair-coloured yarn and size 2mm needles, cast on 30 sts and work 12 rows in ss.

Row 13: (k3, k2 tog) 6 times.
Row 14: p24.
Row 15: (k2, k2 tog) 6 times.
Row 16: p18.
Row 17: (k2 tog) 9 times, then gather these last 9 sts on to a wool needle.

a. With RS tog, fold this piece and sew the 2 side edges. Turn to RS and pad slightly into a dome shape.
b. Fit this cap of hair well back on to the head, off the forehead and well down at the back, see diagram 1. Pin in position and sew all round.

Make a crochet or twisted cord of gold metallic yarn measuring 5cm (2in) long and pin this in a horseshoe shape on top of the forehead, as shown, with the curve just below the hair-line. Sew into the cord with a back stitch to keep it in place.

c. For the headband, with gold yarn cast on 3 sts and knit 10 rows.
   Row 11: inc in first and last sts.
   Rows 12 to 16: k5.
   Row 17: as row 11.
   Rows 18 to 54: k7.
   Row 55: k2 tog, k3, k2 tog.
   Rows 56 to 60: k5.
   Row 61: k2 tog, k1, k2 tog.
   Work 10 more rows on these 3 sts, then cast off.
d. Wrap this band round the lower head, as shown in

diagram 1, with the ends at the top. Pin in place, then sew all round using the tails. Allow the top edge of this band to cover the ends of the gold cord.

e. To make a coil of hair, take a length of the hair yarn measuring 220cm (86in) and fold this five times until it measures approx 40cm (16in) long. Tie yarn tightly round this bundle at both ends to keep it in place.

Make a twisted or crocheted cord of gold metallic yarn the same length as the bundle of hair and sew one end of this into one end of the bundle, using one of the tails. Now twist the cord firmly and evenly about six times round the hair bundle, then sew the other end in.

f. Mark the centre of this coil and pin to the top of the head just behind the headband. Bring the ends together at the back, pinning the coil as you go, to lie just inside the headband. Do not trim the ends of the coil as these will be covered. Just turn up the ends and sew them to the back of the head. Without flattening it, sew the coil on to the head.

g. For the back hair-coil, make a tightly-twisted cord of hair-coloured yarn about 46cm (18in) long and fold this into eight. Tie the centre with a length of yarn, place at the back of the head inside the headband and sew in place like a pony-tail. Now catch the loops up to the back of the head in a loosely arranged bundle, see diagram 1.

h. Sew clusters of tiny seed-pearls all over the headband and also a line of pearls along the edge, to accentuate the shape. Sew a large jewel to match the dress-colour on the top of the headband.

The hair of the Italian Renaissance lady is an elaborate mixture of braids and coils, tied up into a jewelled gold band and topped with a large gold-clasped bead.

Shoes and stockings

These are made all in one piece. Begin with the shoe, and with dress-coloured yarn, size 2¾mm needles, and cast on 24 sts. Work 4 rows of ss.
Row 5: k5, cast off 14 sts, k5.
Cut this yarn and join in white, for stockings.
Row 6: p10, pushing the 2 sets of sts tog on the needle and weaving loose ends in on WS.
Row 7: inc, k3, inc, k4, inc. 13 sts.
Cont in ss for 29 more rows.
Join in metallic gold and k 2 rows. Cut this yarn and work 2 more rows in white, then cast off.

a. Leave the top of the shoe open and use a length of gold to lace it across, beginning at the toe end and tie in a bow. Tie this bow in an extra knot and trim the ends.

b. Sew up the back of the shoe and the stocking. Fit on to the leg and make the sole of the shoe as folls: with shoe-colour, cast on 4 sts and k 17 rows. Cast off and sew this piece to the base of the shoe while in position on the foot, padding a little into the heel. Squeeze into shape.

White underskirt or petticoat

The main skirt piece is made as folls: with white yarn, and size 3¼mm needles, cast on 136 sts and begin at the lower edge.
Work 70 rows in ss.
Row 71: (yfwd, k2 tog) 68 times.
Cast off.
With the same yarn and size 3mm needles, make an edging using border patt No. 3, see page 139, until this is long enough to reach from one side edge to the other, or about 11 pattern reps.

A lace-edged underskirt or petticoat conceals knee-length stockings complete with garters.

a. Sew this border to the bottom of the skirt piece, then pin out the points and press gently.
b. Sew up the back seam.
c. Make a cord to go through the holes at the waist and draw up to fit the figure, or use fine elastic instead. Arrange the fullness towards the back.

Chemise

This long, full-sleeved gown is worn beneath the open-sided patterned brocade overgown, to reveal the knitted-in panels down each side. Only two yarns are required, white for the main part and preferably, a multicoloured variegated one for the pattern, which should either be the same as, or match, the overgown. Use this together with a fine glitter metallic thread which can be knitted in for extra sparkle.

For the skirt section, with white yarn and size 3¼mm needles, cast on 80 sts.

Row 1: join in metallic gold and knit 2 rows, cut the yarn.

To avoid carrying the coloured yarn from one panel to the next, cut 2 longish lengths of this yarn and have them ready to join in at the appropriate place along the first row of the pattern. As one length is used up, knot

another length on and weave ends in on the wrong side. Always twist the 2 yarns together as the new one is picked up to avoid holes appearing where the 2 colours meet.

To work the first row of the pattern, see diagram 2, space the panel as folls:

Row 1: (from chart) in white, k11 sts, join in contrast yarn and work 18 sts from the chart, leave the contrast yarn hanging at the back, k22 white sts, join in second length of contrast yarn and work the 18 sts again, leave this yarn hanging then work the rem 11 sts in white.

Now continue to work the rest of the pattern from the chart, 54 rows in all, to make 2 patterned panels on the white background, then continue in white only for a further 18 rows.

Row 73: (k2 tog) 40 times, to mark the waistline. 40 sts.

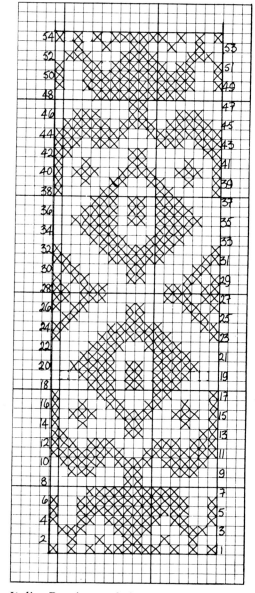

Italian Renaissance lady
Diagram 2
Chart for chemise side panels

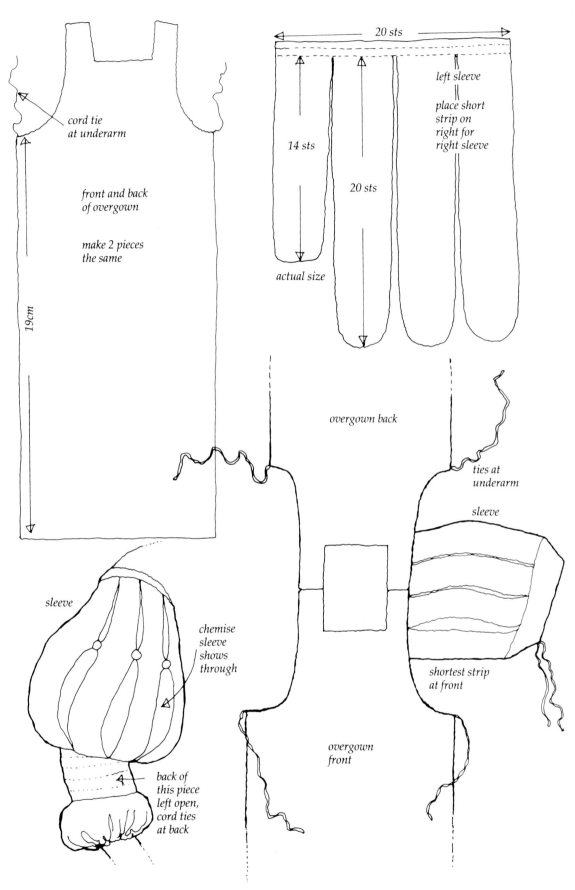

cord tie
at underarm

front and back
of overgown

make 2 pieces
the same

19cm

20 sts

14 sts

20 sts

actual size

left sleeve

place short
strip on
right for
right sleeve

overgown back

ties at
underarm

sleeve

sleeve

chemise
sleeve
shows
through

shortest strip
at front

overgown
front

4

back of
this piece
left open,
cord ties
at back

Italian Renaissance lady
Diagram 3

Shape the bodice as folls:

Rows 74 to 78: work in ss.

Row 79: k9, cast off 2 sts, k18, cast off 2 sts, k9.

Row 80: p9.

Cont on these 9 sts for 11 more rows.

Next row: cast off 4 sts p-wise, p5.

Work 2 more rows on the rem 5 sts, then cast off.

Join yarn to centre 18 sts and work 11 more rows.

Next row: k5, cast off 8 sts, k5.

Next row: p5.

Work 2 more rows on the rem 5 sts, then cast off.

Join yarn to the other front shoulder and work 3 rows. Cast off.

Then join yarn to the back shoulder and work 11 more rows.

Next row: (RS) cast off 4 sts, k5.

Work 2 more rows, then cast off p-wise.

a. Pin skirt and bodice out to shape, then press gently.
b. Sew up skirt section as far as waistline.
c. Sew shoulders.

Sleeves

With white yarn, cast on 30 sts and work in ss for 40 rows.

Row 41: (k2 tog) 15 times.

Cast off k-wise and make another piece the same.

a. With RS tog, sew side edges.
b. Gather the top edge and draw up to fit the armhole.
c. Set sleeve into bodice.
d. Gather wrist edge of sleeve. Fit chemise on to the figure, draw up wrist-gathers and tie snugly.
e. Stitch up back opening from RS.
f. Slightly gather neckline for a loose fit around neck.
g. On the dec row, gather waistline to fit high on the body.

Open-sided overgown

The back and front are worked exactly the same, see diagram 3.

With main colour, plus glitter thread, and size 2¼mm needles, cast on 30 sts and work the open-diamond pattern, see page 141, five complete times. This will measure about 19cm (7½in).

Next row: cast off 4 sts, k to end of row.

Next row: cast off 4 sts p-wise, p to end of row.

Now dec one st at both ends of the next 4 rows. 14 sts. Work 8 rows straight.

Next row: (RS) k4, cast off 6 sts, k4.

Work 5 rows on each of the 4 sts separately to build up the shoulders of the bodice, then cast off.

Make another piece in the same way.

a. With RS tog, join the 2 pieces at the shoulders, pin out flat, WS uppermost, and press very gently. Darn ends in at lower edges,
b. Make 4 short cords and attach these to the 4 underarm points. These will be tied in bows to close the sides.

Sleeves for overgown

Each sleeve consists of 4 narrow strips knitted sideways and joined at the narrow ends to the shoulder and to the lower arm. There is one short strip in each set which is place towards the front to allow for the shortening of the arm when in a bent position, see diagram 3.

With metallic gold yarn and the same needles, cast on 20 sts.

This yarn is used only for the cast on and cast off rows, and you can choose whether to link it with the main yarn up the side of the knitting, or cut it off and join it in for the last stage.

Join in the main dress-colour and knit 6 rows, then cast off in metallic gold. Make three strips in this way, then another one on only 14 sts. Darn all ends in on the WS of each strip.

a. As shown in diagram 3, lay all 4 strips, RS uppermost, side by side. With main yarn, pick up 5 sts from the top edge of each strip in order, (i.e., 20 sts), and knit back across the row. Cast off. This joins the shoulder edges together.
b. Turn the strips the other way up, RS facing, and again pick up 20 sts from the bottom edges of the strips, allowing the longer ones to bend outwards to compensate for the shorter one. This is the lower arm edge.

   Work 4 knit rows on these 20 sts. Now k2 tog at each end of next 4 rows until 12 sts rem. Cont straight for 4 more rows, cut yarn and join in metallic gold to cast off.

   Make the other sleeve in the same way, remembering to reverse the order of the strips.
c. With RS tog, lay each sleeve on top of the bodice, as seen in diagram 3, with the shorter edges tog and sew along the top of the sleeves, leaving the rest of the armhole edge of the bodice open as shown.
d. Crochet or embroider metallic gold round the neckline and attach 2.5cm (1in) cords to each of the lower edges of the sleeves as shown.
e. Fit the gown over the figure and tie the underarm cords. Pull the white chemise sleeve down towards the wrists and pass the wrist-cord under the sleeve of the chemise from one edge of the overgown to the other, leaving a gap of about 2.5cm (1in), (i.e., the length of the cord). The wider points of the 20 sts of the lower sleeves should now be brought together and stitched, to close the sleeves just above the elbows.
f. The sleeve strips can be caught tog at intervals by sewing a small gold bead and sequin across the opening as shown.

Italian Renaissance man c.1450

The model wears a fashionable gown known as a 'houppelande'. This lends itself to many variations, long, medium or short, open-sleeved or closed, high or low-necked. However, for men it was always belted. Following the prevailing whim, this version shows a very high standing collar, pleated bodice, where the pleats were kept in position by inside tapes and full, wide and flowing sleeves with dagged edges. A floor-length skirt of a chequered pattern is knitted all in one with the bodice in a series of straight panels, see the illustration of the back. You may prefer to edge the gown with a fur trim instead of the dagging.

His splendid hat, called a 'chaperone' derives from a previous fashion, when young gallants felt that wearing a long-tailed hood in the conventional manner was too ordinary, so they piled the tail on top of their heads and put their faces through the opening which was formed with the tail, called a 'liripipe', wound round the neck and over the shoulder. (Yes, the fashions were just as crazy then as they are today!) The chaperone can be plain or elaborate, although our version is quite a work of art, with an immensely long liripipe hanging to the floor.

Underneath the houppelande he wears the conventional doublet, shirt and hose, although even these were variable throughout this period of high fashion. The white shirt is a simple high-necked sleeveless one, with a long body reaching to the top of the legs. The hose is divided, (i.e., there is no centre front or back seam), and made to tie on to the doublet, or jacket, with ties called 'points', and the long shirt covers the centre gaps at the back and front, see the illustration of the front. Multicoloured hose were very much in vogue, so oddments of yarn may be used to knit each leg in a different colour, or even chequer them if you wish.

Shoes are made separately, the very long pointed toes of earlier years now having given way to a more natural shape. The doublet in our version is short, although this could vary from waist to thigh-length, and would not be difficult to adapt from the instructions given here. With the short version, the idea was to allow the baggy shirt to puff out in the space between the doublet and hose, rather in the way young people nowadays often wear shirt-tails hanging out. Sleeves on the doublet are very full above the elbow, tighter below, and the bodice opens down the front to expose the shirt but is laced across the lower half. From his belt, the model wears his money-pouch which would have been made of leather, or maybe richly embroidered, stiff fabric.

The shirt, doublet and hose is worn beneath the houppelande. The hose are divided at the front and the back and tie on to the doublet with laces called 'points'. The back view shows how the gathers across the bodice of the houppelande are adjusted to fit the upper figure.

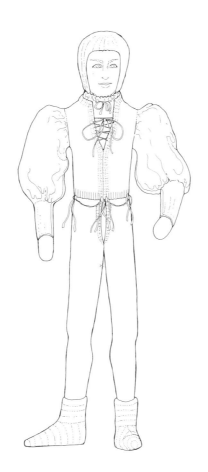

In full dress, the Renaissance man is quite startling. He wears a full-length gown, known as a houppelande, which is knitted in a chequered pattern of colours with sleeves of dagged edges. His splendid hat is known as a chaperone.

Materials

Hair: an oddment of dark brown tweedy 4 ply yarn. Padding.

Shirt: 10gm (½oz) white 4 ply.

Hose: 10gm (½oz) each of 2 different colours in 4 ply.

Jerkin: 20gm (¾oz) pale green 4 ply.

Houppelande: 50gm (2oz) main colour, turquoise, 4 ply. 50gm (2oz) of oddments in contrasting colours 4 ply.

Chaperone: use left-over oddments from the houppelande or, as a complete contrast, make it in black. Approx 15gm (¾oz) 4 ply. Padding.

Belt: oddments of brown 4 ply or a strip of real leather. A tiny shoe buckle adds an authentic touch.

Pouch: brown 4 ply; tiny bead or button to fasten.

Boots: oddments of brown 4 ply, as pouch and belt. Padding.

Needles: sizes 2¼, 2¾ and 3¼mm.

Note: embroider the face with straight dark eyebrows over dark eyes, (though a blonde colouring is just as likely); no ears are required. Beards and moustaches were less in fashion at this time than they had been previously.

Hair

This is a chin-length, smooth bobbed style, with a fringe on the forehead. With dark brown yarn and size 2¼mm needles, cast on 28 sts, leaving a tail of about 25cm (10in).

Work 2 rows in single rib.

Row 3: k28.

Row 4: k1, p26, k1.

Rep rows 3 and 4 six more times.

Row 17: inc, k26, inc.

Row 18: p30.

Row 19: inc, k28, inc.

Row 20: p32.

Row 21: cast on 5 sts, k to end of row.

Row 22: p37.

Row 23: (k1, k2 tog) 12 times, k1.

Row 24: p25.

Row 25: (k2 tog) 12 times, k1.

Row 26: p13.

Gather the last 13 sts on to a wool needle and draw up to form the top of the head.

a. Using the last tail, sew up the side of the fringe.

b. Fit the hair on to the head and use the cast on tail to gather the lower edge of the hair with a running st. Draw up very slightly to fit the nape of the neck as shown.

c. Pad the back of the head with a small piece of padding, and also the fringe, to make a slight overhang on to the forehead. Pin in place all round, pulling the fringe well down and the sides forwards to make a straight line down the sides of the face.

d. Sew the hair all round and squeeze gently into shape.

Shirt

Sleeveless, with back and front alike. With white yarn and size 2¾mm needles, leave a longish tail and cast on 16 sts. Work in single rib for 4 rows. Change to ss and work 12 more rows.

Now inc for the fullness above the waist:

Row 17: (k1, inc) 8 times.

Row 18: p24.

Rows 19 to 36: work straight.

Row 37: cast off 3 sts, k to end.

Row 38: cast off 3 sts, p to end. 18 sts.

Cont straight for 12 more rows.

Row 51: (yfwd, k2 tog) 9 times.

Knit 2 rows g st, then cast off.

Make another piece in the same way.

a. With RS tog, sew both pieces tog down the sides and place over the figure.

b. Pull the shirt well down and catch the back and front tog between the legs to keep it in place.

c. Pull the neck pieces tog at the sides and stitch in place.

d. Make a cord to thread through the holes and tie in a bow at the front or back.

Hose

Make each leg in the same way, using a different colour for each one. Use size 2¾mm needles.

Left leg: **begin at the waist and cast on 15 sts. Keeping a selvedge of 2 knit sts at each end on every row, work in ss for 10 rows.

Row 11: k7, inc, k7.

Row 12: k2, p12, k2.

Row 13: k7, inc. k8.

Row 14: k2, p13, k2.

Row 15: k8, inc, k8.

Row 16: k2, p14, k2.**

Now work 2 rows without shaping.

Row 19: cast on 3 sts, k to end of row. 21 sts.

Row 20: discontinue the selvedge k sts and p21.

Work 12 more rows without shaping.

Row 33: k2 tog, k to last 2 sts, k2 tog.

Work 3 more rows without shaping, then row 33 again.

Rows 38 to 48: work straight.

Row 49: as row 33. 15 sts.

Rows 50 to 70: work straight for 21 rows.

Row 71: as row 33.

Rows 72 to 76: work straight.

Row 77: as row 33. 11 sts.

Work straight for 9 more rows, then gather the last sts on to a wool needle and draw up to form the end of the toes.

Right leg: work from ** to ** as given for left leg.

Row 17: knit.

Row 18: cast on 3 sts, p to end of row, discontinuing the 2 selvedge k sts.

Rows 19 to 32: work straight without shaping.

Now work from row 33 as given for left leg.

a. With RS tog, sew up the foot for 2.5cm (2in), turn to RS and slip on to the foot.
b. Pull the waistline into position over the shirt and pin. Pull the 3 cast on sts through between the legs to the *back*.
c. Pin edges tog down *back* of leg then sew tog from RS as far as the 3 cast on sts. Do not sew up the centre front and back edges as these are left open to show the shirt beneath.
d. The ties (points): make 3 cords, approx 13cm (5in) long for each leg. Thread these half-way through the top edges of the hose and tie the ends tog over the edge to stop them pulling out again. When the jerkin is in position, one tie from each pair of points is threaded through the lower edge of the jerkin and tied to keep the hose up.

Jerkin

With pale green yarn and size 2¾mm needles, cast on 32 sts and work 3 rows in single rib.
Row 4: (WS) k3, p26, k3.
Keeping a selvedge of 3 knit sts at each side, work in ss for 10 more rows, then divide for armholes.
Row 15: k7, cast off 2 sts, k14, cast off 2 sts, k7.
Row 16: working on the first set of 7 sts, k3, p4.
Row 17: k7.
Work 9 more rows in this way, cut yarn and rejoin to

The Italian Renaissance man wears a conventional doublet, shirt and hose.

centre 14 sts. Work 11 rows in ss, cut yarn and rejoin to last 7 sts. Work this side to match the other side but do not cut yarn.
Next row: k across all 28 sts.
Next row: k3, p22, k3.
Next row: k10, k2 tog, k4, k2 tog, k10.
Knit 3 rows then cast off.

Sleeves

Make 2 the same.
Cast on 14 sts and work in ss for 16 rows.
Row 17: inc once into every st to make 28 sts.
Row 18: p28.
Cont in ss but inc one st at each end of every k row until there are 38 sts, then cont straight for 13 more rows.
Cast off 8 sts at beg of next 2 rows.
Next row: k1, (k2 tog, k1) 7 times. 15 sts.
Next row: (p2 tog) 7 times, p1.
Cast off.

a. With RS tog, fold the sleeve in half and sew the side edges tog from cuff to top. Turn to RS.
b. Gather the top half of the sleeve along the edge and draw up to fit the armhole.
c. Pin the sleeve into the armhole and sew in place.
d. Fit the jerkin on to the figure, pull the front edges tog at waistline then stitch upwards approx 2.5cm (1in), leaving the rest open.
e. Make a cord and lace across the bottom of the opening to about half-way up, then tie in a bow.

Houppelande

This large chequered garment is made in easy instalments, the main part being made up of five separate panels of 24 sts each, which are then sewn together, with gaps for the armholes in the joins, see diagram 4. This arrangement simplifies the complex business of either carrying the yarn from one block to the next, or weaving in on the back of the work over 120 sts, or of having separate lengths of yarn for each block to pick up and tie on. However, if you decide to knit a plain fabric rather than a chequered one, you *can* make the piece all in one with slits in the sides for the armholes at the appropriate places. Measurements for this option are given in diagram 4. The panels are joined together at the top before casting off so that the shoulder and collar piece can continue without a join. The sleeves begin with a border of 'dagging', a fashionable decoration of finger-like projections used on the edges of garments at this time. This border is knitted sideways as a separate piece, stitches are then picked up from the straight edge of this, and the sleeve knitted on towards the top. The sleeves are gathered into the armholes for extra fullness.
The tops of the bodice sections at back and front are gathered into tight pleats, as was the fashion. The two front edges have an extra border knitted on as a finishing touch and the garment is kept fastened by

the belt only. The very high collar is a feature of this type of garment, often reaching beyond the ears.

Back and side panels, work all five exactly the same. To make each panel, use the main colour and size 3¼mm needles to cast on 24 sts.

Row 1: k12, join in contrast, k12, leaving main colour hanging on WS and twisting the 2 colours tog at back.

Row 2: k1, p11 in contrast, p11, k1 in main colour. Keeping the 2 colours separate in this way, cont in ss for 13 more rows.

Row 16: k1, p11 in contrast, at change over carry this colour along to the end of the row by weaving in on WS.

Next row: with contrast, begin a new block of 16 rows, carrying main colour along the back to the centre.

Work 6 blocks of colours in this way, 96 rows in all, and leave the sts on a spare needle while the other panels are being made.

a. Sew up the 5 panels as shown in diagram 4, leaving spaces for the armholes at the top of each side panel. This is done while the sts are still on the needle, taking the stitching as far as the last row.

b. Now k2 tog across all sts on needle, including the armhole gaps which will now be closed. 60 sts. Change to size 2¾mm needles and work in single rib for 3 rows for the collar.
   Next row: k2 tog across all sts. 30 sts. Work in single rib for 8 more rows, then cast off in rib.

Sleeves

Begin with the dagged edge as folls: with main colour and size 2¼mm needles, cast on 10 sts and k 4 rows.

Row 5: cast off 5 sts, k to end.

Row 6: k5.

Row 7: cast on 5 sts and k to end.

Rows 8, 9 and 10: k10.

Rep these last 5 rows until 5 'fingers' have been made, then change to contrast colour and rep patt for 5 more fingers.

Make 8 sets of 5 fingers each, then cast off and make another length in the same way. When slightly stretched, each piece will measure about 46cm (18in). These are the wide edges of the sleeves.

To make the upper section, place one border of dagging, RS uppermost, and with size 2¾mm needles pick up 96 sts from the straight edge, that is 12 sts from each set of 5 fingers.

Note: one sleeve begins with the main colour and changes to the contrast half-way up; the other sleeve has a band of the contrast in the centre, but any permutation of colours is acceptable.

Row 1: p96.

Row 2: cast off 8 sts, k to end.

Row 3: cast off 8 sts, p to end.

Rows 4 and 5: keep to ss and cast off 5 sts at beg of rows.

Rows 6 and 7: cast off 3 sts at beg of rows. 64 sts.

Row 8: k2 tog, k to last 2 sts, k2 tog.

Row 9: p62.

Row 10: cut first colour and join in second, weaving ends in on back, k2 tog, k to last 2 sts, k2 tog.

Row 11: p60.

Cont to dec one st at each end of every knit row until 48 sts rem, then purl one more row and cast off.

a. With RS tog, fold piece across centre with pointed ends tog at lower edge,

b. Pin curved side edges tog and sew from cast on edge down to half-way across last fingers of dagging at other end.

c. Fold to RS and squeeze lower pointed edges tog, taking 2 sts at intervals, as shown in diagram 4, through both layers to keep the fabric together.

d. Run a gathering thread along the top half of each sleeve-head and draw up gently to fit the armhole.

e. Fit the sleeve into the armhole, pin in position, then sew from the WS.

f. Front edges: with size 2¾mm needles and RS of main piece facing, use the main colour to pick up 12 sts from the front side edge of each square and 10 sts from the top, shoulder and neck section. 82 sts. Knit 3 rows, cut main colour and join in contrast. Knit one more row, then cast off loosely to ensure an evenly tensioned edge. Work the other edge in the same way.

g. Now gather the back and front bodice; using a continuous length of yarn in the main colour, make 4 rows of gathering sts, evenly spaced, across the *inside* of the back bodice from one armhole to the other. Make the first row along the top edge of the first colour blocks, the fourth row on the colour change at the bottom of the first blocks and the second and third rows evenly spaced between these. This confines the gathers to the top 16 rows only and the threads should be pulled firmly and secured before moving down to make the next row. On the RS, ease the gathers into straight lines, then work the 2 front sections in the same way. Do not include the edgings in the gathers.

Chaperone

This consists of 3 separate pieces, the roundel shaped like a doughnut with a crown in the centre, and a gorget and liripipe piled up on top and allowed to hang down, see diagram 4. Oddments left over from the larger garments can be used for this, or a completely different colour may be used, particularly black.

With main colour and size 2¾mm needles, cast on 18 sts and work in ss until the piece measures 19cm (7½in) × 6cm (2¼in). Either make it in stripes, about 6 rows each, or plain.

a. Fold this piece across its width with RS tog and sew the cast on and cast off edges tog to form a tube.

b. Turn to RS. Enclose a strip of padding inside the tube and fold the long edge over to meet the other

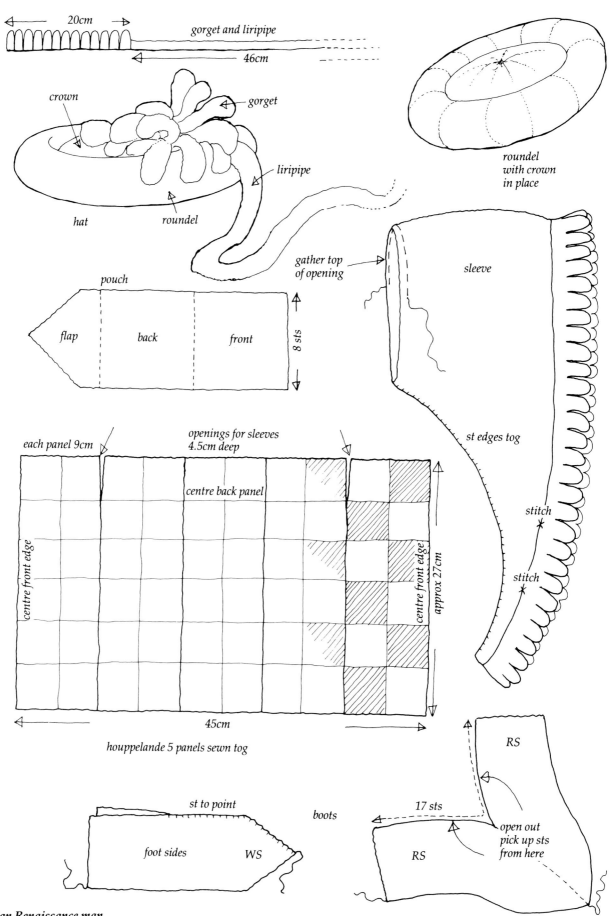

20cm

gorget and liripipe

46cm

crown

gorget

liripipe

hat

roundel

roundel
with crown
in place

gather top
of opening

sleeve

pouch

flap

back

front

8 sts

st edges tog

each panel 9cm

openings for sleeves
4.5cm deep

centre back panel

stitch

centre front edge

centre front edge

approx 27cm

stitch

45cm

houppelande 5 panels sewn tog

st to point

boots

RS

foot sides

WS

17 sts

open out
pick up sts
from here

RS

Italian Renaissance man
Diagram 4

long edge, forming a doughnut shape. Pin the edges.

c. Sew edges tog all round from RS. This forms the roundel.

To make the crown, cast on 28 sts and work 6 rows in single rib.

Row 7: (k2 tog) 14 times.

Row 8: (p2 tog) 7 times.

Gather the last sts on to a wool needle and draw up.

d. Sew the 2 side edges tog to form a flat disc, pulling the edges gently out.

e. Place this disc in the centre of the roundel and match the 2 joins. Sew in place, stitching on the seam of the roundel.

f. Sew the 'brim' of the roundel back into position, so that the cap is near the top. To make the gorget and liripipe in a continuous piece, cast on 10 sts and work the dagged edge patt as for the sleeve borders, see page 47, for 20.5cm (8in). Use any colours for this, changing over as before.

Now dec to 6 sts and cont in g st without shaping for about 46cm (18in) in bands of the same colours. Cast off and darn all ends in neatly.

g. To complete the gorget, run a gathering thread along the straight edge of the dagged border for 20.5cm (8in). Join the end to the beginning, leaving the rest free, and draw up tightly, pulling the dagging into a disorganized heap! Take a few sts into the under-side of this to hold the gathers tog.

h. Arrange the dagging heap slightly to one side of the roundel, check that the join of this is at the back, and pin in place, allowing the liripipe to drape over one edge. References place this at either side of the head, but more commonly on the left.

i. Sew the dagged gorget firmly on to the roundel. The liripipe can now be folded over lengthways and sewn up from the brim of the hat down to its point. Flatten this out, then drape across the front of the body and over the opposite shoulder.

Belt

This can be made in any way you choose, either by plaited cords, flat braid or a narrow strip of real or artificial leather. It should sit fairly low down on the waist or hips and a tiny metal buckle can be used as a fastening.

Pouch

This hangs from the belt and can be made in one piece. With brown yarn and size 2¼mm needles, cast on 8 sts and work in ss with a selvedge of one k st at both sides of every row. Work straight for 26 rows.

Row 27: k2 tog, k4, k2 tog.

Row 28: k1, p4, k1.

Row 29: k2 tog, k2, k2 tog.

Row 30: k1, p2, k1, then cast off.

a. Fold up as shown in diagram 4 and sew the side edges.

b. Make a cord 10cm (4in) long and fold this underneath the flap with the 2 ends attached to the belt. Sew on a bead to keep the flap in place.

Boots

With brown yarn and size 2¼mm needles, cast on 2 sts.

Rows 1, 2 and 3: k2.

Row 4: inc into both sts.

Rows 5, 6 and 7: k4.

Row 8: inc into first and last sts.

Cont in g st for 26 more rows without shaping, then cast off.

Make three more pieces in the same way.

Make the soles, (2), on 4 sts. Work 20 rows in ss.

Row 21: k1, k2 tog, k1.

Rows 22 and 24: k1, p1, k1.

Row 23: k3.

Row 25: k1, k2 tog, pass first st over the k2 tog. Fasten off.

a. As shown in diagram 4, place two upper sections tog and sew from toe half-way along the top edges. Turn to RS and pick up 17 sts from the top edge as shown.

Knit 6 rows then cast off.

b. From the WS, sew up the back heel seams.

c. Darn in the cast off tail of the soles, and use the other tails to sew the soles to the base of the boots with the points at the toe ends. Place a tiny piece of padding inside the heels to fill out the shape.

King Henry VIII of England

Born in 1491 as the second son of the first Tudor king, Henry's larger than life reputation was no doubt partly due to a reaction against his father's extreme stringency, as much as to his own natural ebullience. His marriage to his elder brother's widow, Katherine of Aragon, set the scene for a story of domestic and political intrigue unsurpassed in the history of kings. Unfortunately, his notoriety as the discontented husband of six queens has tended to overwhelm his academic reputation, his ability as a musician and his love of learned discussion, particularly on theology.

He was an exceptionally tall and well-proportioned man, even by our standards, and was renowned for his good looks and athleticism. Indeed, it was his love of jousting which lead to injuries and consequent complications at a time when no treatment was available, this being the cause of his poor health in later years. His death in 1547 no doubt drew a huge sigh of relief from his last wife, Catherine Parr, who was in danger, at one point, of meeting a similar end to previous wives. However, it also sadly paved the way

This shows the sleeves of the overgown puffed out with extra padding and placed just above the top-most jewels of the under-sleeves.

The white and silver tunic is 'smocked' across the front bodice and sleeves, giving the appearance of slashes through which the undershirt appears. The separate skirt is tied on at the waist.

for even more bloodshed during the brief and unsettled reign of the Boy King, Edward VI. Edward's half-sister, the embittered and fanatical Queen Mary I, died in 1558 bringing even greater relief to her subjects than her father's death had done, particularly to Protestants, but even more to her half-sister and successor, Elizabeth.

The model shown here was based, rather loosely, on the portrait after Holbein, in the Walker Art Gallery, Liverpool, England, showing Henry in middle age, while still a fine athletic figure. Men's costume during Henry's reign was designed to draw attention to the wearer's masculinity, hence the exaggerated wide shoulders and chest, the prominently decorated codpiece and the bold stance, with feet wide apart. Clinging hose and short garments revealed strong legs to advantage, and many jewels on richly-patterned fabrics emphasized the puffs of white shirt fabric peeping through the slashed tunic. The sleeves on this model have been adapted somewhat, as they are seen in the portrait as long and hanging, with flaps of braided decoration and a slit towards the top through which the arm emerges, not through the usual opening at the cuff.

Many portraits of Henry can be seen, most of them by unknown artists, offering an interesting array of possibilities to knitters, some quite simple and others relatively complicated.

Materials

Extra padding: 25gm (1oz) white 4 ply. Padding, for measurements, see instructions.

Beard and hair: oddment of speckled chestnut-brown 4 ply. Padding.

Tunic: 50gm (2oz) white or cream 4 ply. 25gm (1oz) silver 4 ply. Oddment of gold 4 ply. 26 red beads and red sewing cotton.

Shoes and hose: 50gm (2oz) white or cream 4 ply. Short lengths gold and black 4 ply for garter. Padding. Oddment of silver 4 ply. Small pieces of stiff card for soles of shoes. Glue.

Robe: 50gm (2oz) red or russet 4 ply. Oddment of gold 4 ply, as for tunic. 25gm (1oz) brown 4 ply for fur border. Padding.

Hat: oddment of black 4 ply. 60 small pearls or silver beads, and 12 larger gold beads. Sewing thread to match. Strips of fur-fabric trimming, about 30cm (12in). Glue.

Chain: gold 4 ply. About 10 each of red, and either silver, pearl or blue beads. Sewing thread to match.

Needles: sizes 2, 2¼ and 2¾mm.

Note: make the ears as given on page 13.

Extra body padding

In this one exception, because of Henry's imposing dimensions, the body is given an extra layer of padding, rather like a long-sleeved vest. So that the basic figure can be re-dressed at a later date, this extra bulk can be removed just as easily as his other clothes. The top of it can just be seen at the neck of the tunic. With white yarn and size 2¼mm needles, cast on 30 sts.

Row 1: k30.
Row 2: k3, p24, k3.
Rep these 2 rows until 50 rows in all have been made.
Rows 51 and 52: cast on 15 sts at beg of each row for the arms, keeping the selvedge of 3 k sts at each end. Now work 12 more rows on these 60 sts.
Row 65: k24, cast off 12 for neck, k24 and work on the 2 sides separately.
Row 66: k3, p21.
Row 67: k24.
Row 68: as row 66.
Cut yarn and rejoin to next set of sts and complete this side in the same way.
Row 69: k24, cast on 12, k24.
Work 11 more rows on these 60 sts.
Cast off 15 sts at beg of next 2 rows, then cont on rem 30 sts for 50 more rows, keeping selvedge of 3 k sts at each end. Cast off.

a. Fold this piece with RS tog and sew side seams all the way round to the sleeve cuffs. Turn to RS and slide on to body, feet first, into neck opening and pull upwards.

b. Cut a piece of padding measuring 30 × 8cm (12 × 3in). Fold this in half and cut a neck opening in the fold. Fit this over the top of the head, (i.e., on top of the knitted vest), and push the padding down the front and back neck openings to lie flat over the shoulders.

Tuck the neckline inside neatly.

c. Begin at *centre back* on lower edge of vest, run a gathering st all round. Take the thread between the legs to the front and catch the front centre edge, pull gently to close the vest at the base to fit snugly round the legs. Fasten off securely, see diagram 5.

d. To close up the neckline, run another gathering thread round the neck opening, beginning and ending at the centre back. Pull up tightly and secure thread.

e. For shoulder padding, cut 2 pieces measuring 5 × 3cm (2 × 1¼in). Hold the figure firmly between your knees, open up the elbow end of the sleeve and use a thick knitting needle to insert one piece of padding up to the top of the shoulder. This should make a nicely rounded 'baseball player' shape at the top of the arm, but this should *not* stand higher than the neckline. Smooth the padding free from wrinkles and do the same at the other side. It is not necessary to sew the edges of the sleeves to the arms.

Beard and moustache

With hair-coloured yarn, and size 2mm needles, cast on 4 sts and k 6 rows.
Row 7: k2 tog, k2.
Rows 8, 9 and 10: k3.
Row 11: k2 tog, k1.
On the rem 2 sts, k 23 more rows then cast off.
Make another piece in the same way.

a. Sew these 2 pieces to the face as shown in diagram 5, and then embroider drooping moustaches to connect with the beard.

Hair

With the same needles and yarn, cast on 12 sts and k 28 rows.
Row 29: k2 tog, k8, k2 tog.
Row 30: k10.
Row 31: k2 tog, k6, k2 tog.
Cast off.

a. Sew this piece to the back of the head as shown in diagram 5, joining the side edges above and below the ears and along the curved top edge. The ears are left exposed and the lower edge of the hair should be left open, so that padding can be inserted to round out the back of the head.

Hose and shoes

The shoes are made in one piece with the waist-length stockings. Each leg is made separately as far as the waist and has padding inserted from the top of the leg to the calf. Begin at the toe as folls:
Right leg: **with cream yarn and size 2¼mm needles, cast on 11 sts and work in ms for 7 rows.

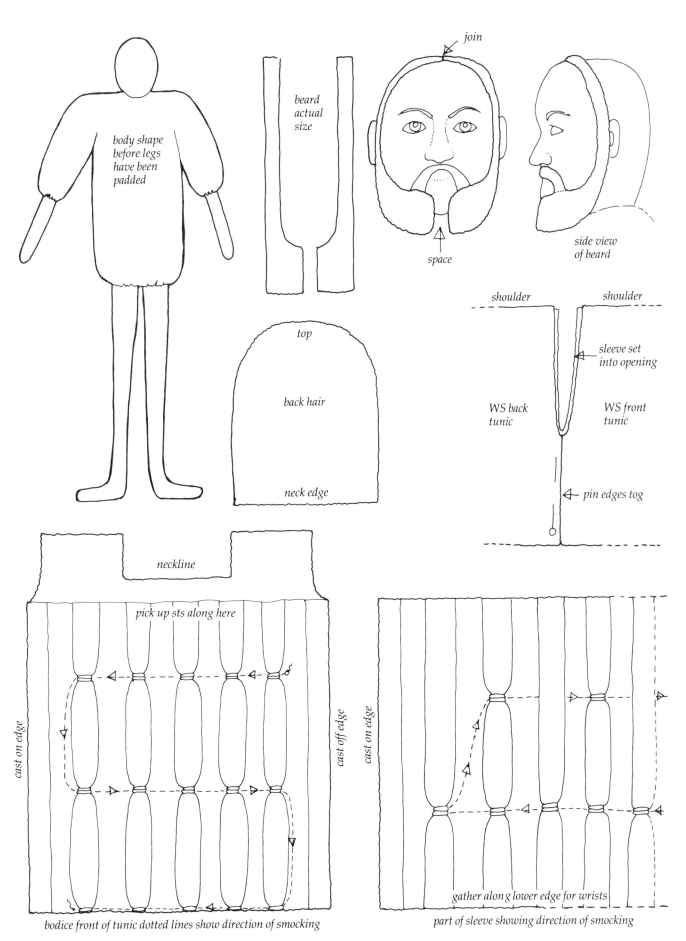

body shape
before legs
have been
padded

beard
actual
size

join

space

side view
of beard

top

back hair

neck edge

shoulder   shoulder

sleeve set
into opening

WS back   WS front
tunic   tunic

pin edges tog

neckline

pick up sts along here

cast on edge

cast off edge

cast on edge

gather along lower edge for wrists

bodice front of tunic dotted lines show direction of smocking

part of sleeve showing direction of smocking

Henry VIII
Diagram 5

Row 8: (k1, p1) twice, k2 tog, (k1, p1) twice, k1.
Row 9: (k1, p1) twice, k2 tog, (p1, k1) twice.
Cont in ms on the rem 9 sts for 5 more rows
Row 15: (k1, p1) twice, cast off the next st then cont in ms to end of row.
Next row: (k1, p1) twice, turn, and work 10 more rows in ms on these 4 sts only.
Cast off and complete the rem 4 sts in the same way.
Pick up 17 sts round the ankle of the shoe, see diagram 6, having 8 sts down each side and one in the centre.
Row 1: (WS) k17.
Row 2: knit.
Row 3: purl.
Rep rows 2 and 3 four more times.
Row 12: inc in first st, k to last 2 sts, inc, k1.
Work straight for 3 more rows.
Rep the last 4 rows once more, then row 12 again. 23 sts.
Now work straight for 13 more rows.**
Row 34: (WS) (k2 tog, k5) 3 times, k2 tog.
Rows 35 and 36: k19.
Row 37: (k3, inc in next st) 4 times, k3.
Row 38: p23.
Row 39: as row 12.
Work straight for 3 more rows
Rep the last 4 rows 5 more times. 35 sts.
Row 63: Cast off 4 sts, k to end of row.
Row 64: cast off 4 sts, p to end of row.
Row 65: as row 12.
Work straight for 3 more rows.
Rep last 4 rows twice more, then row 12 again. 35 sts.
Work straight for 7 more rows.
Next row: (yfwd, k2 tog) 17 times, k1.
Next row: p35.
Cast off.
Left leg: work from ** to ** as given for right leg. 23 sts.
Row 34: (WS) (p2 tog, p5) 3 times, p2 tog, cut cream yarn.
Row 35: join in gold yarn and k19.
Row 36: k19.
Row 37: join in black yarn and knit, weaving gold along back to other end, cut black yarn.
Row 38: pick up gold and p to end of row.
Row 39: p, cut gold yarn.
Row 40: join in cream yarn, (p3, inc in next st) 4 times, p3. 23 sts.
Row 41: as row 12.
Row 42: p25.
Row 43: as row 12. 27 sts.
Work straight for 3 more rows.
Rep last 4 rows four more times. 35 sts.
Now cont from row 63 as given for right leg.

a. With WS tog, use one of the tails and a flat seam to stitch the heels of the shoes, matching the g st at the top of each one. Cont for about 2cm (1in) up the back of the leg and leave the rest open and the thread hanging.

b. Slip the half-garment over the foot and round the leg. Pull the top of the leg together and pin. Using matching thread, stitch the garters tog round the leg at the knee.
   Note: white garter on R leg, black one on L leg.

c. In the opening left between the garter and the ankle, insert a flat piece of padding at the *back* of the leg, to fill out the calf. Push into place, then cont the flat seam up the leg as far as the garter.

d. Run a gathering st, using matching yarn, round the centre of each garter all round the knee, and pull tightly. Secure thread, taking care not to stitch into legs.

e. Sew up rest of hose to top of leg using the flat seam from the RS. Work as far as this on both legs before closing the body seam.

f. Cut 2 strips of padding measuring about 25 × 5cm (9¾ × 2in), one for each leg. Pull the top part of each hose down as far as the garter, and gently wrap each strip of padding round the upper leg only. Carefully replace the hose, easing the padding into place with a knitting needle. Swing the seam to the inside of the leg.

g. From the RS, sew up using a flat seam, between the legs, then the centre back seam, then the centre front seam.

h. Make a white cord and thread this through the holes at the top.
   Leave open for the moment.

i. To complete the shoes, cut 2 pieces of stiff white card for the soles, using the shape in diagram 6 as a template.
   With cream yarn and size 2mm needles, cast on 8 sts and work 10 rows in ss, beg and end every row with a k st.
   Row 11: k3, k2 tog, k3.
   Work 3 more rows straight.
   Row 15: k3, k2 tog, k2.
   Row 16: k1, p4, k1.
   Row 17: k2, k2 tog, k2.
   Row 18: k1, p3, k1.
   Row 19: k2 tog, k1, k2 tog.
   Row 20: k1, p1, k1.
   Row 21: k3.
   Cast off and work another piece in the same way.

j. Darn ends in on WS of sole. Cover one side of card sole with glue and place WS of knitted piece on to this, matching squared toes, and press in position allowing a tiny edge of knitting to extend beyond the card shape.

k. With card on *inside* nearest the foot, pin the sole in place then sew all round from RS.

Codpiece

With cream yarn and size 2¼mm needles, first make the two side pieces. Cast on 9 sts and work 2 rows in ms.
Row 3: k2 tog, (k1, p1) twice, k1, k2 tog.

Row 4: (p1, k1) 3 times, p1.
Row 5: k2 tog, p1, k1, p1, k2 tog.
Row 6: p2 tog, k1, p2 tog.
Cast off rem 3 sts and darn this end in.
Make another piece in the same way.
For the centre strip, use cream yarn to cast on 15 sts and work 1 row in ms. Join in silver yarn and work in ms for 2 rows. Cut silver and work one more row in cream.
Cast off in patt.

a. Sew the curved edges of the 2 side pieces to each edge of the centre strip as shown, using the tail ends. Pad very slightly to keep the shape.

b. Pin the complete codpiece exactly over the centre front seam of the hose about 1cm (½in) from the top edge and sew all round from the RS. Normally, this would have been attached to the hose at the base only, and tied at the top round the waist. Leave the draw-string at the waist untied as you sew and, after re-tying, tuck the ends of the cord back into the hose out of sight.

Tunic

Front bodice, see diagram 5, beginning at side edge.
**With white or cream yarn and size 2¼mm needles, cast on 24 sts and work 2 rows in ss.

Now join in silver yarn and k 6 rows g st, twisting the yarns tog at beg of rows 3 and 5 to carry the loose one up along the edge to row 9.
Rows 9 to 14: with cream yarn, work in ss.
Cont to alternate 6 rows of g st in silver with 6 rows of ss in cream, until 6 bands of each have been worked in all. Work one more k row in cream, then cast off p-wise.**
Work the neckline as folls: with silver yarn and RS facing, pick up 36 sts along one side edge, with the bands running vertically, spacing the sts thus; one st on first cream band, 3 sts on all other bands and 2 sts on last band.
Next row: (WS facing) (k2 tog) 18 times, noting that you may find it easier to do this through the backs of the sts, rather than the fronts.
Next 2 rows: k18.
Next row: k6, cast off 6, k6.
Now work on these 2 sets of sts separately for 5 more g st rows, then cast off.
Back bodice. This piece is not smocked like the front. With cream yarn, cast on 24 sts and work 2 rows in ss.
Row 3: join in silver yarn and knit.
Rows 4, 5 and 6: knit.
Row 7: pick up cream and knit.
Row 8: cream, purl.

The tunic is worked in white (or cream) and silver yarns, and is finished with red beads.

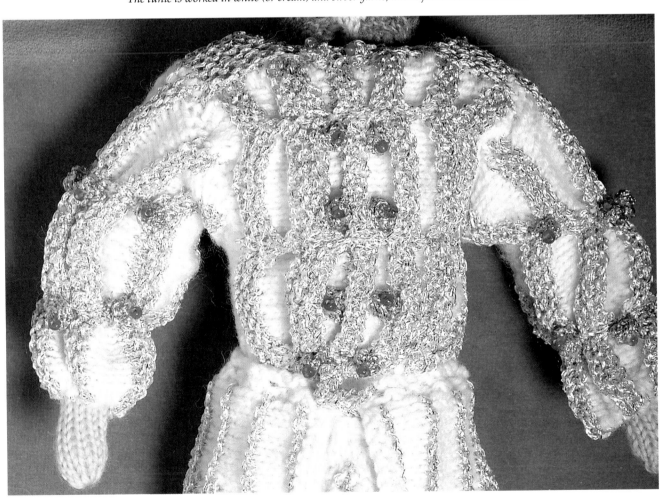

Now cont to alternate 4 rows in silver g st with 2 rows in cream ss, until 6 silver bands have been completed. Work 2 more rows in cream then cast off.

For the neck edge; with RS facing, and silver yarn, pick up 26 sts from one side edge of this piece.

Next row: (k2 tog, k2) 6 times, k2 tog.

Next 2 rows: k19.

Next row: k6, cast off 7, k6.

Work on these 2 sets of sts separately for 5 more g st rows, then cast off.

Sleeves

Work from ** to ** as given for the tunic front bodice. Make two the same.

a. Smock the front bodice as shown in diagram 5 to bring the silver panels together over the top of the cream ones. Thread a wool needle with silver yarn and catch the edges of the panels together, 3 cream sts down from the top edge. Do this also at the lower edge and at a point midway between the two. Fasten off very securely. The dotted line shows how the sts are linked to each other. The cream side panels are left free to be attached to the back bodice.

b. Smock the sleeves in the same way, using the diagram to show where the sts are to be placed. Gather the lower edges of the sleeves with the cast on tails, but do not sew the sides together at this point.

c. Place RS of both bodice pieces tog and pin at lower side edges with one pin, as shown in the diagram. Leave the rest open.

d. With WS tog, fold sleeves in half, open out bodice pieces above pin and align edges of sleeves with bodice side edges, see diagram 5. Pin in position with sleeves open along top edges.

e. Sew the sleeves and bodice tog from one side of shoulder round to the other side. Then sew the lower bodice side seams. Complete the other sleeve in the same way.

f. Turn the garment inside out with the sleeves extended on each side. Pin the top sleeve edges tog and sew from cuffs as far as end of sleeve. *Do not sew up the shoulders.*

g. Front border decoration. The gold and ruby jewels on the tunic bodice may be real ones, perhaps reclaimed from old jewellery, or made from yarn and beads as folls: with size 2mm needles and gold yarn, cast on 3 sts leaving a tail of about 10cm (4in). Knit 3 rows.

Row 4: k2 tog, k1 and pass first st over the other to cast off.

Leave another tail of the same length.

Tie the 2 tails tog, pulling firmly to draw the 2 pointed ends tog, and complete with a knot. This makes a tiny button shape. Now sew a red glass bead on to this button and press it down into the centre.

Leave the tails of yarn for attaching to the tunic. Make 26 of these jewels.

h. Using the tails of yarn, sew the jewels on to the tunic, as shown, eight on each sleeve and ten in pairs down the centre front. More can be added if you wish, but as the upper sleeves are covered by the gown, some may be hidden.

Tunic skirt

This is made in one piece and is open down the front. With cream yarn and size 2¾mm needles, cast on 26 sts and work from side edge to side edge. Knit 1 row.

Rows 2 and 3: join in silver and knit.

Row 4: twist cream and silver yarns at beg of row, k18 and turn.

Row 5: k18 back to beg of row.

Row 6: leave silver yarn hanging, pick up cream and knit to end of row.

Row 7: k1, p24, k1.

Rows 8 and 9: cont in ss with cream, twisting yarns tog at beg of row.

Rows 10, 11, 12 and 13: with silver, rep rows 2, 3, 4 and 5.

Rows 14, 15, 16 and 17: with cream, rep rows 6, 7, 8 and 9.

Cont to rep these 8 rows until 6 silver bands have been completed.

Row 46: k26 in cream.

Row 47: k1, p24, k1.

Row 48: twist the 2 yarns as before, k18, turn.

Row 49: p17, k1.

Rows 50, 51, 52 and 53: in silver, as before.

Cont in this way until 12 silver bands have been completed.

Now work another cream band, as rows 46 to 49, and then work as rows 2 to 9 for 6 more silver bands. 18 altogether.

Cut the silver yarn and k 2 rows in cream.

Cast off but do not cut yarn. Leave the last loop open. To complete the waistband: with RS facing, pick up 52 sts, using last hoop as first st, as folls: 2 sts from first edge: 3 sts from each of the next 6 white panels, (ignore the silver bands): 2 sts from each of the next 6 panels: 3 sts from the next 6 panels, and 2 sts from the last edge.

Row 1: (WS) knit.

Row 2: k1, (yfwd, k2 tog) 25 times, k1.

Cast off.

Make a cord from silver yarn and thread this through the holes. Fit the tunic bodice over the figure, feet first through the neck opening, and pull upwards. Make 2 sts at each side of the neck opening to close, or make a loop and button if the garments are to be removed. Fit the skirt round the waist, (it may need a gentle pressing), tucking the bodice inside. Tie with a bow at the front and arrange the edges of the skirt to fall on either side of the codpiece, see the illustration for the front of the figure.

Henry's gown is made in five separate pieces, with a fur-edged collar and gold borders along the sleeves and gown edge. His hat is a simple affair, pulled down on one side, with the edge trimmed with a feather.

Fur-edged gown

This is made in five pieces, plus two extra pieces in brown for the edgings and collar. The back and side sections are simple rectangles, the two sleeves are shaped and padded. A simple gold border decorates the gown and sleeves.

Main back section. With red yarn and size 2¾mm needles, cast on 60 sts and k 3 rows.

Row 4: join in gold yarn and knit to end of row.

Row 5: k60.

Row 6: (k1 red, 1 gold) 30 times.

Row 7: (p1 red, 1 gold) 30 times.

Rep rows 6 and 7 twice more.

Rows 12 and 13: with gold, k60.

Row 14: cut gold, with red, k60.

Row 15: p60.

Work in ss for 58 more rows.

Row 74: (k2 tog) 30 times.

Row 75: (k2, p2) 14 times, k2.

Row 76: (p2, k2) 14 times, p2.

Rep last 2 rows three more times, then cast off in rib.

Side sections. Both sides are alike. With red yarn, cast on 30 sts and k 3 rows.

Row 4: join in gold yarn and knit to end of row.

Row 5: k30.
Row 6: (k1 red, 1 gold) 15 times.
Row 7: (p1 red, 1 gold) 15 times.
Rep rows 6 and 7 twice more.
Rows 12 and 13: with gold, k30.
Row 14: cut gold, with red k30.
Row 15: p30.
Work in ss for 58 more rows.
Row 74: (k2 tog) 15 times.
Row 75: (k2, p2) 3 times, k2, p1.
Row 76: k1, p2, (k2, p2) 3 times.
Rep the last 2 rows three more times, then cast off in rib.

a. With RS tog, pin pieces tog at side edges and place marker pins 12cm (4¾in) from bottom edge, to mark beg of armholes. Sew up as far as these markers.

Fur borders and collar

With brown yarn and RS facing, begin at lower edge of RHS robe front and pick up 55 sts, see diagram 6.
Row 1: (WS) cast on 10 sts for collar and k65.
Work in ms for 6 rows.
Row 8: cast off 40 sts in patt, then ms to end of row.
Row 9: ms to last 2 sts, p2 tog.
Row 10: cast off 3 sts in patt, ms to end of row.
Row 11: as row 9, but k2 tog.
Row 12: as row 10.
Row 13: as row 9, but k2 tog. 16 sts.
Rows 14 to 19: work straight in ms.
Row 20: p2 tog, ms to last 2 sts, inc, p1.
Row 21: ms.
Row 22: k2 tog, ms to last 2 sts, inc, k1.
Row 23: ms.
Row 24: cast off 4 sts in patt, ms to end of row.
Cast of rem sts and darn ends in.
LHS border and collar. With brown yarn, cast on 10 sts, then, on same needle and with RS facing, begin at top edge of LHS robe front and pick up 55 sts.
Row 1: (WS) k65.
Work in ms for 5 rows.
Row 7: cast off 40 sts in patt, then ms to end of row.
Row 8: ms to last 2 sts, p2 tog.
Row 9: cast off 3 sts in patt, then ms to end of row.
Row 10: as row 8.
Row 11: as row 9.
Row 12: as row 8.
Rows 13 to 18: work straight in ms.
Row 19: k2 tog, ms to last 2 sts, inc, p1.
Row 20: ms.
Row 21: p2 tog, ms to last 2 sts, inc, k1.
Row 22: ms.
Row 23: cast off 4 sts in patt, ms to end of row.
Cast off rem sts and darn ends in.

a. With RS tog, fold the sides over on to the back section and pin the shoulders. Working from the armhole edges, sew only half-way across the shoulders and then secure the yarn. Leave the rest open for the collar.

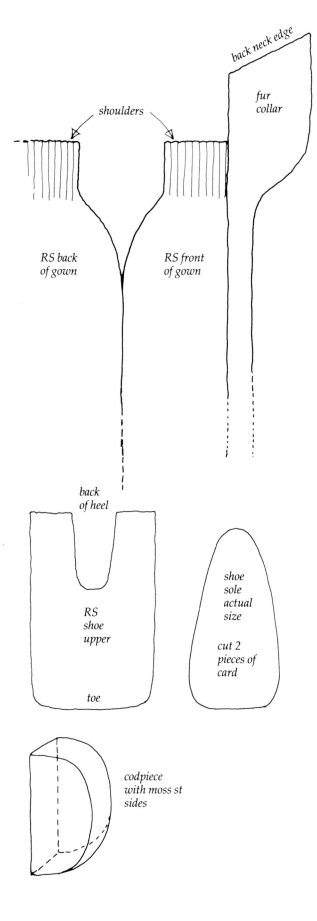

Henry VIII
Diagram 6

58

b. With RS tog, place the 2 back neck edges of the brown collar edge to edge, and pin. Sew these 2 pieces tog with a flat seam.

c. Place collar edge to the neck of the robe and pin in position across the opening from one side to the other to form a continuous collar. It does not really matter whether these are sewn together from the right or wrong sides, as the collar folds over and hides the seam from the outside. Use a flat seam.

Sleeves

Make 2 the same. With red yarn and size 2¾mm needles, cast on 6 sts.

Row 1: k6.
Row 2: k1, p4, k1.
Row 3: inc in first st, k5.
Row 4: k1, p5, k1.
Row 5: inc in first st, k6.
Row 6: k1, p6, k1.
Cont to inc in this way until there are 11 sts, then p one more row.
Row 13: leave red yarn hanging and join in gold, inc in first st, k to end.
Row 14: k12.
Row 15: with gold, inc in first st, k1 red, 1 gold to end of row, ending 1 red.
Row 16: (p1 gold, 1 red) 6 times, 1 gold.
Cont in this chequered patt for 4 more rows, whilst cont to inc one st at beg of every k row. 15 sts.
Rows 21 and 22: as rows 13 and 14, then cut gold yarn.
Row 23: with red, inc in first st, k to end.
Row 24: k1, p to last st, k1.
Rep rows 23 and 24 three more times. 20 sts.
Work straight for 4 more rows.
Now begin to dec by k2 tog at beg of every knit row until only 6 sts rem, as folls:
Rows 35 to 42: work in red only. 16 sts.
Rows 43 to 44: in gold, k both rows. 15 sts.
Rows 45 to 50: chequered patt as before. 12 sts.
Rows 51 to 52: as rows 43 and 44, cut gold yarn.
Rows 53 to 62: red only.
Work 2 more rows in ss without shaping then cast off rem 6 sts.

a. Pin the two sleeve pieces out flat and press gently.

b. With gold yarn, from RS of *curved edge* begin at extreme point and pick up sts as folls: 12 sts along lower red edge; 7 sts along chequered border edge; 14 sts along centre section as far as gold border; 7 sts along chequered border edge, and 12 sts along last red edge as far as point. 52 sts.
Knit 1 row then cut gold and join in brown.
Knit 2 brown rows then cast off.

c. The sleeve seams are only joined on the tiny brown edges. Pin, then sew. Place this seam on the underarm side seam of the gown. Pin the sleeves in place all round, then sew in place with the fullness at the top.

d. Turn to RS and place a small piece of padding inside each sleeve and fit the gown on to the figure with the padding at the *side* of the shoulder.

e. To tighten the lower edges on to the tunic, gather them with brown yarn and tie underneath out of sight. Puff the tops out evenly and arrange the sleeve edges to sit just above the higher set of jewels, see illustration of back of figure.

Hat

This is a very shallow style, with a turned up brim. Made in one piece, it has beads sewn on all round and a white feather lying round the edge to hang down slightly at one side, but this can be made from anything furry or feathery. Coarse chenille yarn will do perfectly.

With black yarn and size 2¼mm needles, cast on 60 sts and knit 3 rows.
Row 4: (k2 tog, k1) 20 times.
Rows 5 and 7: k40.
Row 6: p40.
Row 8: (p2 tog) 20 times.
Rows 9, 10, 11 and 12: work straight in ss.
Row 13: (k2 tog) 10 times.
Gather the rem sts on to a wool needle and draw up to form the crown of the hat.

a. Stitch the 2 edges tog from top of crown to edge of brim. Press the crown down a little to flatten it and ease the brim out to lie flat. Stiffen into shape if necessary, see page 138 for details.

b. Sew clusters of tiny pearl beads all round the under-side of the brim, see photograph, with one gold bead between each cluster.

c. Glue or sew a narrow strip of white nylon fur fabric, or alternative, all round the outer edge of the brim to hang down very slightly at one side.

d. Arrange the hat on the head at a slight angle and pin in place with black glass-headed pins, or sew, or glue.

Chain

To make the heavy gold chain which lies over the gown, use any gold yarn to produce a thick cord. Use several cords plaited or twisted tog, or crocheted, and sew this into a circle of the required size. Then sew at intervals of about 1cm (½in) beads of red, with either silver, pearl or blue ones between. You may have to use a few hidden sts at front, back and shoulders to keep the chain in place.

Queen Elizabeth I of England

As the daughter of Anne Boleyn and King Henry VIII, Elizabeth's chances of being in her father's good books were slim, although her brightness, intelligence and sheer determination to survive in the face of all odds enchanted others who knew her well and who came, in time, to worship her. Not surprisingly, the traumas of her dangerous childhood left deep scars and she refused to marry, although this was also partly to avoid the very complicated political and religious repercussions which would no doubt have followed a sharing of power. There were few, if any, eligible princes or kings who would not somehow make life difficult as the husband of the Queen of England, and having reached a comparitively secure position for the first time in her life, she naturally felt no great urgency to jeopardize it by making unnecessary decisions of a long-term nature.

Her learning and accomplishments are legendary; her wardrobe is even more so. Throughout her life she led fashion, introduced her favourite colours, dyed her hair red when the natural colour began to fade, in middle age wore mostly black, (which suited her), and in later years wore nothing but white and silver. There was, apparently, an unwritten agreement that her personal ladies-in-waiting should also wear white, and the effect must have been stunning. Favourite colour-combinations were russet reds, tawny browns, orange, peach, black, white, silver and gold with an abundance of jewels, metal-thread encrusted fabrics and liberal sprinklings of pearls, embroidery, lace, bows and braids on ruffs, handkerchiefs, scarves and fans. To a knitter, this is an invitation to improvise and have fun.

The clothes worn by this model are a compilation taken from various portraits, in an attempt to keep the pattern within the bounds of possibility for average-to-good knitters. But more complex styles could be tackled by use of card stiffening and glue, and perhaps wires too. Obviously, access to a bead shop, or a mail order supply, is a must for anyone who wishes to knit Elizabeth, but meanwhile, save tiny jewels and bits of fine lace, feathers and fur for trimmings, and, most important of all, do lots of research, drawings and notes.

She wears a very full-skirted gown over two full petticoats. These would normally have been held out by a farthingale, but our version relies solely on bulk and a hip-pad which is tied on to the figure over the hips. The gown is worked in a diaper pattern of gold, silver and cream or white yarn, but here the WS of the pattern is used as the RS, although this is entirely optional, see page 141. The fashionable long sleeves hang empty almost to hem level, the arm appearing through one of the openings towards the top.

The jewelled shoulder roll is seen just underneath the wide lace collar, or ruff. Pearls and other jewels adorn every surface; this can hardly be overdone though on a model as small as this it is important to comply with the rules of proportion and scale, see the illustration of the front of the figure.

Materials

Hair: 15gm (¾oz) orange/brown 4 ply. Padding.
Hair ornaments: oddments gold metallic 4 ply; an assortment of tiny jewels, pearls, beads and sequins, and a large drop pearl for the centre.
Hip-pad: oddment of white 4 ply. Padding.
Underskirt: 50gm (2oz) white 4 ply. Fine elastic.
Full petticoat: 50gm (2oz) white of cream 4 ply. Fine elastic.
Gown: 100gm (3½oz) white or cream 4 ply. 2 to 3 × 50gm (2oz) balls metallic gold of various tones, see pattern notes, or less if you choose to use only one tone. White coton à broder or crochet cotton. About 100 tiny pearls for the skirt edges, (these can be bought in continuous strips), and 6 more for the sleeves. For the waist, 44 tiny pearls and 1 large drop pearl. Padding for shoulders and sleeves. Extra decorations, see pattern notes on page 66.
Collar or ruff: white crochet cotton of 3 ply thickness.

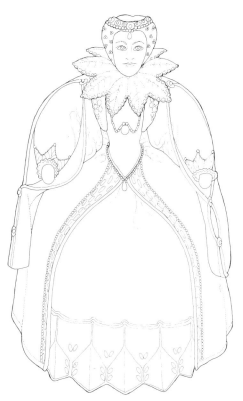

The drawing clearly shows the shoulder rolls which were part of every fashionable woman's dress at this time. The long hanging sleeves are merely decorative and often hung longer than this.

Stockings and shoes: oddments of gold metallic and white 4 ply.

Needles: sizes 2, 2¼, 2¾, 3 and 3¼mm.

Have some extra padding to hand.

Note: Embroider the face with eyes in mid-brown, finely arched eyebrows, high forehead and small pink mouth. No ears are required.

Hair

With orange/brown yarn and size 2¼mm needles, cast on 28 sts and work in single rib for 6 rows.

Row 7: inc in first st, k to last st, inc.

Row 8: purl.

Rep rows 7 and 8 until there are 38 sts.

Cont straight for 9 more rows.

Next row: (k2 tog) 19 times, gather last sts on to a wool needle and draw up tightly.

a. Fold this piece across noting that the p side is the RS, and place padding at each side of the centre. Sew up into a pointed sausage shape as shown in diagram 7. Pull the gathering thread and secure tightly.

b. Place the fold towards the front of the head, pull the points down towards the position of the ears, and pin in place.

c. Stitch the hair round the face.

d. Make a bun for the back of the head as folls: cast on 40 sts using the loose cast on method. Work in ss for 4 rows.

Row 5: (k2 tog, k2) 10 times.

Row 6: p30.

Row 7: k28, turn.

Row 8: p26, turn.

Row 9: k24, turn.

Row 10: p22, and cont to leave 2 extra sts at the end of every row until the last row reads p10, turn, then k to end of row.

Next row: p30.

Next row: (k2 tog) 15 times.

e. Gather the last 15 sts on to a wool needle and fasten off securely. Sew the 2 short edges tog to form a dome. Pad this slightly, then run a gathering thread through the cast on loops and draw up tightly. Form a flattened doughnut shape with the central dimple towards the top. Pin this in position at the back of the head as shown, then sew all round, see diagram 7. The hair ornaments are attached later.

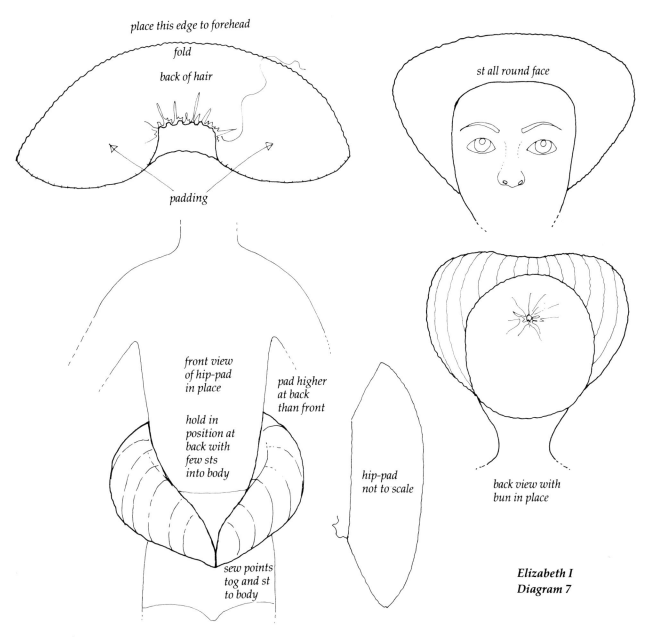

place this edge to forehead

fold

back of hair

padding

st all round face

front view
of hip-pad
in place

pad higher
at back
than front

hold in
position at
back with
few sts
into body

hip-pad
not to scale

back view with
bun in place

sew points
tog and st
to body

**Elizabeth I
Diagram 7**

Hip-pad

With white yarn and size 3mm needles, cast on 30 sts and work in ss for 2 rows.

Row 3: inc at each end of this and every row until there are 38 sts.

Now dec at each end of every row until 22 sts.

Last row: k2 tog, cast off to last 2 sts, k2 tog and fasten off.

a. Fold piece over lengthways with padding inside, see diagram 7, and sew up 2 edges.

b. Squeeze into shape and fit to body as shown.

Underskirt

With white yarn and size 2¾mm needles, cast on 133 sts and work border pattern No. 4 for 10 rows, see page 140 then cont in ss for 50 more rows. Work a line of picot holes, see page 138, then cast off and pin the piece out flat, pulling the bottom edge into points.

a. Press gently under a damp cloth.

b. Sew up the side edges and thread fine elastic or a cord through the holes at the waist.

c. This underskirt is fitted over the top of the hip-pad.

Full petticoat

This is the one which shows under the gown. Make 2 pieces in the same way.

With white or cream yarn and size 3¼mm needles, cast on 112 sts and work border pattern No. 2, see page 139, complete with the last 2 rows of rev ss.

Now work in ss for 40 more rows.

Row 41: (i.e., of ss part), (k2 tog) 56 times.

Rows 42, 44 and 46: purl.

Row 43: (k2 tog) 28 times.

Row 45: (yfwd, k2 tog) 14 times.

After row 46, cast off.

a. Sew one side seam. Pin the piece out flat, pulling the points into shape, and press gently.

63

b. Sew the second side seam.

c. Thread the elastic through the holes at the waist and tie.

d. Slip the petticoat on to the figure over the hip-pad, and adjust the gathers towards the sides and back, leaving the front as flat as possible.

Gown

This is made in four main sections; the skirt, the bodice, the under-sleeves and the outer hanging sleeves.

For the skirt in this version, the diaper pattern, see page 141, is used with the reverse side as the RS. The following instructions will ensure that this is how your skirt will look, but if you wish to use the other side of the fabric instead, you must knit with this in mind, and make sure that all ends are on the WS.

Gold in various tones is used as the contrasting colour on the skirt for the first 24 rows of the pattern, then silver for 4 rows, then pearly-white for 4 rows. After that, the pearly-white is continued as the contrast as far as the waist, which is 8 more complete repeats. this brings the total of pattern repeats to 12. Begin with the gold border, as folls: with gold yarn, (B), and size 3¼mm needles, cast on 125 sts and knit 3 rows. Cut gold, (because it will be at the wrong end), and join in white.

Next row: knit, weaving in loose ends on the side of the fabric you are using as the back.

Now begin the patt by joining in the gold again. This will be the WS. Work row 1, then go on to row 2, and so on.

At the end of the 96th row of patt, cut the contrast yarn and cont the decreases in white only, as folls:

Next row: (k2 tog) 62 times, k1.

Next row: p63.

Next row: (k2 tog) 31 times, k1.

Cast off p-wise.

For the front gold and white borders, use size 3mm needles, gold yarn and with the RS facing, begin at the hem edge and pick up 68 sts.

Row 1: knit.

Row 2: (RS) join in white yarn, *k3, yfwd, sl 3 p-wise, yb* to last 2 sts, k2.

Row 3: p2, *yb, sl 3 p-wise, yfwd, p3*, to end of row.

Rows 4 and 5: with gold yarn, k both rows.

Row 6: with white yarn, k6, *yfwd, sl 3 p-wise, yb, k3*, to last 2 sts, k2.

Row 7: p5, *yb, sl 3 p-wise, yfwd, p3*, to last 3 sts, p3. Cut white yarn, k 2 rows in gold, then cast off.

To work the other border, have the RS facing and pick up 68 sts beginning at the waist end. Continue as before.

a. Darn all ends in and press borders gently on the WS.

b. Sew about 50 pearls down each side edge, along the joins of each border.

c. With double yarn, run a gathering st through the cast off edge of the waistband and draw up very tightly.

d. Fit the skirt over the petticoat and adjust the gathers towards the back and sides. Stitch the top front edges tog and secure the gathering thread.

Bodice

With white yarn and size 2¼mm needles, cast on 3 sts.

Row 1: knit.

Row 2: purl.

Row 3: inc in first and third sts to make 5.

Row 4: k1, p3, k1.

Row 5: inc in first and last sts to make 7.

Row 6: k1, p5, k1.

Cont inc in this way until there are 13 sts.

Work one more p row.

Row 13: cast on 8 sts, k to end of row, working into back of 9th st.

Row 14: cast on 8 sts, p into back of 9th st, p to last st, k1.

Work in ss on these 29 sts for 8 more rows.

Row 23: k5, cast off 3, k13, cast off 3, k5.

Work on these 3 sets of sts separately as folls: on the first 5 sts work 11 rows, then with RS facing, inc one st on sleeve edge of next 3 k rows. P one more row. 8 sts. Cast off and cut yarn.

Join yarn to centre 13 sts and work 11 rows in ss.

Now inc one st at both ends on the next 3 k rows.

Cast off p-wise.

Work the last section in the same way as the first.

a. Fold with the RS tog and sew across the shoulders, leaving one third of the centre portion open for the neck.

b. Turn the bodice upside-down, (point at the top) and RS facing. From the RHS back edge, and using gold yarn, pick up 19 sts as far as the front point. Knit one row, then cast off but do not cut yarn.

c. With one st still left on needle, pick up the next st on one side of the gold edge just made, then 18 more from the other edge. 20 sts. Knit one row then cast off.

d. To make the centre back panel, use white yarn and size 3¼mm needles and cast on 6 sts. Work in g st for 10 rows.

Row 11: k2, k2 tog, k2.

Knit 15 more rows, then cut white yarn and join in gold.

Knit 1 row, then cast off. The last row is the bottom edge of the bodice.

e. Sew this piece, (from the WS) to one side edge of the back bodice, leaving the other side open until all other sections are completed.

Under-sleeves

With white yarn and size 3¼mm needles, cast on 36 sts.

Work 2 rows in single rib, then cont in ss for 16 more rows.
Row 19: (k2 tog, k10) 3 times.
Row 20: p33.
Row 21: (k2 tog, k9) 3 times.
Rows 22, 24, 26, 28 and 30: purl.
Row 23: (k2 tog, k8) 3 times.
Row 25: (k2 tog, k7) 3 times.
Row 27: (k2 tog, k6) 3 times.
Row 29: (k2 tog, k5) 3 times.
Row 31: (k2 tog, k1) 6 times.
Row 32: p12, cut white yarn.
Row 33: join in gold, inc in every st to make 24.
Row 34: work in single rib, then cast off in rib.
Make another sleeve in the same way.

a. With RS tog, fold the sleeves and sew the side edges tog. Turn to RS.
b. Run a gathering thread all round the top edges.
c. Turn the bodice inside out and set the sleeves into the armholes, then turn to RS. Match the under-arms with care.

Hanging sleeves

With white yarn and size 3mm needles, cast on 35 sts and work in ss for 2 rows.
Using one of the gold metallic yarns as a contrast, join this in on the next row and work 12 complete patt repeats as for the skirt, beg on row 1. 96 rows of pattern in all.
Cut white yarn and work (k2 tog, k1) 11 times, k2 tog, in gold.
Next row: p23.
Next row: k23.
Cast off but do not cut yarn.
With RS facing, keep the last st on the needle and pick up 53 more sts from the side edge. Knit 1 more row, then cast off.
Now pick up 54 sts from the other edge, beg at the top. Complete in the same way.

a. On the gold border, stitch the 2 bottom corners together.
b. Slide the hanging sleeve over the top of the under-sleeve to the shoulder. Adjust so that the join of the hanging sleeve lies just in front of the bodice shoulder seam and pin in position.
c. Sew all round on top of the sleeve and bodice seam. To make the cuffs, use fine white or cream crochet cotton and size 2mm needles to cast on 35 sts. Using border pattern No. 2, see page 139, work the first 6 rows then cast off.
d. Join the edges to form a tube and sew this with the point uppermost to the sleeve cuff above the gold edge. Gathering is done later.
e. Using double sewing cotton, sew tiny pearls to the three points, holding them to the sleeve as you do so. Make another cuff to match.

Elizabeth's gown is worked in a diaper pattern of gold, silver and cream (or white) yarns. Notice the long sleeves, which hang almost to the hem.

Shoulder rolls

Make 2 the same. With white yarn and size 2¼mm needles, cast on 30 sts.
Work 4 rows in double rib.
Row 5: k5, (yfwd, k2 tog) 10 times, k5.
Row 6: p30.
Rep rows 5 and 6 once more, then work 4 more rows in double rib. Cast off in rib.

a. Cut a tiny piece of padding about 6 × 1cm (2½ × ¼in), and fold this lengthways into the centre of the knitting. Fold this over with the ridge on the outside, and stitch the 2 long edges together.
b. Mark the centre of the roll with a pin and place this on the bodice shoulder seam. Pin in position and sew the roll on to the shoulder seams to cover the top edge of the hanging sleeve. The roll does not extend to the underarms.

c. Now close the edges of the hanging sleeves just below the inner sleeve cuff, leaving gaps between the closures. Close the edges again between this and the cuff. This will be decorated at a later stage.

d. Edge the lower part of the bodice with pearls to accentuate the point and use the large drop pearl in the centre.

e. Fit the completed bodice on to the figure and adjust the sleeves. Before closing the back bodice, place a little padding into each under-sleeve to fill them out.

f. Pin the back bodice, matching gold borders, and sew up. This should fit neatly on top of the gathered skirt without stitching.

g. Stitch the front point lightly in position on the skirt between the two borders.

h. Squeeze the shoulder rolls gently and ease them over towards the sleeves.

i. Run gathering threads round the cuffs and fix close to the wrists.

Extra decorations

Having attached pearls down the skirt borders and the base of the bodice, a combination of beads and sequins can be used to cover the sleeve fastenings, see the illustration of the front of the figure for details of this. Make one or more long necklaces reaching to the waist, using tiny assorted beads of pearl, gold and silver, and sew a drop pearl to the lowest point. More tiny beads and/or sequins can be added to the wrists, sleeves and bodice, but these have been omitted from this version so that the construction can more clearly be seen.

Hair ornament

With gold metallic yarn and size 2¾mm needles, cast on 40 sts.
Kit 2 rows then cast off.

a. Join the 2 ends to form a circlet and use this as the base on which to sew tiny jewels, beads and sequins. Finish off with a large drop pearl in the centre of the forehead.

b. Sew 2 pearls and 1 gold bead in triple clusters all over the hair, 9 sets at each side.

Shoes and stockings

Made all in one piece. With gold metallic yarn and size 2¾mm needles, cast on 24 sts.
Work in ss for 4 rows.
Row 5: k5, cast off 5, k4, cast off 5, k5.
Row 6: p5, cut yarn and rejoin to centre 4 sts, p4, turn and work 4 more rows in ss on these 4 sts.
Next row: cut yarn and join in white, then add 4 more rows to the centre 4 sts.
Next row: (RS) knit the centre 4 sts again, then the 5 sts rem on the LH needle, weaving the loose gold end in on the WS.
Next row: p across 9 white sts and then across 5 gold sts, pulling all 3 sections tog into one row of 14 sts.
Now cont in ss for 28 more rows for the stocking. Join in gold again and work 2 knit rows for the garter, then pick up white again and knit 2 more rows. Cast off.
Make another piece in the same way.

a. Join the back of the heel with gold yarn, then sew up tops of shoes from WS. You may find it more convenient to place the shoe over the foot and sew it in this position. Don't sew it to the foot though!

b. Turn to WS and sew back stocking seam.
Turn to RS and fit on to leg, then make the sole of the shoe on 4 sts and 17 rows of g st. Sew this piece to the base of the shoe, and place a tiny piece of padding into the heel end before closing up completely.

Collar or ruff

With white crochet cotton and size 2¾mm needles, cast on 133 sts loosely and knit 3 rows.
Now work 9 rows of border pattern No. 4, see page 140.
Next row: (WS) (k2 tog) 66 times, k1.
Next row: (k2 tog) 33 times, k1.
Gather the last row on to a wool needle and draw up.

a. Pin the piece out flat, pulling the points into shape, then press gently under a damp cloth.

b. Sew the 2 short side edges tog from the WS. Run a gathering thread along the top edge.

c. Fit the collar over the neck of the figure and draw up to fit the neck snugly without gaps.

d. Arrange the points symmetrically, then secure the thread.

Seventeenth century

Unlike the Spaniards, who went to America as conquerors, the English went as settlers, although the eastern coast of North America offered no easy path to comfort or riches. The religious, political and economic problems of the seventeenth century encouraged thousands to flee from England and Holland between the years 1620 and 1660, and these early arrivals became known as the Pilgrim Fathers. Conditions at home, particularly unemployment and religious persecution, made many people look with longing to a continent which could offer them fresh opportunities and freedom of conscience.

The Pilgrim Fathers started a great wave of emigration, but economic motives were also important to those who had become shareholders in these new colonies. The subsequent manipulations to have minor offenders transported to work on the new estates were nothing short of horrendous. Nevertheless, our two pioneering figures are full of hope and faith as they set sail from Bristol aboard the Mayflower, as part of the original settlement of thirty-five passengers from Leyden in Holland and sixty-six from London and Southampton, to found the settlement of Plymouth in Massachusetts. It is estimated that, by the end of the movement, no less than 60,000 people left England to become settlers in America.

Those whose prime motive for leaving their homeland was to find religious freedom were mostly Protestants, and so strong was their distaste for the outward trappings of finery worn by those in high society that they reverted to the plainest possible clothing, entirely devoid of all ornament. They became known as Puritans and extreme members wore only dark colours, mostly black, in modified versions of the fashion of the day without lace, frills, bows, feathers or other decoration. Many Puritans, however, decided on a middle way between ostentation and severity and our two models were of this mind.

Mrs Pilgrim

Mrs Pilgrim wears an under-dress of violet, a sober enough colour, fully sleeved and with a high neckline, for no Puritan lady would show bare arms or neck in public, see diagram of front of figure. An overdress of homespun charcoal-grey wool, with three-quarter length sleeves is bunched up in front partly to show the hem of her under-dress, and partly to keep it out of the mud along the quayside.

Her hair is neatly covered out of sight by a white cotton, starched coif and for outdoors she wears the tall-crowned hat, peculiar to both men and women at this time. Her huge collar, starched white and almost plain, covers her shoulders, a remnant of the high lace ruff of earlier times. This matches her cuffs of white cotton. Out of sight is her waist petticoat, though in reality this would no doubt have been a full-length chemise with sleeves. She wears white knee-stockings and black shoes with fashionable flaps on the tops.

Materials

Hair: oddment of dark brown 3 or 4 ply. Padding.
Waist-length underskirt: 25gm (1oz) white 4 ply.
Under-dress: 50gm (2oz) violet 4 ply, 3 tiny matching buttons.
Overdress: 50gm (2oz) charcoal-grey sock wool 4 ply. 1 matching button.
Cuffs, coif and collar: 25gm (1oz) white 4 ply.
Hat: 15gm (¾oz) black 4 ply. Thin card and glue.
Muff: oddments of any common fur-colour, and white or grey 4 ply.
Stockings: oddment of white 4 ply.
Shoes: oddment of dark grey, black or brown 4 ply. Padding.
Needles: sizes 2, 2¾ and 3¼mm.
Note: make the lower half of the body and the legs completely white.
Embroider the face, as shown on pages 14–15, using dark brown sewing cotton.

Hair

With dark brown yarn and size 2mm needles, cast on 28 sts and work 18 rows in ss.
At beg of next 2 rows, cast on 2 sts. 32 sts.
At beg of next 2 rows, cast on 3 sts. 38 sts.
Row 23: (k2 tog) 19 times.
Row 24: (p2 tog) 5 times, p1, (p2 tog) 4 times.
Gather the last sts tog on to a wool needle and draw up for the top of the head.

a. Sew the 2 short centre edges tog and place this on to the centre crown of the head. Pin high up on the forehead.
b. Gather the cast on edge with the same yarn and draw up to fit the back of the head. Pin in position with the fullness at the back of the neck and with sides gently curving over the ears, see diagram 1.

Mrs Pilgrim wears a simple violet under-dress and grey knitted overdress, with her hair hidden inside a coif beneath a tall-crowned hat. She carries a muff.

c. Before stitching down, place a little padding into the fullness at the back of the head. Sew firmly all round.

d. To make the bun, cast on 10 sts and work 12 rows in ss.

Cast off.

Run a gathering thread round all 4 sides and draw up. Place padding into the centre, squeeze flat and stitch the bun to the top or back of the head.

Waist-length white underskirt

With white yarn and size 2¾mm needles, cast on 136 sts and work in ss until the piece measures 16.5cm (6½in), approx 76 rows. Make picot holes for the waist, then cast off.

Make a border of border pattern No. 3, see page 139, long enough to go round the lower edge, and sew this on. Make a cord, or use elastic for the waist and fit the garment on to the figure.

Violet under-dress

With violet yarn and size 3¼mm needles, cast on 80 sts and work in ms for 4 rows.

Continue in ss for 66 rows, or about 19.5cm (7¾in) from the cast on edge. Change to size 2¾mm needles.

Row 71: (k2 tog) 40 times.

Rows 72 and 74: k4, p32, k4.

Row 73: k40.

Row 75: k to last 3 sts, yfwd, k2 tog, k1, to make first buttonhole.

Row 76: as row 72.

Work 4 rows straight, (i.e., with 4 g st selvedge), then rep row 75, (second buttonhole).

Row 82: as row 72.

Row 83: k8, cast off 4, k16, cast off 4, k8.

Now work on these 3 sets of sts separately as folls:

Beneath her petticoat, Mrs Pilgrim wears knee-stockings and black shoes with fashionable flaps on top.

Rows 84 and 86: k4, p4.

Row 85: k8.

Row 87: k5, yfwd, k2 tog, k1, (third buttonhole).

Row 88: cast off 4, p to end of row.

Work 6 more rows on the rem 4 sts, then cast off.

Join yarn to centre sts and work in ss for 3 rows.

Next row: k4, cast off 8, k4.

Now work on these 2 sets of 4 sts separately for 5 rows each, then cast off.

Rejoin yarn to last 8 sts.

Next row: p4, k4.

Work 2 more rows, then on next row (RS) cast off 4 and k to end.

Work 5 more rows, then cast off.

To finish the neckline, sew the shoulders tog and darn ends in. With RS facing and using size 2¾mm needles, pick up 4 sts from g st edge at back, 12 sts over shoulder to front neck, 8 sts across front neck, 12 sts over other shoulder to back neck and 4 sts across g st edge at back. 40 sts.

Work 2 rows in single rib then cast off in patt.

Sleeves

Make 2 the same. With size 2¾mm needles, cast on 24 sts.

Row 1: knit.

Row 2: purl.

Row 3: k to last 2 sts, turn.

Row 4: p to last 2 sts, turn.

Row 5: k to last 4 sts, turn.

Row 6: p to last 4 sts, turn.

Cont in this way, leaving 2 extra sts at each turn until 8 unworked sts are left at each end.

Next row: k16.

Next row: p24.

Cont in ss for 26 more rows.

Next row: (k2 tog) 12 times.

Cast off p-wise.

a. Fold each sleeve with RS tog and sew up side edges. Turn to RS.

b. Set sleeves into armholes and sew in.

c. Press skirt hem gently then fold with RS tog and pin edges to form back seam, marking the top edge with a pin 5cm (2in) down from the gathers at the waist. Sew the edges tog, leaving the rest open above the pin.

d. Sew tiny buttons down one back edge, fit the dress on to the figure over the white underskirt and button up.

e. Run a length of yarn round the cuffs and gather tightly to the wrists, tie in a knot and trim the ends.

Grey overdress

With charcoal-grey yarn and size 2¾mm needles, cast on 80 sts and work in ss for 5 rows.

Row 6: knit.

This makes a rev ss ridge which becomes the turn-up line for the hem of the dress.

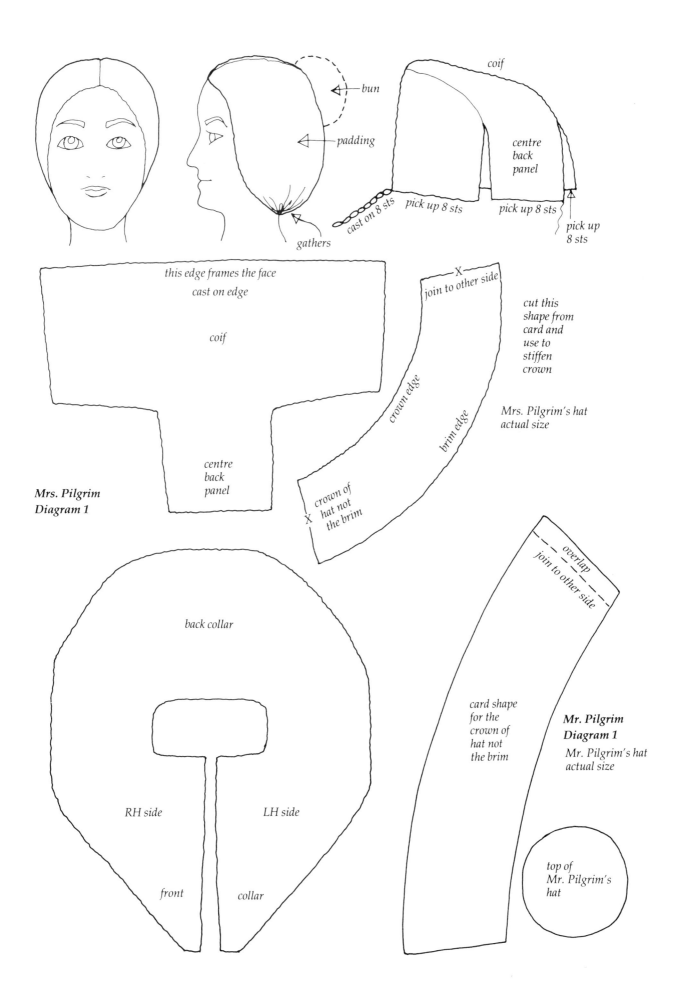

bun

padding

coif

centre
back
panel

gathers

cast on 8 sts

pick up 8 sts

pick up 8 sts

pick up
8 sts

this edge frames the face

cast on edge

coif

centre
back
panel

**Mrs. Pilgrim
Diagram 1**

X
join to other side

crown edge

brim edge

crown of
hat not
the brim

X

cut this
shape from
card and
use to
stiffen
crown

*Mrs. Pilgrim's hat
actual size*

back collar

RH side

LH side

front

collar

card shape
for the
crown of
hat not
the brim

overlap
join to other side

**Mr. Pilgrim
Diagram 1**

*Mr. Pilgrim's hat
actual size*

top of
Mr. Pilgrim's
hat

Work in ss for 78 more rows.

Row 79: k2 tog across all sts.

Row 80: p40.

Row 81: (yfwd, k2 tog) 20 times, for waistline draw-string holes.

Work in ss for 5 more rows.

Row 87: k8, cast off 4, k16, cast off 4, k8.

Now work on these 3 sets of sts separately as folls: on the first set of 8 sts, work in ss for 10 rows then, on next row (WS) cast off 4 sts.

Work 2 more rows on rem 4 sts and cast off.

Join yarn to centre 16 sts and work 5 rows.

Next row: (shape neckline and shoulders) k4, cast off 8, k4.

Work on the first set of 4 sts for 6 rows, then cast off p-wise, then complete the second set.

Join yarn to last set of 8 sts, work 9 rows then, on next row (RS) cast off 4 sts. Work 2 more rows on rem 4 sts and cast off p-wise.

To neaten the neckline, pick up 40 sts spaced evenly round the neck and shoulders as given for the under-dress, rib one row then cast off in rib.

Sleeves

Make 2 the same. Cast on 24 sts and work 26 rows in ss. Cast off.

Pin out and press gently.

a. With RS tog, place the 2 side edges tog, pin, and sew as far as the waist-holes.
b. Pin up the hem on the rev ss ridge and slip stitch in place.
   Press the back seam.
c. Sew the shoulder edges tog.
d. Fold each sleeve in half and sew side edges tog.
e. Set into armholes of bodice, pin and sew.
f. Fit dress on to figure, make a cord for the waist and thread this into the waist-holes. Draw up and fasten.
g. Make a buttonhole loop at the back neck opening and sew a tiny button to the other side. Fasten.
h. Run a gathering thread round the lower openings of the sleeves and push the sleeves up the arm a little, so that they reach just below the elbows. Draw the thread tightly, tie in knots and trim the ends.

Cuffs

Make 2 the same. These fit over the sleeves of the violet under-dress.

With white yarn and size 2¾mm needles, cast on 18 sts.

Row 1: knit.

Row 2: purl.

Row 3: (inc, k5) 3 times.

Row 4: p21.

Row 5: (inc, k6) 3 times.

Row 6: p24.

Row 7: (inc, k7) 3 times.

Cast off k-wise.

a. With RS tog, fold each cuff across and sew the side edges tog. Turn to RS and slip them on to the wrists over the violet sleeves with the widest parts at the top. A crochet edge may be worked round the top of the cuff if you wish.
b. Neatly stitch round the lower edge only, using white yarn.

Collar

With white yarn and size 2¾mm needles, begin at the front point on the RHS of the figure, see diagram 1. Cast on 3 sts.

Row 1: k3.

Row 2: p3.

Row 3: k1, inc, k1.

Row 4: inc, p3.

Row 5: k3, inc, k1.

Row 6: inc, p5.

Row 7: k5, inc, k1.

Row 8: inc, p7.

Row 9: k9.

Row 10: inc, p8.

Row 11: k10.

Row 12: inc, p9.

Cont to inc one st at beg of every p row until there are 14 st, then work straight for 2 more rows.

Row 21: cast off 5, k to end of row.

Work straight on the rem 9 sts for 7 more rows, then leave these sts on the needles, cut the yarn and begin the other side.

Cast on 3 sts.

Row 1: k3.

Row 2: p3.

Row 3: k1, inc, k1.

Row 4: p3, inc.

Row 5: inc, k4.

Row 6: p4, inc, p1.

Row 7: inc, p6.

Row 8: p6, inc, p1.

Row 9: k9.

Row 10: p7, inc, p1.

Row 11: k10.

Row 12: p8, inc, p1.

Cont to inc one st at end of every p row until there are 14 st, then work straight for 3 more rows.

Row 22: (WS) Cast off 5 sts, p to end of row.

Work straight on rem 9 sts for 6 more rows.

Row 29: k9, turn and cast on 10 sts, turn back and knit the 9 sts from the first set of sts left on the needle.

Work 3 rows straight across all 28 sts.

Now dec one st at each end of every k row until 20 sts rem, (i.e., k1, sl 1, k1, psso, k to last 3 sts, k2 tog, k1).

Row 40: p20.

Cast off 2 sts at beg of next 2 rows. Cast off 3 sts at beg of next 2 rows. Cast off rem 10 sts.

a. Darn all ends in, pin out and press gently. Fit on to figure as shown.

b. Thread a short length of yarn through the neck corners, tie in a bow and trim the ends.

c. If you wish, crochet a fine narrow border around the curve edges. To prevent the collar from standing away from the shoulder line too stiffly, and to mould it more roundly into the body, run a tiny gathering st all round the extreme edge of the collar *excluding* the two centre front edges. Draw up very slightly and adjust to the figure fastening off.

Coif

With white yarn and size 2¾mm needles cast on 28 sts and work in ss for 16 rows, see diagram 1.

Row 17: cast off 7 sts, k2 tog and cast one more st off, k 9 more sts from LH needle, (making a total of 10 sts on RH needle) k2 tog and cast this and the rem 9 sts off, leaving 10 sts in the centre.

Next row: p10.

Work 10 more rows on these sts, then cast off.

Fold the centre section down as shown, see diagram 1, cast on 8 sts, pick up 8 sts from the bottom/side edge, 8 sts from centre back panel, then 8 sts from the other bottom/side edge. 32 sts.

Next row: (WS) k8, (k2 tog) 4 times, k16. 28 sts.

Next row: cast off 8, k20.

Cast off k-wise.

a. From the WS, sew up the 2 slits at the back of the coif and darn ends in.

b. To fasten, use either a press-stud, button and loop, or a length of yarn threaded through the end of the bar and into the other side. Tie this in a bow and trim the ends.

Hat

With black yarn and size 2¾mm needles, begin at the crown and cast on 36 sts. Work in ss for 2 rows.

Row 3: (k2 tog, k10) 3 times.

Row 4: p33.

Row 5: (k2 tog, k9) 3 times.

Row 6: p30.

Row 7: (k2 tog, k8) 3 times.

Row 8: p27.

Row 9: (k2 tog, k7) 3 times.

Row 10: k24, (rev ss).

Row 11: (k2 tog) 12 times.

Row 12: p12.

Gather the last sts on to a wool needle for the top of the hat.

a. Sew up the side edges and top.

b. Flatten the top and cut a shape from thin card as shown in diagram 1. Curve the card into the shape of the crown and glue the edges tog. Do not glue this into the knitted shape yet.

For the brim, cast on 7 sts and knit 2 rows.

Row 3: k5, turn.

Row 4: k5 back to beg of row.

Rows 5 and 6: k7.

Rep these 4 rows until the piece is long enough to make a complete circle round the brim. Cast off.

c. Sew the 2 edges tog to form the brim and pin to the crown from the top side, matching the 2 seams at the back.

d. Sew the brim and crown tog from the under-side.

e. Make a cord of violet yarn and tie this round the brim with the bow at the back.

Muff

With fur-coloured yarn and size 2¾mm needles, cast on 24 sts and k 30 rows. Cut yarn.

Change to white or grey yarn and work 22 more rows. Cast off.

a. With RS tog, join the white edge to the fur-coloured edge to make a tube.

b. Insert a piece of padding.

c. Fold the piece up with the white or grey lining inside and sew the 2 lining edges tog.

d. Now sew the 2 outer edges tog from the RS.

e. Roll the shape into a tube and attach this to one hand of the figure.

Shoes and stockings

These are made all in one piece. Make 2 the same.

With black, or other shoe-coloured yarn, and size 2¾mm needles, cast on 24 sts and work 4 rows in ss.

The grey dress is full-length but it was fashionable to tuck it up in front as shown here, keeping at least one garment clear of the dirt. The hat has been stiffened in a sugar solution, see page 138, and the violet under-dress buttons at the back.

Row 5: k5, cast off 5, k4, cast off 5, k5.
Row 6: p5, cut yarn and rejoin to centre 4 sts, p4.
Now work 4 more rows of ss on the centre 4 sts.
Cut black yarn and join in white. Cont in ss for 4 more rows.
Next row: k across the 4 sts once more then k the 5 sts from the LH needle.
Next row: p across all 14 sts, pulling the 3 sections tog into one piece.
Cont in ss for 26 more rows, then work 2 rows of single rib.
Cast off in rib.

a. With RS tog, sew up the back of the shoe, then run a gathering thread all round the lower edge. Leave open.
b. Sew up the top of the shoe at each side.
c. Sew the back seam of the stocking.
d. Turn to RS and make the front tab as folls: with black yarn, cast on 5 sts and k 2 rows.
   Row 3: k2, inc, k2.
   Cont in g st for 3 more rows, then cast off.
e. Sew the narrow end of the tab to the top of the shoe and take a few sts along each side, leaving the top part free.
f. Draw up the bottom edges of the shoes and sew down the centres, inserting a tiny piece of padding into each heel.

Mr Pilgrim

Mr Pilgrim wears a white collared, long-sleeved shirt which is laced part-way down the front, see the illustration, right. Over this is his hip-length leather jerkin, which ties at the front in three places and the bottom edge of which is slashed. His warm close-fitting trousers are calf-length, the tops just nestling inside his bucket-top boots of brown leather which wrinkle into soft folds around his ankles. On the top of each boot is a butterfly-shaped piece of leather, to cover the spurs, although Mr Pilgrim does not wear his today.

Overall, he wears his travelling cloak of thick homespun wool, with a large collar and front tie fastening. Like his wife, his hat is of the high-crowned, wide-brimmed style made of felted wool.

Materials

Hair: an oddment of straw-coloured 4 ply.
Breeches: 20gm (¾oz) neutral 4 ply.
Shirt: 15gm (½oz) white or cream 4 ply.
Jerkin: 20gm (¾oz) brown sock wool 4 ply.
Cloak: 25gm (1oz) brown, black or grey 4 ply.
Stockings: oddment of white or cream 4 ply left over from shirt.
Boots: 15gm (½oz) tan 4 ply, or any other leather colour. Padding.
Hat: oddment of dark grey or black 4 ply.

Piece of bendy card, (a postcard will do), and glue.
Needles: sizes 2¼, 2¾ and 3¼mm.
Note: embroider the face as shown on pages 14–15, using colours to match the hair. In England at this time, most Puritan gentlemen were clean-shaven.

Hair

With hair-coloured yarn and size 2¼mm needles, cast on 28 sts and work 2 rows in single rib.
Rows 3 and 4: rib to last 4 sts, turn.
Rows 5 and 6: rib to last 8 sts, turn.
Row 7: rib to end of row.
Row 8: rib 28.
Rep rows 3 to 8 once more.
Rows 19 and 20: inc in first st, rib to last st, inc. 32 sts.
Rows 21 and 22: cast on 5 sts, rib to end, working into back of 6th st.
Row 23: (k2 tog) 21 times.
Row 24: p21.
Row 25: (k2 tog) 5 times, k1, (k2 tog) 5 times.
Gather the last sts on to a wool needle and draw up for the top of the head.

a. Sew up centre fringe edges from WS.
b. Pin hair piece to the head, pulling side edges well forwards on to the face, and pull the fringe on to the forehead. If necessary, place a little padding on top of the head, and also at the back.
c. Sew the hair all round the face but leave the lower edge free to sit on top of the collar.

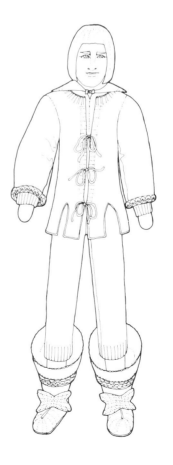

Without the hat, the model's hair-style can clearly be seen. The jerkin is fashionably tabbed at the bottom and ties down the front. Bucket-top boots are worn over three-quarter length breeches.

Mr Pilgrim wears a thick travelling cloak with large collar and front tie-fastening to protect him against the cold weather.

Breeches

With neutral yarn and size 2¾mm needles, cast on 18 sts. Working from the waist downwards, cont in ss for 18 rows.

Row 19: cast on 2 sts, k to end of row.
Row 20: cast on 2 sts, p to end of row. 22 sts.
Work in ss for 36 more rows.
Row 57: (k2 tog, k5) twice, k2 tog, k4, k2 tog. 18 sts.
Work 5 rows in single rib, then cast off in rib.
Make another piece in the same way.

a. With WS tog, fold each piece in half and sew up the inside leg seams from ribbing to 2 cast on sts.
b. Place both pieces tog, matching centre front and back seams and sew up. Turn to RS and thread a cord through the waistline, or make a narrow belt.

Shirt

With white or cream yarn and size 2¾mm needles, cast on 20 sts for the front.
Work 8 rows in single rib followed by 21 rows in ss.
Row 30: p8, k4, p8.
Row 31: k20.
Row 32: as row 30.
Row 33: k10, turn and work on the 2 sides separately.
Row 34: k2, p8.
Keeping to this stitch pattern, work 14 more rows in ss, then cast off 6 sts and leave the rem 4 sts on a safety-pin.
Cut yarn and rejoin to rem 10 sts.
Next row: k10.
Next row: p8, k2.
Work 13 more rows in ss in the same way.
Next row (WS) cast off 6 sts p-wise and leave the rem 4 sts on a safety-pin. Cut the yarn.
For the back, cast on 20 sts and work 8 rows in single rib followed by 48 rows in ss.
Rows 49 and 50: cast off 6 sts at beg of rows.
Leave rem sts on needle and cut yarn.

a. With RS tog, place back and front sections tog, with the back piece still on needle, and sew shoulder edges. Turn to RS.
b. Slide 4 sts from RHS front section on to point of needle alongside the back neck sts. Now make the collar on these neck sts.
    Beg on the under-side of the collar:
    Row 1: k2, p10, slide rem 4 sts from front section on to the free needle, p2, k2.
    Row 2: k2, inc, k10, inc, k2. 18 sts.
    Rows 3, 5 and 7: k2, p to last 2 sts, k2.
    Row 4: k2, inc, k12, inc, k2.
    Row 6: k2, inc, k14, inc, k2.
    Row 8: k2, inc, k16, inc, k2.
    Knit 3 rows then cast off.

Beneath his cloak, Mr Pilgrim wears a long-sleeved shirt covered with a leather jerkin.

Sleeves

Lay the front and back sections out flat and measure 3cm (1¼in) from each side of the shoulder seam. On the RS mark this centre 6cm (2¼in) section with pins. With RS facing, pick up 20 sts between the 2 pins. On these 20 sts, work 31 rows of ss, followed by 10 rows of single rib. Cast off in rib.

a. With RS tog, fold the piece across the shoulders and sew up sleeve and side seams.
b. Make a cord for the neck opening and lace the opening across from side to side.

Jerkin

With brown yarn and size 2¾mm needles, begin by making the six separate sections for the slashed bottom edge as folls: Cast on 6 sts.
Rows 1, 2 and 3: k2 rows, then p the next row.
Cont in ss for 10 more rows, then cut yarn and leave the sts on the needle.
Make five more tabs in the same way, casting the new sts on to the free needle each time. Leave all the tabs on one needle facing the same way, but do not cut the yarn after the sixth tab. 36 sts.
Row 14: k6, inc in next st, (i.e., the first st of the second set), k5, (inc, k5) 4 times. 41 sts.
Row 15: k2, p37, k2.

Cont in ss with a selvedge of 2 k sts at each side for 24 more rows.

Row 40: k9, cast off 2, k19, cast off 2, k9.

Work on these 3 sets of sts separately as folls:

Row 41: k2, p7.

Cont in ss for 11 more rows, keeping the selvedge on the front border as before.

Row 53: (WS) cast off 5 sts p-wise, p to end of row.

Work 6 more rows on rem 4 sts, then cast off.

Rejoin yarn to centre 19 sts and work in ss for 15 more rows.

Next row: k4, cast off 11 sts, k to end.

Work 3 more rows on both sets of sts then cast off.

Rejoin yarn to last 9 sts and work in ss, keeping selvedge as before, for 11 more rows.

Next row: (RS) cast off 5 sts, k to end.

Work 6 more rows on rem 4 sts then cast off.

a. Press the body section gently, blocking tabs and shoulders.
   Sew shoulder edges tog.
b. To neaten the neck edge, beg on RS of front border and pick up 37 sts all the way round the neckline. Work 2 rows in single rib, then cast off in rib.

Sleeves

Make two the same. Cast on 30 sts.

Row 1: k28, turn.
Row 2: p26, turn.
Row 3: k24, turn.
Row 4: p22, turn.

Cont in this way, leaving 2 extra sts at the end of every row until there are 8 unworked sts at the end of the last 2 rows.

Next row: k22.
Next row: p30.

Cont in ss for 25 more rows.

Next row: (WS) knit, then cast off p-wise.

a. With RS tog, fold sleeves and sew side edges. Turn to RS.
b. Pin each sleeve into armholes, then sew from WS.
c. Make 3 pairs of cords about 8cm (3in) long for the front ties. Sew these to the front edges of the jerkin, equally spaced, as shown in the illustration on page 74. Fit on to the figure and tie.

Cloak

With brown yarn and size 3¼mm needles, begin with the back section and make the cloak in three main sections.

Cast on 47 sts and k 2 rows.

Row 3: purl.

Cont in ss for 54 more rows.

Row 58: (RS) k1, sl 1, k1, psso, k19, k2 tog, k20, k2 tog, k1.

Rows 59, 60 and 61: work in ss, and for all other rows between shaping rows.

Row 62: k1, sl 1, k1, psso, (k18, k2 tog) twice, k1. 41 sts.

Row 66: k1, sl 1, k1, psso, k16, k2 tog, k17, k2 tog, k1.
Row 70: k1, sl 1, k1, psso, (k15, k2 tog) twice, k1.
Row 74: k1, sl 1, k1, psso, k13, k2 tog, k14, k2 tog, k1.
Row 78: k1, sl 1, k1, psso, (k12, k2 tog) twice, k1.
Row 82: k1, sl 1, k1, psso, k10, k2 tog, k11, k2 tog, k1. 26 sts.
Row 86: (k2 tog, k2) 6 times, k2 tog.
Row 87: purl.

Cut the yarn and leave the rem 19 sts on a spare needle until the 2 front panels have been made.

**Cast on 20 sts for the left front and k 2 rows.

Row 3: purl.

Cont in ss for 54 more rows.**

Row 58: (RS) k1, sl 1, k1, psso, k to end of row.

Cont without shaping for 3 rows.

***Rep the last 4 rows six more times, 13 sts.

Row 86: (k2 tog, k2) 3 times, k1.

Row 87: purl. ***

Cut yarn and leave rem sts on same needle as back panel.

For the right front, work from ** to ** as given for left front.

Row 58: (RS) k to last 3 sts, k2 tog, k1.

Cont without shaping for 3 rows.

Now work from *** to *** as given for left front.

Do not cut yarn but knit back across the last 10 sts of the right front, then across the 19 sts of the back, then across the 10 sts of the left front. Weave the cut ends in on the back as you go.

Next row: (WS) change to size 2¾mm needles, p18, p2 tog, p19. 38 sts.

Next row: (k2, k2 tog) 9 times, k2.

Next row: k29.

Next row: (this is where the collar turns over on to the RS), inc in first st, p to last st, inc.

Next row: inc in first st, k to last st, inc.

Cont to inc one st at both ends of every row until there are 41 sts.

Next row: p41.

Knit 2 rows in g st then cast off p-wise.

To make the edging down each side, use size 3¼mm needles and, with the RS of the left front facing you, pick up sts, beg on the under-side of the collar, as folls: 9 sts from the collar edge, and 47 sts from the front edge of the cloak.

Knit 2 rows, then cast off.

Work the other side to match.

a. Pin the sections tog down the sides and sew.
b. Pin out and press gently on seams and edges.
c. Fold collar down, make 2 cords about 20cm (8in) long and sew these to each side of the neck opening.
   Place the cloak on the figure and tie the cords at the neck.

Stockings

Make two the same. With white or cream yarn and size 2¼mm needles, cast on 14 sts and work 4 rows in single rib.

Now change to ss and work 18 more rows.

Row 23: k7, turn and p back to end of row.
Row 24 and foll alt rows: purl.
Row 25: k6, turn and p back.
Row 27: k5, turn and p back.
Row 29: k4, turn and p back.
Row 31: k3, turn and p back.
Row 33: k14.
Row 34: p7, turn and k back.
Row 36: p6, turn and k back.
Row 38: p5, turn and k back.
Row 40: p4, turn and k back.
Row 42: p3, turn and k back.
Row 44: p14.

Cont in ss for 10 more rows then gather the last sts on to a wool needle and draw up for the end of the toe.

a. With RS tog, fold each stocking piece in half and pin the edges tog, then sew from toe to top. Turn to RS.

Bucket-top boots

With tan yarn and size 2¼mm needles, cast on 30 sts and work 6 rows in ss.

Row 7: k14, k2 tog, k14.
Row 8: p12, p2 tog, p1, p2 tog, p12. 27 sts.
Row 9: k10, cast off 7 sts, k10.
Row 10: Push all sts tog across the gap and p20.
Row 11: inc in first st, k18, inc.
Rows 12, 13 and 14: work straight.
Row 15: inc in first st, k5, (inc, k4) twice; inc, k5.
Rows 16, 17 and 18: work straight on these 26 sts.
Rows 19 and 22: purl.
Rows 20 and 21: knit.
Row 23: k11, inc, k2, inc, k11. 28 sts.
Row 24: (WS) knit.
Rows 25 and 26: purl.

Mr Pilgrim's bucket-top boots.

Row 27: k12, inc, k2, inc, k12.
Row 28: purl.
Row 29: (k1, inc) 15 times. 45 sts.
Rows 30, 31 and 33: knit.
Row 32: purl.
Row 34: (WS) knit (this makes the last rev ss ridge). Work 4 more rows in ss then cast off.

Make the spur-leathers as folls: cast on 11 sts and work in ms for 2 rows.

Rows 3 and 4: cast off 2 sts at beg of row, patt to end.
Rows 5 and 6: cast on 2 sts at beg of row, patt to end.

Cast off and make another one in the same way.

To make the soles, cast on 5 sts for each one and k 23 rows. Cast off.

a. With RS tog, fold boot in half and sew up the back, carefully matching the ridges. Leave the sole open, but sew up the space on top of the boot.

b. Fold down the wide top edge of the boot along the last rev ss ridge, and slip st all round to hold in place.

c. Gather the centre of each spur-leather and pin in place on top of the boot as shown. Stitch in place.

d. Fit boots, minus soles, on to the figure over the stockings, pin the soles in place, then sew. Take care not to stitch them to the feet! Place a tiny piece of padding into each heel to make a better foot shape.

Hat

With dark grey or black yarn and size 2¾mm needles, begin with the crown of the hat. Cast on 41 sts and work 2 rows in ss.

Row 3: (k2 tog, k11) 3 times, k2.
Rows 4, 6, 8 and 10: purl.
Row 5: (k2 tog, k10) 3 times, k2.
Row 7: (k10, k2 tog) twice, k11.
Row 9: (k9, k2 tog) 3 times.
Row 11: (k2 tog, k8) 3 times.
Row 12: k27, (rev ss).
Row 13: (k2 tog) 13 times, k1.
Rows 14 and 15: k14.

Gather the last sts on to a wool needle and draw up to form the top.

a. Sew up the side edges.

b. From a piece of bendy card, make the crown stiffener as shown and glue this to the inside of the knitted crown before adding the brim, leaving a tiny strip of knitting projecting beyond the card at the lower edge, see diagram 1, page 71.

c. To make the brim, cast on 6 sts and k 2 rows.
   Row 3: k5 and turn.
   Row 4: k5 back to beg of row.
   Rows 5 and 6: k6.
   Rep these 4 rows until the piece is long enough to go all the way round the crown without distorting, then cast off.

d. Sew the brim to the crown, matching the joins at the back.

Lady of *c.*1625 to 35 (Colonial American style)

The early settlers in America were not all Puritans. Some were wealthy merchants and owners of estates, whose prime concern was commerce, and a desire to supply Europe with the commodities which it needed. Many families transported their entire household belongings across the Atlantic, found plentiful local servants and were eager to have their portraits painted to prove their success and affluence.

Their dress reflected the desire to be abreast of fashion, although inevitably there was a time-lag. Contemporary portraits highlight subtle differences, not only in the styles imposed by the painters themselves, but in the slightly plainer and more servicable dress, such as the white cotton head-coverings worn by almost all women at one time, both indoors and out, and a more apparent formality of demeanour. Puritans had their portraits painted too,

and gradually allowed themselves a little lace here and there.

The model illustrates a typical costume worn in England around 1625 to 1635 and in America slightly later. Portraits of this period, especially those by the Flemish painter, Sir Anthony van Dyck, show sumptuous gowns of satins and silks, much lace and ribbon and often with long skirts trailing on the ground. Our version is a little more restrained for everyday wear. Whilst some gowns of this period would still be open in front to reveal the decorated undergarment, called an 'open gown', a later tendency was to close the gown completely and to allow the huge lace collar of the previous Stuart period to descend over the shoulders, exposing the neck completely. European fashions intermingled more than ever at this time especially after the accession of Charles I and his French-born wife, Henrietta Maria, which led to an exchange not only of French fabrics, but of fashion details and style.

Our model wears the typically high-waisted, one-piece bodice with tabs, the stomacher point appearing at the front as a central tab. The sleeves are wide, although they were often slashed to reveal the under-sleeve, and the lace-edged ruffles of the undergarment show below them at three-quarter length, leaving the lower arm bare. Colonial American ladies of the same period are shown wearing open gowns, as in the portrait of Elizabeth Freake and Baby Mary Freake *c.*1670, which can be seen in Worcester Art Gallery, England, with additional aprons and indoor hoods of cotton and lace. The sleeves and collar are similar to the ones shown here. A pattern for the hood and also for Baby Mary Freake are included for those wishing to follow that portrait more closely. The colours are mainly greyish-green and yellow with red ribbon decorations.

Underneath the cream garment with the decorated border and ruffled sleeves, our model wears a plainer waist-skirt with a lacy patterned border and three-quarter length white drawers, with divided legs attached only by the draw-string around the waist. The burgundy bodice and skirt are in separate pieces, the skirt tying at the back with a draw-string and the bodice sewn up the front to close. It can be laced or snap-fastened instead if you wish to make it easier to remove. The shoes are gold-coloured with pink rosettes or bows on top, although it is quite likely that tiny heels would have been worn.

Here is the back view of the bodice and skirt, with the lace collar in position. Baby Mary is being held on leading-strings which were at this time made from the same fabric as her gown and attached to the shoulders.

Materials

Colonial lady.

Hair: 10gm (½oz) deep gold 4 ply. Padding. Tiny pearls for the chignon.

Drawers, waist-length underskirt and collar: 50gm (2oz) white 4 ply.

Sleeved chemise: 50gm (2oz) white or cream 4 ply and a total of 15gm (¾oz) in oddments of rose, metallic gold and yellow 4 ply.

Gown: 50gm (2oz) burgundy 4 ply and an oddment of matching textured glitter 4 ply or similar. Copper or purple metallic 4 ply, about 10gm (½oz), but these border colours can be anything you prefer of the correct thickness.

Hood: (optional) 10gm (½oz) white 4 ply.

Shoes: oddments of any matching or contrasting yarn.

Needles: sizes 2, 2¼, 2¾, 3 and 3¼mm.

Baby Mary.

Body: 10gm (½oz) flesh-coloured 4 ply, oddments of white 4 ply and some padding.

Dress: 10gm (½oz) pale yellow 4 ply.

Pinafore and bonnet: 10gm (½oz) white 4 ply.

Needles: sizes 2 and 2¼mm.

Note: For both models, embroider the faces in colours to match the hair, see pages 14–15.

Colonial lady

With deep gold yarn and size 2mm needles, cast on 28 sts for the hair and work in ss for 18 rows.

Cast on 2 sts at beg of next 2 rows. Cast on 3 sts at beg of next 2 rows.

Row 23: (k2 tog) 19 times.

Row 24: (p2 tog) 5 times, p1, (p2 tog) 4 times. 10 sts.

Gather the last sts on to a wool needle and draw up for the top of the head.

a. Sew the 2 short edges tog in the centre, place on head and pin in position.
b. Sew forehead piece straight across, then sew down sides.
c. Gather cast on edge to fit back of neck. Pad inside back of hair to form a rounded shape to the head; pull hair down to back hair-line (the back neck is left bare) and pin. Sew down securely.
d. To make the plaited coil for the back of the head, cut a strand of yarn 178cm (70in) long and fold this into 4. Fold this piece again into 3 and tie one end to keep all the strands together before plaiting begins. Separate into 3 equal sets and plait the strands together firmly to make a piece about 19cm (7½in) long. Tie the bottom and trim ends.
e. Coil this plait to make a chignon of about 2.5cm (1in) in diameter and pin to the back of the head, with its top edge level with the top of the head. Tuck ends in and sew from the outer edges, in a spiral, towards the centre.
f. To make ringlet bunches for each side of the head, measure lengths of yarn 305cm (120in) long and make into 2 twisted cords measuring about 64cm (25in) long. Fold each cord into 8 and tie round the centres to make clusters. This centre tie is now fixed at the side of the face on a level with the eyes and sewn in position. The base of the ringlets will just reach the shoulders. A circlet of tiny pearls encloses the chignon, see diagram 2.

Waist-length underskirt

With white yarn and size 3mm needles, cast on 134 sts

Beneath the decorative border of the cream gown can be seen a plainer waist-skirt with lacy patterned border, three-quarter length white drawers, and gold-coloured shoes with tiny pink bows on top.

and work border pattern No. 2, see page 139. Then continue in ss until the piece measures 18cm (7in), about 60 rows from the top of the border.

Next row: (yfwd, k2 tog) across all sts, then cast off.

a. Press lightly and sew the sides together.
b. Make a cord for the waist, thread this through the holes, fit on to the figure and tie at the back.

Three-quarter length drawers

With white yarn and size 2¾mm needles, cast on 30 sts and work 4 rows in single rib.

Change to size 3mm needles and work in ss for 34 rows as far as the top of the leg.

Now cont in ss, but leaving a selvedge of 2 knit sts on every row. Work 20 more rows from top of leg to waist, then make a row of picot holes as folls:

Next row: (yfwd, k2 tog) 15 times.

Cast off and make another piece in the same way.

a. With RS tog, fold each piece in half lengthways, and sew the inside leg seams from the ribbing as far as the selvedge of 2 k sts. Leave the centre front and centre back seams open. Turn to RS.
b. Either make a cord to go through the holes at the waist or thread fine elastic through and tie firmly.
Note: the 2 legs are joined only at the waistline, without a crotch, as was the method at this time.

Sleeved chemise

With yellow yarn and size 3¼mm needles, cast on 100 sts and knit 3 rows. Cut yellow and join in metallic gold.

Rows 4 and 5: k, cut yarn, this part forms the hem to be turned under.

Rows 6 and 7: join in rose, knit, then cut yarn.

Row 8: join in white and yellow, k 2 white, 2 yellow to end of row.

Row 9: p 2 yellow, 2 white to end of row.
Rows 10 and 11: as rows 8 and 9 but reverse the order of the colours to produce a chequered effect, cut yarns.
Row 12: join in rose, (k2, sl 2 white sts) to end of row.
Row 13: (sl 2, k2) to end of row, cut yarn.
Rows 14 and 15: join in metallic gold, knit to end of row, cut yarn.
Rows 16 and 17: join in yellow, knit to end of row, cut yarn.

Join in white or cream and work 4 rows in ss then 4 rows double ms, leave yarn hanging.

Join in metallic gold and k 2 rows, cut yarn and pick up white. Work 4 more cream rows in double ms, then 26 rows in ss.
Next row: (k3, k2 tog) 20 times.
Next row: p80.
Now work 20 more rows in ss, then change to size 2¼mm needles.
Next row: (k2 tog) 40 times.
Next row: p40.
Make holes for the draw-string waistband.
Next row: (yfwd, k2 tog) 20 times.
Next row: p40.
Cont in ss for 10 more rows.
Divide for armholes.
Next row: k8, k2 tog, then cont to work on these sts only for 14 more rows, then cast them off p-wise.
Rejoin yarn to rem sts, k2 tog, k16, k2 tog.
Work on these 18 sts for 14 more rows, then cast off p-wise.
Rejoin yarn to last 10 sts, k2 tog, k8 and complete as first section.

Sleeves

With RS facing, pick up 10 sts down first armhole edge, 2 sts across base of armhole and 10 more sts from second edge.
Row 2: p22.
Row 3: (k1, inc in next st) 11 times.
Row 4: p33.
Cont on these sts for 10 more rows in ss.
Row 15: k16, turn.
Rows 16, 18, 20, 22, 24, 26, 28: p to end of row.
Row 17: k14, turn.
Row 19: k12, turn.
Row 21: k10, turn.
Row 23: k8, turn.
Row 25: k6, turn.
Row 27: k4, turn.
Row 29: k33.
Next row: p16, turn, then k back to the end of the row. Complete other side of same sleeve in the same way from rows 17 to 28, but leaving the 2 extra sts in the centre on every p row. The last row reads, k4.
Row 30: p33.
Cont in ss for 8 more rows.
Row 39: (yfwd, k2 tog) 16 times, k1.
Row 40: (k1, p1) 16 times, inc in last st.

Cont in single rib for 6 more rows then cast off in patt. Work another sleeve in the same way.

a. Pin skirt section out and press gently.
b. With RS tog, fold sleeves along top and sew up from edge of cuff to half-way across back bodice pieces.
c. With RS tog, fold skirt section in half and sew centre back seam from hem to waistline, matching borders carefully.
d. Turn up hem of skirt on first row of metallic gold and hem st on inside.
e. Turn to RS and fit on to figure. Pin back bodice edges tog and sew from waist to neck.
f. Make cords for waist and sleeves. Tie waist cord at back, and sleeve cord on outer edges just below the elbow.

Burgundy overgown skirt

Use the main contrast colour, (textured glitter yarn) and size 3¼mm needles and cast on 90 sts.
Rows 1, 2 and 3: knit.
Row 4: (RS) purl.
Row 5: knit, cut yarn.
Row 6: join in burgundy and knit.
Row 7: purl, do not cut yarn.
Row 8: join in copper or purple metallic, knit.
Row 9: knit.
Row 10: with burgundy, knit.
Row 11: purl.
Row 12: with metallic, knit.
Row 13: knit, cut metallic.
Row 14: with burgundy, (k2, sl 1) 30 times.
Row 15: (sl 1 , p2) 30 times.
Rows 16 and 17: k90, (at this point a fine gold thread was used with the burgundy on row 17).
Row 18: knit.
Row 19: purl.
Row 20: k2, *yfwd and round needle, p1, p3 tog, p1, yfwd, k2*, to last 4 sts, yfwd and round needle, p2 tog, p2.
Row 21: purl.
Rep rows 18, 19, 20 and 21 twice more and, if you choose, run the fine gold thread along the last patt row.

At this point, you may *either* cont the pattern until the piece measures approximately 21cm (8½in), or work in ss, as on this figure, to the same length. This will take the skirt to slightly above the natural waistline.
Next row: change to size 2¾mm needles, k2 tog across all sts, 45 sts.
Next row: make picot holes for elastic; (yfwd, k2 tog) 22 times, k1.
Next row: k45.
Cast off.
Work front bands as folls: with size 3¼mm needles, and RS facing, use main colour to pick up 62 sts from the side edge of the skirt.
Next row: p62, cut main colour.

Next 2 rows: with metallic, (as before) knit, cut yarn. With main contrast border-colour, (i.e., first colour used on hem) knit 2 rows, then cast off p-wise in the same yarn.

a. Darn all ends in to neaten corners.
b. Press the skirt gently and ease into shape.
c. Place on figure over top of the chemise, pulling the waistline above that of the chemise.
d. Sew tog the top corners at the waistline to join the open skirt at the front.
e. Thread fine black elastic through the holes and pull tightly, tie at the back and ease the fullness away from the front.

Overgown bodice

Use the burgundy yarn and size 2¾mm needles and cast on 10 sts to begin the centre back panel.
Row 1: knit.
Row 2: purl.
Row 3: inc one st at each end.
Row 4: p12.
Row 5: as row 3.
Cont to inc at each end of every k row until there are 24 sts, then work one p row.
Work without shaping for 2 more rows.
Row 19: k7, cast off 10, k7.
Work on the first set of sts, leaving the other set on a spare needle or pin.
Rows 20 to 24: work in ss.
Row 25: cast on 5 sts, k10, k2 tog.
Row 26: p11.
Row 27: k9, k2 tog.
Row 28: p10.
Cont to dec on outside edge of every k row until 5 sts rem.
Work 2 more rows straight, then cast off.
Return to the other set of 7 sts, join in the yarn and work 4 rows in ss without shaping.
Next row: cast on 5 sts, p10, p2 tog.
Cont to dec one st at outside edge at end of every p row until 5 sts rem. Work 2 rows straight, then cast off.
For the underarm bodice gussets, see diagram 2, cast on 6 sts and work 4 rows in ss.
Row 5: k2 tog, k4.
Row 6: p3, p2 tog.
Row 7: k2 tog, k2.
Row 8: p1, p2 tog and pass first st over second.
Make another piece in the same way.
To make the second pair of gussets, cast on 6 sts and work 4 rows in ss.
Row 5: k4, k2 tog.
Row 6: p2 tog, p3.
Row 7: k2, k2 tog.
Row 8: p2 tog, p1 and pass the first st over the second.
Make another piece in the same way.
To make the tabs for the base of the bodice, in burgundy yarn, cast on 6 sts and k 12 rows in g st.
Cut yarn and leave each set of sts on the same needle

until 6 more tabs have been completed, but do not cut yarn after the 7th tab.
Now k 2 rows across all 42 sts, then cast off.
Darn all loose ends in neatly and securely.

a. To set the tabs on to the bodice, with RS tog, pin to lower edge of bodice, so that the left edge projects by half a tab and the right edge is inset by this amount, as shown in diagram 2. This is to centralize the front tab.
b. Sew tabs on to the bodice from WS, then press gently into position.
c. With metallic yarn, work a narrow edging of buttonhole st all round the tabs, spacing the sts evenly and close tog.

Sleeves

Make 2 the same. With burgundy yarn and size 2¾mm needles, cast on 40 sts and work 14 rows in ss.
Rows 15 and 16: join in metallic yarn, as before and k both rows, cut yarn.
Rows 17 and 18: with burgundy, work in ss, cut yarn.
Rows 19 and 20: join in main contrast border-colour and knit both rows, cut yarn.
Row 21: join in metallic and knit.
Cast off k-wise.

a. From WS, sew sleeve pieces into tubes and turn to RS.
b. Gather all round top edges and draw up to fit armholes of bodice.
c. Fit sleeves to armholes and pin, with most gathers on shoulder edges.
d. Sew in place.
e. With metallic yarn, embroider lines of chain st from each side of front tabs, following the bodice and sleeve seam over the shoulders and down the back seams as far as the tabs.
f. Fit the bodice on to the figure, pin the front edges closed and sew up from the RS.
g. To decorate the bodice with bows, use any contrasting yarn colour and make 2 cords, each 10cm (4in) long. Fold each one into 4 and tie round the centre with another piece of the same yarn. Sew these bundles on to the bodice, using the yarn ends.

Elizabeth Freake and Baby Mary Freake. The clothing designs and features have been taken from a portrait of the same in Worcester Art Gallery, England.

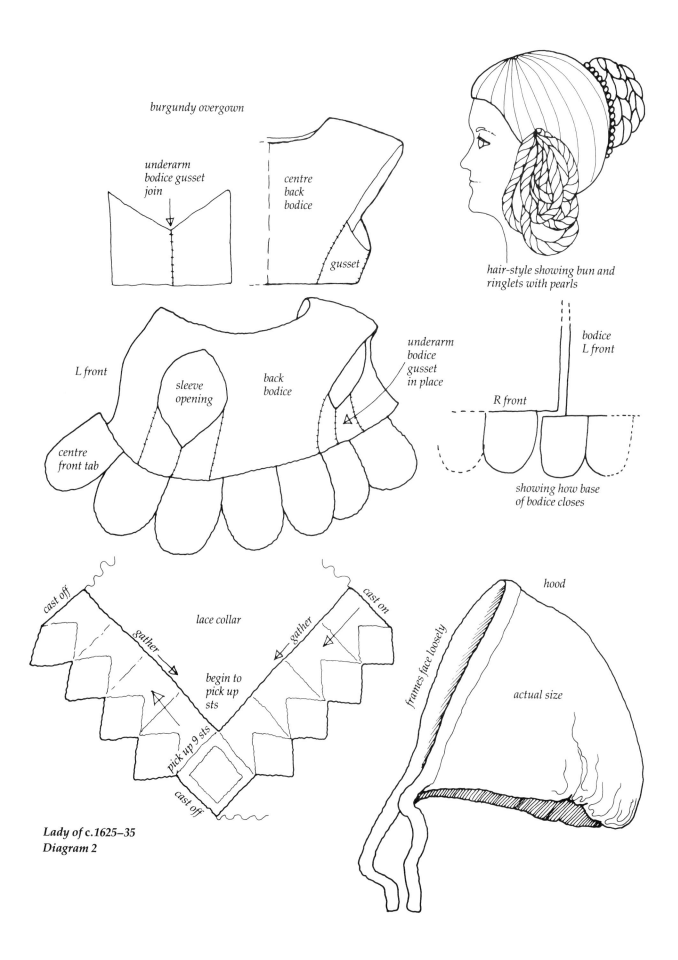

burgundy overgown

underarm
bodice gusset
join

centre
back
bodice

gusset

hair-style showing bun and
ringlets with pearls

L front

sleeve
opening

back
bodice

underarm
bodice
gusset
in place

centre
front tab

bodice
L front

R front

showing how base
of bodice closes

cast off

cast on

lace collar

gather

gather

begin to
pick up
sts

pick up 9 sts

cast off

hood

frames face loosely

actual size

**Lady of c.1625–35
Diagram 2**

84

Lace collar

With white yarn and size 2¼mm needles, cast on 9 sts and work border pattern No. 3 four times, see page 139, finishing on row 12.

Row 49: k9.
Row 50: (yfwd, k2 tog) 4 times, yfwd, k1.
Row 51: k10.
Row 52: k1, yfwd, k2 tog, k4, yfwd, k2 tog, k1.
Rep rows 51 and 52 five more times.
Row 63: k10.
Row 64: (yfwd, k2 tog) 5 times.
Cast off.

With pointed edges towards you and with RS facing, pick up 9 sts from the top edge of this last square section, see diagram 2, and work 4 more repeats of border patt No. 3.
Cast off.

a. Use the cast on and cast off tails to gather along the 2 neck edges towards the back point. Draw up to fit the neck snugly and tie the 2 ends tog. Darn these into the WS at the back.
b. Fit the collar to the neck and stitch to under the chin, at the top of the collar only. Pull the front and back points gently downwards.

Hood

The portrait of Elizabeth Freake in Worcester Art Gallery, England, shows her wearing a hood of fine lawn, which was usual for ladies of this period in America, both indoors and out. Our model is not wearing hers, but see the drawing in diagram 2.
With white yarn and size 2¾mm needles, cast on 60 sts.
Rows 1 and 2: cast off 8 sts, k to end of row.
Row 3: cast off 2 sts, p to end of row.
Row 4: cast off 2 sts, k to end of row. 40 sts.
Cont in ss for 7 more rows.
Row 12: keeping the side edges straight, begin to dec in centre as folls: k16, k2 tog tbl, k4, k2 tog, k16.
Row 13: p38.
Row 14: k15, k2 tog tbl, k4, k2 tog, k15.
Row 15: p36.
Cont to dec in this way on every k row, keeping the 4 sts in the centre between decreases, until only 20 sts rem. Work one more p row.
Next row: (k2 tog) 10 times, gather last sts on to a wool needle to form the back of the hood, take the needle twice through the sts and secure.

a. Gather lower edge of hood (i.e., side edges of knitting) from half-way along, and across back gathers, to other half-way point. Adjust gathers and secure.
b. Place hood centrally on head, well forward, and tie ends in a knot under chin, allowing the back to pouch evenly.

Shoes

Small amounts of any contrasting yarn can be used.
Use size 2¾mm needles and cast on 24 sts.
Work 5 rows in ss then cast off k-wise.

a. Fold across and sew the 2 short side edges tog. Turn to RS and slip on to foot with the cast on edge to the sole.
b. Take a few sts through the heel of the shoe and foot tog, to prevent the shoe from slipping off.
c. Make the sole on 4 sts with 17 rows of g st. Sew this to the under-side cast on edge of the upper, while the shoe is on the foot. It may be necessary to pad a little under the heel before closing the sole.
d. Close the top of the shoe with a few sts and make 2 bunches of contrasting yarn for the top of the shoe. Make another shoe in the same way.

Baby Mary Freake

For materials, see page 80. Measurements, before clothing, 11cm (4¼in). See illustration showing front of figure, page 79.

Body and head

With flesh-coloured yarn and size 2¼mm needles, cast on 18 sts and work in ss for 28 rows.
Row 29: (k2 tog) 9 times.

a. Gather the last sts on to a wool needle for the top of the head and draw up tightly. From the WS, sew down the 2 edges to form a tube. Leave the bottom open.
b. Turn to the RS. Slip this tube on to your finger and count down 9 rows from the top. Mark this point with a pin or thread. Place padding into the end above this point.
c. Run a gathering thread around this row to mark the neck, then draw up gently and wrap round once or twice.
Fasten off.
d. Pad the rest of the body, fold across the opening with the seam at the centre back and stitch the edges together to close.

Legs

Make two the same. With yarn and needles as for body, cast on 10 sts and work in ss for 8 rows.
Change to white yarn and work 2 more rows.
Row 11: k2 tog, k6, k2 tog.
Work 7 more rows in ss then gather all sts on to a wool needle for the end of the foot.

a. With RS tog, fold this piece across and sew up the side edges from white sock to top.
b. Turn to RS and pad. Sew across top to close.

c. Sew to base of body with seams on inside, or at back.

Arms

Make 2 the same. With yarn and needles as for body, cast on 8 sts and work in ss for 14 rows. Cast off

a. Use the cast on tail to gather the cast on row for the end of the hand. Draw up tightly and cont to sew up the two edges from the RS.
b. Pad the arm gently.
c. Close the open end (the cast off row) and sew this flat to the shoulder just below the neckline so that the top of the arm forms a line continuous with the top of the body. The end of the hand should reach almost to the bottom of the body section, see diagram 3.
d. Embroider the face and work a few sts of brown hair on to the forehead, to show just underneath the bonnet.

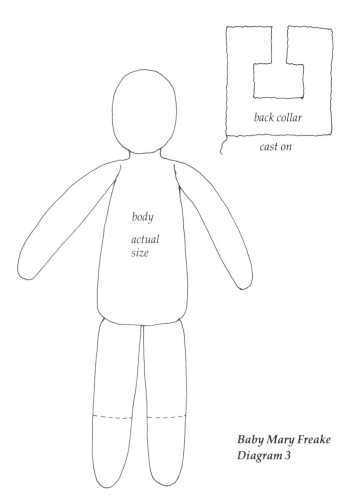

back collar

cast on

body

actual size

Baby Mary Freake Diagram 3

Dress

The portrait shows Baby Mary Freake wearing a long gown of pale yellow, with short cuffed sleeves over a white chemise, the sleeves of which are tied with yellow ribbons. Over her gown she wears a white pinafore with a front and back sleeveless bodice and, like her mother, a large lace collar. As the dress bodice is completely hidden, our version shows only the white one as a continuation of the lower skirt. Her lower pinafore ties at the back. Our sleeves are knitted in one piece to reduce the bulk. The little bonnet also has a band of lace all round, through which the yellow fabric shows, but our version is rather more dense and the front band turns back on to the bonnet.

With pale yellow yarn and size 2¾mm needles, cast on 40 sts and k 2 rows.

Row 3: purl.

Cont in ss for 36 more rows.

Row 40: (k2, k2 tog) 10 times.

Row 41: p30, cut yellow yarn.

Rows 42 and 43: join in white yarn and work 2 rows in ss.

Row 44: divide for armholes as folls: k7, cast off 1, k14, cast off 1, k7.

Work on these 3 sets of sts separately.

Next row: p5, p2 tog.

Work 6 more rows on these 6 sts, then cut yarn and slide sts on to a st holder.

Join yarn to centre 14 sts.

Next row: p2 tog, p10, p2 tog.

Work 6 more rows on these 12 sts, then cut yarn and slide them on to a stitch holder.

Join yarn to last 7 sts.

Next row: p2 tog, p5, then complete as first side, but keep sts on needle.

Next row: on same sts, (k2 tog) 3 times, then slide other 2 sets of sts on to the free needle and k2 tog across these also. 12 sts.

Next row: p12.

Cast off.

Sleeves

With yellow yarn, cast on 20 sts and work 6 rows in ss.

Row 7: purl, then cut yellow.

Row 8: join in white, then purl.

Work 4 more rows in ss.

Row 13: (yfwd, k2 tog) 10 times, this makes the lacy edge.

Cast off k-wise.

a. With WS tog, join sleeve edges to form a tube.
b. With yellow yarn, run a gathering st round the cast on edge, (top of sleeve), and draw up to fit armhole.
c. Use same thread to sew sleeve into armhole.
d. Make second sleeve in same way, then use double yellow yarn and thread this through the knitting on the second white row below the yellow, *above* the holes, not into them.

Pinafore or apron

With white yarn and size 2¾mm needles, cast on 18 sts.

Work in ms for 3 rows, then, keeping a border of 3 sts in ms at each side, cont in ss for 26 more rows.

Row 30: (k2 tog) 9 times.

Row 31: (k1, p1) 4 times, k1.

To make the tie at one side, cast on 30 sts and cast them off again on the next row. P the foll 8 sts, to make 9 altogether then turn and cast on another 30 sts. Cast them off again on the next row and k across the foll 8 sts.

Cast off p-wise.

Collar

Begin at the back and with white yarn, cast on 11 sts and work 6 rows in ms, see diagram 3.

Row 7: ms 3, cast off 5, ms 3.

Work in ms on these 2 sets of sts as folls: cont in ms for 5 more rows for the side of the neck, then cast on 2 more sts on the inside edge, remembering to k into back of 3rd st on first row after casting on. Complete 4 more rows then cast off in patt.

When working on the second set of sts, one more row of 3 sts must be worked to be able to cast on the 2 sts on the *inside* edge at the beginning of the row.

Darn all ends in on one side.

a. To make up the dress, first press all pieces gently. Turn main dress piece to WS and sew up from hem to end of yellow knitting.

b. Turn to RS and slip on to the figure, then sew white back bodice from RS as far as neck.

c. Tie apron to figure well up under arms. Place one or two sts at front band to keep in position.

d. Place collar round neck and stitch under chin. Tie sleeve threads and trim ends.

Bonnet

With white yarn and size 2mm needles, cast on 22 sts.

Rows 1, 2, 4, 6, 7 and 9: knit.

Rows 3, 5, 8 and 10: purl.

Cut white and join in yellow.

Row 11: (RS) knit.

Row 12: purl.

Work 6 more rows in ss.

Row 19: k6, (k2 tog) 5 times, k6.

Row 20: purl.

Row 21: k4, (k2 tog) twice, k1, (k2 tog) twice, k4.

Gather last sts on to wool needle and draw up to form back of bonnet.

a. Run a white gathering thread round last white row and draw this up slightly to frame the face. Fasten off.

b. Fold the white border back on to the yellow part and sew across the 2 bottom edges.

c. Draw up the back of the bonnet to close, secure thread.

d. Fit bonnet on to head and pad space at back. Sew up gap at back of neck. Pull 2 front edges tog and stitch in place under chin.

Gentleman *c.*1670s

A gentleman of this period would probably wear a costume more highly decorated than a lady's of the same period. Although our model wears fewer ribbons and bows than he might, it would be quite in order to add more to your version, especially clusters of ribbons on the sleeves and down the sides of the breeches. These would probably be of a contrasting colour. The shirt would be ruffled down the front with a froth of lace at the neck. Our cravat is a relatively sober affair, but real lace oddments can be used if you wish. His short jacket has sleeves with split seams; sometimes these were tied together with ribbons too. The shirt is designed to show between the short jacket and breeches, which are very full and knee-length, ending with a full ruffle of lace at the calf. Many men of fashion wore overskirts, called 'rhinegraves', but this is an option.

Colours worn by gentlemen were bright, almost gaudy, as were the women's. Jacket, breeches and rhinegrave would be of the same colour with matching accessories, or contrasting ribbons, bows and edgings. Shirts were always white, and most men wore their

Here our model shows the rhinegrave, a type of overskirt sometimes worn over the full breeches. Many portraits of this period show men wearing versions of this garment.

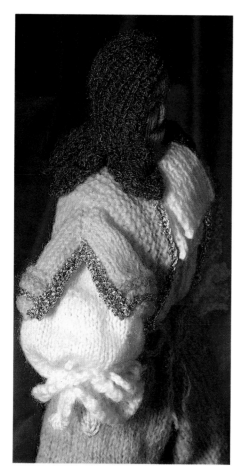

This side view shows the distinctive split seams on the sleeves of the gentleman's jacket.

Hair

With dark brown yarn and size 2¼mm needles, cast on 10 sts and work 10 rows in single rib.

Row 11: (k2 tog) 5 times.

Row 12: (k1, p1) twice, k1.

Row 13: (p1, k1) twice, p1.

Cut yarn and make another piece in the same way on the same needles, (cast sts on to *free* needle), and leave these sts alongside the first set.

Make a third piece, this time with 14 rows instead of 10. Complete in the same way as the others and leave on same needle.

Make 2 more pieces in the same way as the first 2, but do *not* cut yarn after last piece. 25 sts.

With 5 sets of sts on needle, cont as folls:

Row 14: (k1, p1) 12 times, k1.

Row 15: (RS) (p1, k1) 12 times, p1.

Rep rows 14 and 15 ten more times.

Last row: (p2 tog) 12 times, p1.

Gather last 13 sts on to a wool needle and draw up to form top of head.

a. Sew short edges tog at centre crown, see diagram 4.

b. Darn all loose ends in except top one.

c. Fit wig to head and pad at top to raise hair a little. Pin and sew centre front edge, as shown in diagram 4, then stitch down sides of face as far as cheeks. Leave rest open and thread hanging.

d. Place padding at back of head under wig to fill out back of head. Keep in place with 2 or 3 sts on to the hair.

e. The fixing of the front side pieces is to be left until the costume is fitted to make handling easier. Run a gathering thread down the extreme edge on each side of the wig bordering the face, (not across the bottom edge), and draw up as tightly as possible. Secure with 1 or 2 back sts, then stitch the inside of the 'bunch' to the sides of the face.

Shirt

With white yarn and size 2¾mm needles, cast on 40 sts and work 4 rows in single rib.

Row 5: (k1, inc in next st) 20 times. 60 sts.

Row 6: k4, p52, k4.

Keeping the g st borders of 4 sts, cont in ss for 14 more rows.

Divide for armholes:

Row 21: k13, k2 tog, turn.

Row 22: p2 tog, p8, k4.

Cont as before on these 13 sts for 17 more rows.

Next row: cast off 5 sts p-wise. 8 sts.

Next row: k4, (k2 tog) twice, cut yarn.

Rejoin yarn to rem sts.

Next row: k2 tog, k26, k2 tog, turn.

Next row: p2 tog, p24, p2 tog.

Cont on these 26 sts for 16 more rows.

Next row: cast off 5 sts, k to end.

Next row: cast off 5 sts p-wise, (p2 tog) 7 times, p1.

Next row: (k1, p1) 4 times, k1, cut yarn.

Rejoin yarn to last 15 sts.

own natural hair long, or wore wigs of a natural colour or greyish-white.

Men's shoes were made of leather but often had coloured heels and trims around the tops. Ribbons and bows would be attached here too. A cane or walking-stick was often carried, and this too would have a ribbon tied to it.

Materials

Hair: 10gm (½oz) dark brown 4 ply.

Shirt: 25gm (1oz) white 4 ply. Fine white elastic, (optional).

Breeches: 20gm (¾oz) deep yellow 4 ply and oddments of white and metallic gold 4 ply for frills.

Rhinegrave (overskirt): 20gm (¾oz) bright yellow 4 ply and oddments of contrast for stripes.

Short jacket: 20gm (¾oz) bright yellow 4 ply, oddments of deep yellow and metallic gold 4 ply.

Stockings: oddments of white 4 ply.

Shoes: oddment of dark brown 4 ply and a little contrast for the bows.

Cravat: oddment of white 4 ply.

Needles: sizes 2¼, 2¾, 3¼ and 4mm, and a crochet hook size 2.00 or 2.50mm, (optional).

Note: work the features in the usual way, see pages 14–15, but add a short moustache in the same colour as the hair. No ears are needed for this figure.

Gentlemen of this period were renowned for their brightly coloured clothing, usually wearing matching jacket and breeches as shown here.

Next row: k2 tog, k to end of row.
Next row: k4, p8, p2 tog.
Cont on these 13 sts as before for 16 rows.
Next row: cast off 5, k to end.
Next row: k4, (p2 tog) twice, turn.
Next row: (p1, k1), 3 times.
Next row: (p1, k1), 10 times, k1.
Cast off in rib. Sew shoulders together.

Sleeves

Make two the same. Cast on 30 sts and work 4 rows in ss.
Row 5: (k2, inc in next st) 10 times.
Row 6: p40.
Cont in ss for 12 more rows.
Row 19: (k3, inc in next st) 10 times.
Row 20: p50.
Cont in ss for 20 more rows. The extra length makes the sleeve fuller than usual.
Row 41: (k2 tog) 25 times.
Row 42: p25.
Row 43: (yfwd, k2 tog) 12 times, k1.
Row 44: p25.
Row 45: (k1, p1) 12 times, k1.
Row 46: (p1, k1) 12 times, p1.
Change to size 4mm needles and rep rows 45 and 46 twice more.
Row 51: inc into every st to make 50 sts.
Cast of loosely.
To make the second layer of frilling above the first, work as folls: with RS facing and cuff at top, use size 2¾mm needles to pick up 24 sts just above the picot holes. (You may find this easier if you use the crochet hook and slip the sts off the straight end directly on to the needle.)
Work 1 row of single rib, then change to size 4mm needles and work 2 more rows. Rep row 51 as above to make 48 sts, then cast off loosely.
Push this frill downwards on top of the first one.

a. Fold the sleeve piece with RS tog and sew the smaller frill edges first. Now sew the edges of the larger frill, pin the rest of the sleeve and sew up to the top.
b. Turn sleeve to RS and insert into armhole of bodice, placing sleeve seam at base. Pin in position; it should fit without gathering. Sew all round and fit shirt to figure.
c. Make 2 cords to thread through sleeves and tie with bows. Gather the frills evenly and pouch sleeves over the tops.
d. From RS, sew up front opening using invisible seam. Thread fine white elastic through bottom edge of shirt, (optional).

Breeches

With white and metallic gold yarns together and size 4mm needles, use a loose cast on to make 48 sts. Then cut gold yarn and proceed as folls on white alone:

Row 1: (k1, p1) to end of row.
Change to size 2¾mm needles.
Rows 2, 3 and 4: single rib.
Row 5: (k2 tog, p2 tog) 12 times. 24 sts.
Row 6: (k1, p1) 12 times.
Row 7: to make holes, (yfwd, k2 tog) 12 times.
Row 8: p24, cut white yarn.
Row 9: join in deep yellow yarn, inc into every st to make 48 sts.
Row 10: p48.
Change to size 3¼mm needles and cont in ss for 40 more rows.
Cast off 6 sts at beg of next 2 rows.
Row 53: k2 tog, k to last 2 sts, k2 tog.
Row 54: purl.
Rep rows 53 and 54 twice more. 30 sts.
Cont straight without shaping for 4 more rows.
Row 63: (yfwd, k2 tog) 15 times.
Row 64: p30.
Cast off and make another piece in the same way.

a. Place RS tog and pin the 2 pieces at front and back edges from waist to cast off 6 sts at top of legs. Sew both edges.
b. With front and back seams sewn, fold the piece across in the other direction so that the seams are now central and the legs separated. Pin together along inside edges of both legs then sew all round, including frills.

Rhinegrave (overskirt)

Contrast stripes are not included in the instructions as these are optional, see the illustration for the front of the figure.
With bright yellow yarn and size 2¾mm needles, cast on 90 sts and knit 2 rows.
Row 3: purl.
Cont in ss for 20 more rows.
Row 24: (k3, p1) 22 times, k2.
Row 25: p2, (k1, p3) 22 times.
Rows 26 and 27: as rows 24 and 25.
Rows 28 to 33: double rib.
Row 34: (k2 tog, p2 tog) 22 times, k2 tog. 45 sts.
Row 35: (p1, k1) to last st, p1.
Row 36: (yfwd, k2 tog) to last st, k1.
Row 37: p45.
Cast off.

a. With RS tog, place edges of skirt tog and pin, Sew centre back seam.
b. Make a cord to thread through the waistline and tie in a large bow.

Short jacket

The bodice is made in g st and the sleeves in ss, see diagram 4.
With metallic gold yarn and size 2¾mm needles, cast on 18 sts and k 2 rows. Cut gold and join in bright yellow.
Row 3: (k7, k2 tog) twice.

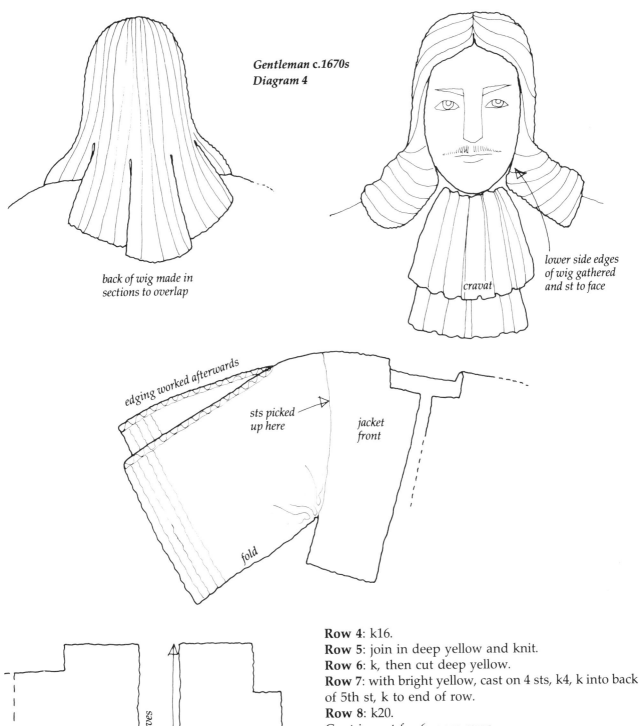

Gentleman c.1670s
Diagram 4

back of wig made in
sections to overlap

lower side edges
of wig gathered
and st to face

cravat

edging worked afterwards

sts picked
up here

jacket
front

fold

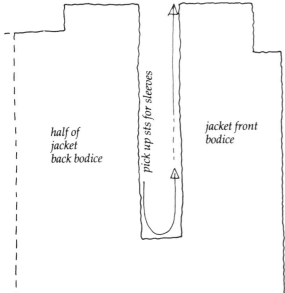

half of
jacket
back bodice

pick up sts for sleeves

jacket front
bodice

Row 4: k16.
Row 5: join in deep yellow and knit.
Row 6: k, then cut deep yellow.
Row 7: with bright yellow, cast on 4 sts, k4, k into back
of 5th st, k to end of row.
Row 8: k20.
Cont in g st for 6 more rows.
Row 15: cast off 16 sts, k to end.
Row 16: k4.
Knit 6 more rows on these 4 sts.
Row 23: cast on 16 sts, k20.
Knit 7 more rows.
Row 31: cast off 3 sts, k to end.
Knit 17 more rows.
Row 49: cast on 3 sts, k to end.
Knit 7 more rows.
Row 57: as row 15.
Row 58: as row 16.
Knit 6 more rows on these 4 sts.
Row 65: as row 23.

Knit 5 more rows.
Row 71: cast off 4, knit to end.
Row 72: k16.
Join in deep yellow and k 2 rows, then cut this yarn.
Knit 2 rows in bright yellow and cut this yarn.
Join in metallic gold.
Next row: (k7, inc), twice.
Knit one more row, then cast off.

Sleeves

Make 2 pieces the same. With size 2¾mm needles, bright yellow yarn, and with RS of bodice facing, pick up 16 sts from along RHS of bodice sleeve opening, 4 sts across base and 16 sts from back edge of bodice sleeve opening.
Row 2: p36.
Row 3: (RS) inc in first st, k to last st, inc.
Cont to p on all alt rows, and inc as on row 3 until there are 42 sts. Work straight for 10 more rows.
Next row: (WS) knit.
The rest of the sleeve is worked in g st.
Join in deep yellow yarn and k 2 rows, then cut this yarn.
With bright yellow, k 2 rows.
Join in metallic gold, k 2 rows, cut this yarn.
With bright yellow, k 2 rows.
Cast off.

a. The two side edges of the knitting form the false opening along the top edge of the sleeve, while the shoulder is sewn in the usual way. With RS tog, pin the shoulders of the bodice and sew tog, then proceed 2cm (¾in) along the increase edge of the sleeves. Turn to RS.
b. To make a gold edging for the sleeves, pick up 17 sts from one open edge towards the shoulder seam, then 17 more sts down the other side towards the border. 34 sts.
   Row 1: k16, k2 tog, k16.
   Row 2: k15, k2 tog, k16.
   Cast off as folls; cast off 15, k2 tog then complete cast off to end of row.
c. To edge the jacket with gold, pick up 42 sts round the lower edge and k 2 rows, then cast off. Alternatively, this can be crocheted using a size 2.00 or 2.50mm hook.
d. To edge the neckline, pick up 32 sts and k one row. On the second row, k2 tog on the first 2 and last 2 sts, then cast off.

Stockings

With white yarn and size 2¼mm needles, cast on 14 sts and work in ss for 46 rows.
Row 47: (k2 tog) 7 times.
Gather the last sts on to a wool needle and pin side edge tog from WS. Sew up and turn to RS. Slip this on to the foot and insert a small wad of padding inside the heel.
Make another one in the same way.

This detail shows the ruffled edges of the breeches, which are tied with bows. The shoes are also trimmed with bows.

Shoes

With dark brown yarn and size 2¼mm needles, cast on 28 sts and work in ss for 5 rows.
Cast off.

a. With RS tog, fold, and sew back heel edge.
   Slip this piece on to foot with cast off edge on top.
b. While still on foot, close shoe over top of foot with a few sts.
c. Make shoe sole as folls: cast on 6 sts and k 22 rows.
   Row 23: k2 tog, k2, k2 tog.
   Cast off. This end is the heel.
d. Keep the shoe on the foot and sew the sole to the upper all round from the RS. Squeeze gently into shape.
e. Make large bows for the top of the shoes using either the same colour as the suit, or a contrast.
   Cast on 5 sts and k 16 rows. Darn both ends in and tie tightly round the middle with gold metallic yarn. Sew these to the top of the shoes.

Cravat

With white yarn and size 3¼mm needles, cast on 14 sts and work in single rib for 10 rows.
Change to size 2¼mm needles and work 6 more rows.
Row 17: (k2 tog) 7 times.
Rows 18, 19 and 21: p7.
Row 20: k7.
Row 22: (k1, p1) 3 times, k1.
Row 23: inc into every st. 14 sts.
Rows 24, 25, 26 and 27: (k1, p1) 7 times.
Change to size 3¼mm needles and cont in single rib for 7 more rows, then cast off in rib.
Fold this piece across the narrow part so that the top layer lies just a little shorter than the lower one. Sew this to the neckband of the shirt as shown in diagram 4.
The side pieces of the wig can now be fixed into place.

Eighteenth century

The style of ornamentation which we now know as 'rococo', was created in France and flourished in the 1720s, during the reign of Louis XV. Originally it applied to interior decoration and furniture, but its influence was also eventually reflected in fashionable clothes, especially at court where dressmakers, milliners, textile designers and wig-makers would use every opportunity to advertise their skills. The style is recognizable by its use of shell-shaped ornament, by 'S' and 'C' shapes and no straight lines anywhere. In costume design, fanciful and frivolous festoons of gathered lace, ribbons and bows, artificial flowers, ruching, frills and flounces were extensive.

The French fashion industry was given a boost by the production in Lyons of fine silk fabrics, a state-supported industry which became world-famous. The king's mistress, Madame Jeanne de Pompadour, became an influential leader of fashion and her portraits by the artists of the day convey an essence of extreme feminity and glamour. Her elegant coiffure, which was re-introduced almost unchanged in the 1890s and at later dates, perfectly complemented the profusion of lace, bows, ribbons and ruffles. The style of hair ornament which she introduced in the mid 1740s consisted of a small spray of flowers, feathers or jewels placed in the centre, or to one side, of the head, and in England this was called a 'pompon'. It was sometimes worn with a tiny lace cap, as many English portraits show.

Madame de Pompadour, 1721 to 1764

In this version of her costume, Madame de Pompadour wears two underskirts. Originally, the top one, the petticoat, could have been quilted instead of frilled, to hold out her gown in place of a cone-shaped hoop. Her open gown shows the deeply flounced petticoat, in this case a false front panel, with the wide neckline of the bodice sloping to a point at the waist and revealing a stomacher, decorated with a ladder-like row of bows called 'echelle'. Although her shoes are decorated with rose-buds, as her garters, she would also have worn embroidered silk high-heeled slippers but strictly for indoor wear!

It was at this time that fashion dolls were used to show overseas clients what the leaders of fashion in France and England were wearing. Our model resembles one of these dolls, which were not used as toys but rather as illustrations for dressmakers and their clients. Fashion journals were introduced in the second half of the eighteenth century and these showed subscribers what was currently high fashion, *not* what would be worn in the future.

Materials

Hair: 10gm (½oz) pale brown 4 ply used with a fine silver metallic thread, of machine embroidery thickness. Padding.
A tiny sprig of fabric flowers and matching cotton.
Underskirts: 75gm (3oz) white 4 ply. Fine white elastic.
Gown: 50gm (2oz) main colour, (pinky-mauve), 4 ply used with 1 bobbin of fine pink glitter thread, as for hair. 50gm (2oz) paler pink 4 ply for centre panel and sleeve under-frills. 25gm (1oz) deeper pink 4 ply for upper sleeve frill, but this is optional, as the main colour can be used instead, and also for the gown hem frill. 8 press-studs, with matching sewing cotton.
Stockings and shoes: oddments of dress-colour with glitter thread, and white 4 ply. 2 fabric flowers.
Neck frill: about 30cm (12in) fine cream nylon lace, no wider than 1cm (½in) and sewing cotton to match.
2 tiny pearls for earrings.
Needles: sizes 2¼, 2¾, 3¼ and 4mm.
Note: the body should begin with white underpants and continue for the upper body and arms in the palest skin-colour available. The legs should be all white, to suggest all-in-one stockings and pants, thus avoiding the bulk of an extra pair of drawers under the two underskirts.

Madame Jeanne de Pompadour festooned with ruches, frills and flounces.

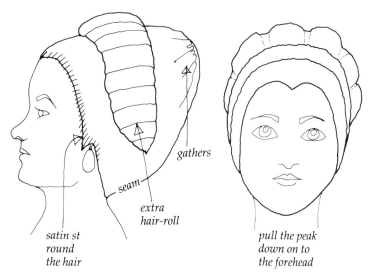

satin st round the hair

seam

gathers

extra hair-roll

pull the peak down on to the forehead

Madame de Pompadour
Diagram 1

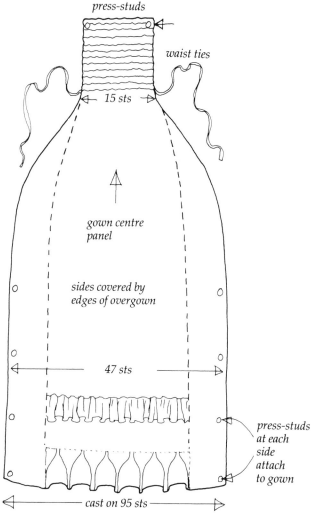

press-studs

waist ties

15 sts

gown centre panel

sides covered by edges of overgown

47 sts

cast on 95 sts

press-studs at each side attach to gown

Hair

With pale brown yarn, metallic thread and size 2¼mm needles, cast on 40 sts and work in ss for 6 rows.
Row 7: (k2, k2 tog) 10 times.
Work 3 more rows without shaping.
Row 11: k2 tog, k to last 2 sts, k2 tog.
Cont in ss but rep row 11 on every knit row until 18 sts rem.
Next row: (k2 tog) 9 times.
Gather the last sts on to a wool needle and draw up to form the top of the head.

a. Pull sts firmly tog, then sew 2 side edges tog to form a dome.
b. Pad cavity inside the dome and pin this to the head with the seam at back. Pull well down on to the nape of the neck.
c. Sew all round with tiny sts, then go over front and side hair-line again with evenly spaced, but *irregular lengths* of satin sts to form a 'widow's peak' in the centre of the forehead.
d. Make an extra hair roll as folls: cast on 30 sts.
   Row 1: (k2, p2) to last 2 sts, k2.
   Row 2: (p2, k2) to last 2 sts, p2.
   Cast off 2 sts at beg of next 4 rows, keeping rib intact.
   Cast off in rib.
e. Pin this piece well back on the head as shown in diagram 1, and sew down, bunching 2 edges tog slightly to give a rounded effect.
f. Sew earrings to sides, on a level with the mouth.

Underskirt 1

With white yarn and size 2¾mm needles, cast on 136 sts and work in ss for about 60 rows 14.5cm (5½in). Finish the top with a row of picot holes, see page 138, then cast off.

Make a border strip for the bottom edge, using border pattern No. 3, long enough to fit all the way round the hem.
Sew this on, then press gently. Sew up the sides and thread fine elastic through top holes.

Underskirt 2

With the same yarn and needles, make this version *either* in the same way as before, or choose another border pattern and cast on the appropriate number of sts. This version is worn over the top of the previous one, so should be a little longer.

Gown

The side edge frill of the gown is made and fixed at a later stage in the construction.
With pink yarn, fine glitter thread and size 3¼mm needles, cast on 100 sts and work in ss for 80 rows, leaving a selvedge of 4 knit sts on every row.
Change to size 2¾mm needles.
Row 81: k4, (k2 tog) to last 4 sts, k4.
Row 82: k4, (p2 tog) to last 4 sts, k4. 31 sts.
Row 83: k31.
Row 84: k4, p23, k4.
Rep the last 2 rows three more times.
Row 91: k5, cast off 3, k15, cast off 3, k5.

A detail of Madame de Pompadour's gown, showing her deeply flounced petticoat.

Now work on these 3 sets of sts separately as folls: on the first 5 sts, k 11 rows g st, then cast off.

Rejoin yarn to centre 15 sts and work in ss for 7 rows.

Next row: k6, cast off 3, k6.

Next row: p4, p2 tog.

Work 2 more rows in ss on these 5 sts, then cast off.

Rejoin yarn to other 6 sts, p2 tog, p4. Work 2 more rows in ss, then cast off.

Rejoin yarn to last 5 sts and k 11 rows. Cast off.

a. Darn in unwanted ends and sew shoulders tog.

b. Make frill for lower edge of skirt as folls: with deep pink yarn and size 4mm needles, cast on 200 sts and work 2 rows in double rib.
   Change to size 2¼mm needles and (k2 tog, p2 tog) to end of row. Cast off.

c. Sew cast off edge to lower edge of gown. Pin out flat and press *seam only*, not the frill, very gently.

Sleeves

With deep pink yarn and size 2¼mm needles, begin at lower edge with wide frill. Cast on 87 sts and work flounce patt as folls:

Row 1: (RS) p3, *k9, p3*, to end of row.

Row 2: k3, *p9, k3*, to end of row.

Row 3: p3, *sl 1 k-wise, k1, psso, k5, k2 tog, p3*, to end of row.

Row 4: k3, *p7, k3*, to end of row.

Row 5: p3, *sl 1 k-wise, k1, psso, k3, k2 tog, p3*, to end of row.

Row 6: k3, *p5, k3*, to end of row.

Row 7: p3, *sl 1 k-wise, k1, psso, k1, k2 tog, p3* to end of row.

Row 8: k3, *p3, k3*, to end of row.

Row 9: p3, *sl 1 k-wise, k2 tog, psso, p3*, to end of row. 31 sts.

Rows 10 and 12: k3 *p1, k3*, to end of row.

Row 11: p3, *k1, p3*, to end of row.

Next row: (k1, k2 tog) 10 times, k1.

Next row: k21, (rev ss).

Cont in ss without shaping for 8 more rows.

Cast off 2 sts at beg of next 2 rows.

Next row: k2 tog, k13, k2 tog.

Next row: p15.

Next row: k2 tog, k11, k2 tog.

Next row: p13.

Cont to dec one st at each end of every k row until 7 sts rem.

P 1 row then cast off.

a. Sew up sleeve seam as far as the 2 cast off sts.

b. Make extra under-frill as folls: with pale pink yarn and size 4mm needles, cast on 60 sts and work 6 rows in double rib. change to size 2¼mm needles and work one more row.
   Next row: (k2 tog, p2 tog) to end of row.
   Cast off.

c. Turn sleeve inside out and slide pale pink frill over this so that the narrow edge sits on top of the decrease row on the under-side of the sleeve. The lower edges will be level at this point and both seams together. Pin in place then slip st all round. Turn to RS.

d. To make the tiny bows, use dress-coloured yarn and glitter thread on size 2¼mm needles. Cast on 8 sts and knit 4 rows. Cast off, then wrap yarn once

The centre panel is attached to the sides of the open gown with hidden press-studs; the frills and bows are sewn on top. The flounce pattern at the lower hem is repeated on the sleeves, topped by tiny bows.

The wide-frilled sleeves of Madame de Pompadour's gown are worked in a flounce pattern. Her elegant coiffure is a mixture of pale brown and fine silver threads.

or twice round the centre of this piece and secure the thread. use the same thread to sew bows to top of ruffle, 4 for each sleeve.

e. Set sleeves into bodice armholes, see page 138.

Gown centre panel

With pale pink yarn (no glitter thread as most of this area will be covered) and size 2¾mm needles, cast on 95 sts, see diagram 1.

Row 1: k10, (p3, k9) 6 times, p3, k10.

Row 2: p10, (k3, p9) 6 times, k3, p10.

This establishes the central position of the flounce on the bottom edge of the panel. Keeping 10 sts in ss at each side of this panel, cont in flounce patt as for sleeves, beginning on row 3, which will read:

Row 3: k10, p3, *sl 1 k-wise, k1, psso, k5, k2 tog, p3*, rep to last 10 sts, k10.

Work all 12 rows of flounce patt, now reduced to 47 sts and then cont in ss for 60 rows.

Row 73: (k3, k2 tog) 9 times, k2.

Row 74: p38.

Row 75: k2 tog (k16, k2 tog) twice.

Row 76: p35.

Cont to dec one st at each end of every k row until 27 sts rem.

Row 85: (k2 tog, k7) 3 times.

Row 86: p24.

Row 87: (k2 tog, k2) 6 times.

Row 88: p18.

Row 89: (k2 tog, k6) twice, k2 tog.

Row 90: p15.

Cont in g st for 20 rows then cast off.

a. Pin the panel out under a light tension (i.e., from top to bottom, not sideways) and press gently, except the flounce.

b. Darn ends in and make 2 cords which should be sewn, as shown in diagram 1, to each side of the waist section on the lowest row of g st. These cords are tied round the waist and the ends tucked underneath the top underskirt to reduce bulk.

c. This central panel is the foundation on to which are sewn separate flounces, frills and ruffles. Make as many or as few as you wish and sew them one above the other as shown in the illustration of the front of the figure. Bought fabric rose-buds can also be used here.

Sew the frills across the width, as the knitted in flounce on the lower edge, leaving the 10 sts at each side free to tuck under the sides of the overgown. This is marked with a dotted line on diagram 1.

Deep flounce (make 4): with the same pink yarn, and the glitter thread, use size 4mm needles to cast on 60 sts. Work in double rib for 4 rows.

Row 5: change to size 2¾mm needles,
(k2 tog, p2 tog) 15 times.

Cast off in single rib.

Run a gathering st along one edge and draw up to fit the central panel well within the side edges. Sew these in position, one above the other, across the tops and sides.

d. Top flounce: with the same yarn and size 2¾mm needles, cast on 71 sts.

Row 1: k10, (p3, k9) 4 times, p3, k10.

Row 2: p10, (k3, p9) 4 times, k3, p10.

Cont in flounce patt, as given for sleeves beginning on row 3.
Complete all 12 rows, then cast off.

e. Bow (make 10): the top flounce edge is covered by 6 tiny bows, made in the same way as those for the sleeves. Sew them on at a slight angle, as shown in the illustration. Make a vertical row down the front bodice with the 4 rem bows.

f. Arrange the centre panel and gown on the figure over the 2 underskirts, and mark 3 points down each side of the front edges of the gown, where press-studs will be required to just cover the extreme edges of each flounce and frill. Mark with pins, then attach press-studs on gown edge and centre panel, see diagram 1. Do the same at the top corners of the centre panel bodice and on the corresponding part of the gown. Sewing marks will be covered by the outer frill, not yet attached, but keep them well back from the edge of the gown. Use matching sewing cotton for this.

g. Now remove the gown and make the edge frill. With pale pink yarn, glitter thread and size 4mm needles, cast on 180 sts and work one row of double rib. Cast off. Make another piece in the same way. Make a gathering thread along the cast on edges and draw up to fit from back neck to hem, one frill at each side, placing the gathered edge along the extreme edge of the gown, frill facing backwards. Pin in place, then sew on with the same yarn, joining the 2 lengths tog at back of neck. Where the frill protrudes towards the front, make a little stitch here and there to hold it in place.

h. With pale pink yarn, make a cord about 25cm (10in) long and thread this through the waistline of the gown, with the 2 ends coming out from underneath the side frills.
Fit the gown on to the figure, over the centre panel, and tie the cord firmly round the waist in a double bow. Trim ends if necessary.

Neck frill

This is made by gathering a narrow length of cream lace on to matching sewing cotton and joining the ends at the back of the neck. A knitted version of this may be made if preferred, although the effect may be too clumsy.

Hair ornament

The hair ornament is a bought machine-embroidered rosette, of the kind used to decorate bridesmaids' dresses, but you may prefer to either knit or crochet this.

Rose-buds decorate the shoes and stockings, which are hidden beneath layers of petticoat.

Shoes and stockings

With dress-colour and glitter thread (optional), and size 2¾mm needles, cast on 24 sts and work 4 rows in ss.
Row 5: (RS) p5, cast off 5 k-wise, k4, cast off 5, p5.
Row 6: p5, cut yarn and join to centre 4 sts, p4.
Turn and work 3 more rows in ss on these 4 sts.
On the 4th row, knit, making a rev ss ridge on RS.
Next row: cut yarn and join in white for stockings and work 4 more rows on the centre 4 sts.
Next row: (RS) k the 4 centre sts again, then 5 rem sts on LH needle, weaving loose colour in on WS.
Next row: p across 9 white sts and then across rem 5 coloured sts, pulling all 3 sections tog into one row of 14 sts.
Now cont in ss for 28 more rows.
Join in a length of main colour and knit 2 rows for the garter, then pick up white again and k 2 more rows. Cast off. Make another piece in the same way.

a. With main colour, join back of heel, then sew tops of shoes from WS.

b. Run gathering st round lower edges of shoe and draw up to fit foot, then sew across from RS, keeping base flat.

c. Turn to WS and sew back stocking seam, then turn to RS and fit figure.

d. Make 2 tiny bows, as for front bodice, and sew one to front of each shoe.

e. Two more bows may be fixed to the side of each garter, or, alternatively, use 2 fabric ones as for the hair ornament.

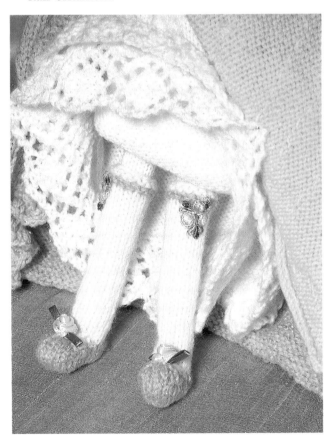

Young girl c.1750 (American)

Until relatively recent times, there was no distinction in the style of dress worn by children, but merely scaled-down versions of adult fashions. Indeed, very young boys and girls were dressed more or less alike, until they reached four or five years old, when boys would then be dressed in breeches. Girls wore the same styles as their mothers from an early age, including stiffened bodices, although this applied less to children of poorer parents than to those whose parents followed the rules of fashion.

At this time, especially in America, girls, like their mothers, wore lacy caps indoors and out and, more often than not, white aprons over their gowns. Lace and frills were to be seen round the necklines and falling over the lower arms, and although panniers would hold out the skirts of adults, young girls, such as our model, would wear several underskirts instead. This particular style of dress spans several years before and after 1750 in many European countries, as well as America and, with a few variations, can suggest clothing worn by children dancing round a maypole, or being led along by the Pied Piper of Hamlin.

The flounce pattern is used again on the hem of this dress; an apron is worn over the top, as was the fashion. The little mob-cap was also worn indoors and out at this time.

Materials

Hair: oddment of reddish-orange 4 ply.
Underskirt: 25gm (1oz) white 4 ply.
30cm (12in) fine white ribbon, (optional).
Dress: 30gm (1¼ oz) pale pink 4 ply and oddments of white 4 ply for cuffs and neckline.
Apron and cap: 15gm (¾oz) white 4 ply, with an optional oddment of white, pink or green for the borders. Padding.
Shoes and stockings: (all in one piece) 10gm (½oz) pink or yellow 4 ply. 10gm (½oz) white 4 ply.
Needles: 2¼, 2¾, 3¼ and 4mm.
Note: the body has knitted in white underpants as part of the skin.
For the face, embroider 2 large eyes with dark edges, fine eyebrows and a pink mouth. No ears needed.

Hair

With reddish-orange yarn and size 2¼mm needles, cast on 17 sts and work in ms for 16 rows.
Row 17: inc in first and last sts.
Row 18: work straight in ms.
Rep rows 17 and 18 twice more. 23 sts.
Row 23: (k2 tog) 5 times, k1, (k2 tog) 6 times. 12 sts.
Gather the rem 12 sts on to a wool needle and draw up to form the top of the hair.

a. Sew cap of hair along edges at top to close crown.
b. Fit to head and sew all round face.
c. For lower hair, make 2 twisted cords each about 75cm (30in) long, noting that about 3.5m (4yd) is needed for each one.
   Fold each cord up 3 times and tie the bunch in the centre.
d. Pin centre tie of each bundle to each side of the back of the head. Arrange curls round the face, with ends resting on shoulders. Stitch across back of head and on to the front neck.

Underskirt

With white 4 ply and size 4mm needles, cast on 90 sts and work the first 8 rows of the open-diamond pattern, see page 141, reading row 2 as k1, p88, k1.
Row 9: (RS) change to size 3¼mm needles, (p2 tog, p1) 30 times.
Row 10: k1, p58, k1.
Row 11: (yfwd, k2 tog) 30 times to make holes for ribbon above border.
Row 12: knit.
Now cont in ss for 34 more rows.
Next row: (k2 tog) 30 times.
Next row: (yfwd, k2 tog) 15 times to make holes at waist.
Cast off.

a. Press bottom and side edges gently.
b. With RS tog and beginning from bottom edge, sew half-way up sides to close centre back. Secure thread, leaving top half open. The underskirt and

dress will later be joined together and one cord will be passed through both sets of holes at waist.

c. Thread a cord, or fine white ribbon through holes above border and tie in a tiny bow at the front, gently drawing in the flounce as you do so.

Dress

With pink yarn and size 3¼mm needles, cast on 147 sts and work rows 1 to 8 of flounce pattern, as given for sleeves of Madame de Pompadour's gown, see page 97.

Row 9: (RS) purl 75 to form rev ss ridge.

Row 10: purl.

Now cont in ss for 38 more rows as far as the waist.

Row 49: (k2 tog) 37 times, k1.

Row 50: (p2 tog, p2) 4 times, p6, (p2, p2 tog) 4 times. 30 sts.

Row 51: (yfwd, k2 tog) 15 times for holes at waist.

Row 52: p30.

Change to size 2¾mm needles and work 8 rows in ss on the rem 30 sts.

Row 61: k7, cast off next st, k14, cast off next st, k7.

Row 62: p7.

Work 7 more rows on these 7 sts, then cast off p-wise. On the centre 14 sts, work 2 rows, then cast off p-wise. Work the last 7 sts as the other side, then cast off.

Sleeves

Make 2 the same, beginning at the top of the sleeve. With pink yarn and size 2¾mm needles, cast on 20 sts and work in ss for 13 rows.

Finish off the lower edge of the sleeve with 4 rows of g st, then cast off.

a. From WS, sew up side edges of sleeve pieces to form tubes.

b. Turn to RS and match sleeve seam with underarm point of sleeve-opening on bodice. Pin tog along edge of back bodice and the few rows of the front bodice as far as the front neck edge, leaving rest of sleeve unattached. This leaves almost the whole of the top edge of the sleeve free.

c. Neckline: with pink yarn and size 2¾mm needles, pick up sts from neckline and top of sleeves as folls: with RS facing, pick up 6 sts from back of left bodice, 9 from top of left sleeve, 14 from front edge of neckline, 9 from top of right sleeve and 6 from back of right bodice. 44 sts.
Next row: p44.

d. Change to white yarn and k2 tog across all sts. Cast off.

e. With RS tog, pin back edges of dress and sew 11.5cm (4½in) from hem upwards, leaving the rest open.

f. Turn to RS and place underskirt inside dress, matching openings and holes at waist. Pin tog at waist then, from RS, sew the 2 garments tog round the openings below the waist.

This young American girl wears a lacy cap and a white apron over her gown.

g. Make a pink cord and thread this through both sets of holes, dress and underskirt tog, to tie at back when sleeves are completed.

h. Sleeve frills, make 2: with white yarn and size 2¾mm needles, cast on 40 sts and work in double rib for 4 rows.
Rows 5 and 6: cast off 6 sts in rib at beg of rows, rib to end.
Rows 7 and 8: cast off 8 sts in rib at beg of rows, rib to end.
Cast off in patt the rem 12 sts.

i. Darn cast off end in and use other tail to sew 2 side edges tog. The straight edge should be gathered to fit the lower edge of the sleeve, then sewn in place from WS. The deepest part hangs at the back, see illustration of the front of the figure.

Apron

With white, pink and green, or plain white yarn and size 2¾mm needles, cast on 37 sts and work border pattern No. 5 for 3 complete repeats, see page 140.
Change to plain white and cont in ss for 30 more rows.
Row 43: k1, (k2 tog, k1) 12 times.
Row 44: p25.
Row 45: k1, (k2 tog, k1) 8 times.
Rows 46 and 47: p17 to make rev ss ridge.
Row 48: k17.
Cast off.

a. Pin out and press gently.
b. Make 2 cords and attach these to each end of the waistband.

Cap

With white yarn and size 2¾mm needles, cast on 28 sts, using the loose cast on method.
Row 1: (yfwd, k2 tog) 14 times.
Row 2: k28 to form rev ss ridge.
Row 3: (RS) k2, yfwd, k2 tog, k20, k2 tog, yfwd, k2.
Row 4: k2, p24, k2.
Rep rows 3 and 4 eight more times, then row 3 once more.
Next row: k28.
Next row: as row 1.
Cast off k-wise, loosely.

a. This produces a rectangle measuring about 9 × 6cm (3½ × 2¼in). Darn all ends in.
Run a gathering thread all round the rectangle just *inside* the border and draw up to fit the top of the head.

b. Fit to head with short edges at sides and longer edges at front and back. Pad slightly at the back of the head inside the cap, but not on top. Back stitch the cap to the hair all round, leaving the frill to stand away from the head.

Shoes and stockings

Made all in one piece. With pink or yellow yarn and size 2¼mm needles, cast on 24 sts and work 4 rows in ss.
Row 5: (RS) p5, cast off 5 k-wise, k4, cast off 5, p5.
Row 6: p5, cut yarn and join to centre 4 sts, p4, then turn, and work 3 more rows in ss on these 4 sts then on the 4th row, knit, making a rev ss ridge on RS.
Next row: cut yarn and join in white for stockings and work 4 more rows on the centre 4 sts.
Next row: (RS) knit the centre 4 sts again, then the 5 rem sts on LH needle, weaving loose colour in on WS.
Next row: p across 9 white sts and then across 5 coloured sts, pulling all 3 sections tog into one row of 14 sts.
Now cont in ss for 14 more rows, then cast off.
Make another piece in the same way.

a. With shoe-colour, sew up back heel from WS. Begin again at top of stocking and, with white yarn, sew back seam down to shoe.
b. From WS, sew tops of shoes, then turn to RS.
c. Run a gathering thread round bottom edge of shoe and draw up. Fit shoe and stocking to foot and leg.
d. Stitch base of shoe to close, and flatten gently.
e. With double shoe-coloured yarn, begin at front of ankle and run gathering thread all round top edge of shoe omitting the top of foot. Pull tightly, tie in double bow and snip ends.

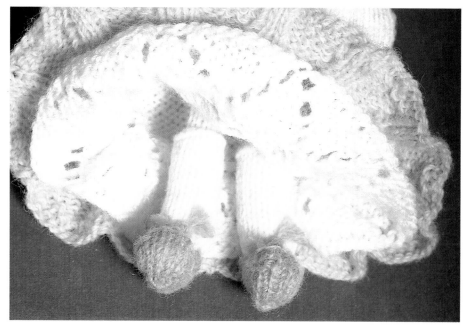

Beneath her underskirt, the young girl wears shoes and stockings knitted all in one.

French Gentleman *c.*1760

The three-piece suit of coat, waistcoat and breeches was, at this time, the most usual form of dress for gentlemen in European countries. Although details changed, ornate decoration decreased and fabrics darkened, the suit continued its way until modern times.

The coat was full-skirted and open at the back to facilitate riding and to accommodate a sword, which was often worn. Our version slopes away at the front, is quite collarless and is worn unbuttoned. The sleeves have huge buttoned cuffs, below which can be seen the lace frills of the white shirt. Men's costume made much use of rich fabrics, silks, velvets, satins and brocades, with elaborate embroidery down the front edges, round the pockets, cuffs and neckline. Our model's coat simulates a rich brocade by combining a random-dyed multicoloured yarn with a fine glitter thread of the type used for machine embroidery, to add sparkle. It is edged with a deep, lime green which is echoed in the shoes. The waistcoat, only slightly shorter than the coat, is pale green with a gold spot-pattern knitted on the front sections only. The ties of the cravat can be seen at the opening of the waistcoat, although at this time the cravat tended towards a plainer style than that worn by the typical 'Prince Charming' of Cinderella fame.

The breeches fit the legs closely and are made here in a paler random-dyed yarn but can, if you prefer, be made in the same yarn as either the waistcoat or the coat. White breeches are also quite in order, especially for evening-wear. They fasten just below the knee with tiny gold buttons or beads and are worn over white silk stockings, although the two items are, in our case, made all in one piece.

The wig can be made in at least three different styles, with or without the extra roll on top of the head. This version is tied at the back with a large bow, which was usually made of some dark fabric, but it would also be correct for your model to wear his 'queue' in a black bag, which was intended to prevent the white hair-powder from falling on to the coat. This style was known as a 'bag-wig'. The ties of the bag would be hidden by a large black bow, the ends of which were sometimes brought round to the front of the neck and tied over the top of the cravat. This was known as a 'solitaire'.

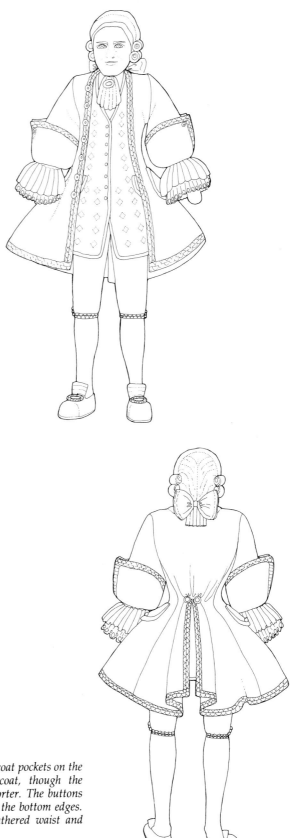

The front view shows the waistcoat pockets on the same level as those on the coat, though the waistcoat hem is somewhat shorter. The buttons on both garments do not reach the bottom edges. In the back view, note the gathered waist and button decoration.

103

Materials

Wig: oddment of white 4 ply used with fine glitter thread. Padding.

Shirt: 25gm (1oz) white 4 ply, oddment of white crochet cotton for cravat and extra frills. Fine white elastic. Tiny gold or pearl buckle, and 5 or 6 white press-studs.

Breeches and stockings: 20gm (¾oz) pastel-coloured 4 ply. 10gm (½oz) white 4 ply. Fine elastic. 6 tiny gold beads for buttons.

Waistcoat: 20gm (¾oz) pale green 4 ply used with 10gm (½oz) greenish-gold metallic yarn. 5 transparent press-studs. 12 tiny gold beads for buttons.

Coat: 40gm (1½oz) 3 ply used with fine glitter thread. The colour used on the model is a random-dyed blue, green and red mixture. Edgings require 15gm (½oz) matching or contrasting yarn. 13 small gold buttons or beads.

Shoes: oddment of same yarn as used for edgings, or black. Padding and 2 gold buckles.

Hair bow: 4 ply usually black, but any oddment of a dark colour,

Needles: sizes 2¼ and 2¾mm.

Note: embroider the face using a medium brown thread for the outline of the eyes and for the eyebrows. Outline the top of the eye with black or dark brown for greater definition. They eyes are dark blue but need bear no relationship to the colour of the wig, which is heavily powdered. Keep the mouth very pale.

Wig

With white yarn and fine glitter thread, as used for machine embroidery, and size 2¼mm needles, cast on 36 sts and work 8 rows of ss.
Now begin the back shaping.
Row 9: k12, sl 1, k1, psso, k8, k2 tog, k12.
Next and all alternate rows: purl.
Row 11: k12, sl 1, k1, psso, k6, k2 tog, k12.
Row 13: k12, sl 1, k1, psso, k4, k2 tog, k12.
Row 15: k12, sl 1, k1, psso, k2, k2 tog, k12.
Row 17: k12, sl 1, k1, psso, k2 tog, k12.
Row 19: k11, sl 1, k1, psso, k2 tog, k11.
Row 21: k10, sl 1, k1, psso, k2 tog, k10.
Cont to dec 2 sts in centre of every k row as before until 14 sts rem, then p one more row.
Next row: (k2 tog) 7 times.
Next row: (k1, p1) 3 times, k1.
Cont in rib on these 7 sts for 10 more rows, then cast off in rib.
Make the 4 side-rolls as folls: cast on 8 sts and work 10 rows in ss. Cast off and make 3 more.

a. Roll each piece into a neat sausage shape with the cast on edge inside, see diagram 2. Sew up gently, gathering the ends tog with one or two sts to neaten.

b. Lay the main wig section out flat and run a gathering thread all the way round the V-shape, (not the hair-line edge), as shown in diagram 2.

c. Mark the centre point of the hair-line of the wig with a pin and place this at the centre point of the forehead. Pin in position. Arrange the sides of the wig around the face, round to the back of the neck, and pin.

d. Place padding on top of the head under the wig and ease this towards the front with the points of the scissors. Now place more padding into the cavity at the back of the head as shown and arrange this evenly to fill out the shape. Draw up the gathering thread as you do this, to contain the padding.

e. Using a long sharp needle threaded with the same yarn, catch the 2 corners of the wig together at the back of the neck underneath the queue, and, leaving a gap of about 1cm (½in), stitch these points together and into the back of the neck to hold the wig in place.

f. Now with the same yarn and needle, continue to sew the wig to the head all round the face making a squared effect across the top of the forehead and down the sides, as shown in the diagram.

g. Using a satin stitch, go over the hair-line again to define the shape and to give a more positive sharp edge to the wig.

h. The folds at the back of the head should be arranged symmetrically, see diagram 2, and stitched together to close up any spaces. Stitch the queue firmly down at the back, leaving the nape of the neck free to accommodate the bow at a later stage.

i. Arrange the 4 hair rolls level with the eyes as shown and pin in place. Check for complete symmetry at all stages. Sew in place along top and lower edges of each roll.

j. Finally, make 2 rolls for the top of the head, although these can be omitted if you prefer: Cast on 22 sts and work 2 rows in ss. Now cast off 2 sts at beg of next 2 rows. Cast off 3 sts at beg of next 2 rows.
Row 7: sl 1, k1, psso, k8, k2 tog.
Row 8: purl.
Row 9: sl 1, k1, psso, k6, k2 tog.
Cast off p-wise and make another piece in the same way.
Fold each piece across, lengthwise with WS tog and sew up, like a pointed sausage, from RS. Place each piece over top of head reaching from one side roll to the other, close tog with folds at front.
Sew in place as shown.

Shirt

With white yarn and size 2¾mm needles, cast on 34 sts and work 6 rows in single rib, then change to ss and work 30 rows.
Row 37: k7, cast off 3, k14, cast off 3, k7.
Cont on each set of sts separately for 13 rows each. Do not cast off but leave each set on the needle, cut the yarn and rejoin it to the next set. At the end of the last set, do not cut yarn.

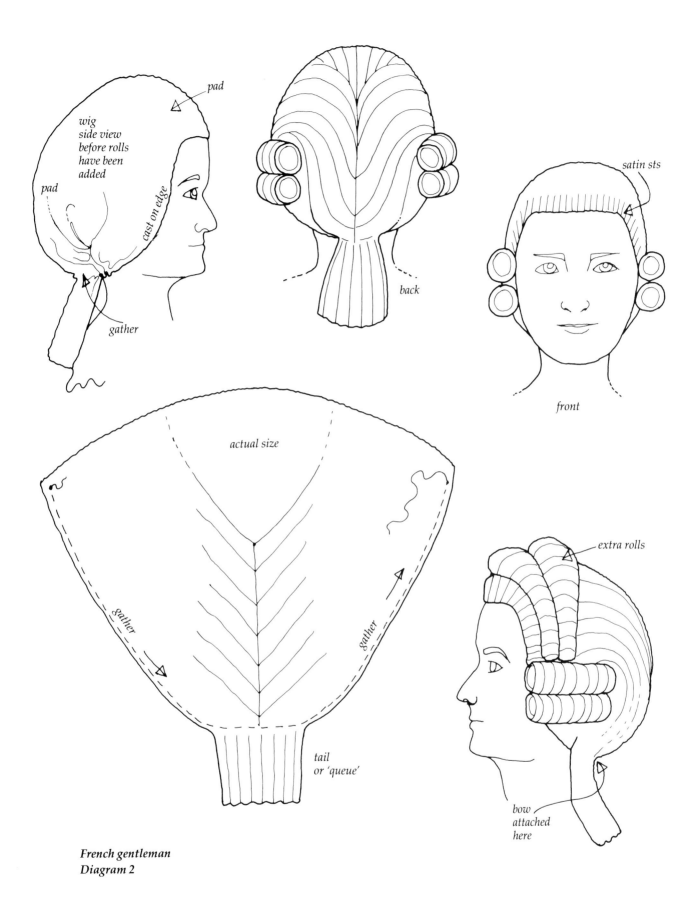

pad

wig
side view
before rolls
have been
added

pad

cast on edge

gather

back

satin sts

front

actual size

gather

gather

tail
or 'queue'

extra rolls

bow
attached
here

French gentleman
Diagram 2

Next row: k across all 28 sts, weaving ends in on WS.
Next row: (WS) k5, (k2 tog) twice, (k2, k2 tog) twice, k2, (k2 tog) twice, k5.
Knit 2 more rows on these 22 sts, then cast off k-wise, but keep the last st on the needle. Do not cut yarn. Point the needle down the side edge of shirt front and pick up 30 sts, (including one on the needle).
Without knitting any rows, cast off *very loosely*, or use a size larger needle. Do the same on the other side.

Sleeves

Both the same.
With white yarn, cast on 40 sts.
Row 1: (yfwd, k2 tog) 20 times.
Row 2: knit.
Rows 3 and 4: (k1, p1) 20 times.
Row 5: purl.
Row 6: as row 1.
Row 7: purl.
Rows 8, 9, 10, 11 and 12: as rows 3 and 4.
Row 13: (k2 tog) 20 times.
Row 14: as row 1.
Row 15: k20.
Row 16: p20.
Cont in ss for 28 more rows.
Rows 45 and 46: cast off 3 sts at beg of rows.
Row 47: k1, sl 1, k1, psso, k to last 3 sts, k2 tog, k1.
Row 48: purl.
Rep last 2 rows three more times until 6 sts rem, then cast off.

a. From WS, sew up sides of lace cuffs and sleeves. Turn to RS and pin into armholes. Extra lace cuff is optional: see e. below.
b. Sew sleeves into shirt bodice. Make 2 cords and thread these through tops of lace cuffs, or use fine white elastic.
c. Press front edges of shirt gently.
d. Sew 5 press-studs down edges from neck to hem.
e. For extra lace cuffs, use a fine white crochet cotton and size 2¾mm needles. Cast on 40 sts loosely and work in double rib for 8 rows. Cast off in patt and sew side edges tog. Gather cast off edge and fit round sleeve just below holes of existing frill. Sew in place.

Cravat

With fine white crochet cotton and size 2¾mm needles, cast on 10 sts loosely and work in double rib for 8 rows.
Row 9: (k2 tog, p2 tog) twice, k2 tog.
Cast off p-wise.
Sew the narrow edge to the top of the front neckline to hang freely just inside the 'V' of the waistcoat. Sew a tiny pearl or gold buckle to the cravat if you wish, but this is optional.

Breeches and stockings

Made all in one piece. With pastel-coloured yarn and size 2¾mm needles, cast on 15 sts and work in ss for 2 rows.
Row 3: inc into every st to make 30 sts.
Row 4: purl.
Cont without shaping for 14 more rows.
Rows 19 and 20: cast on 3 sts at beg of rows.
Row 21: k1, sl 1, k1, psso, k to last 3 sts, k2 tog, k1.
Row 22: purl.
Rep last 2 rows five more times until only 24 sts rem. Cont without shaping for 14 more rows.
Row 47: (k1, k2 tog) 8 times.
Row 48: k16, cut yarn.
Join in white yarn for stockings and work straight for 34 rows.
Row 83: (k2 tog) 8 times.
Gather last sts on to a wool needle and draw up for end of foot.
Make another piece in same way.

a. Fold each piece with RS tog and pin inside legs from crotch to toe. Sew each piece to form upper legs and stockings, matching colours.
b. With RS tog, pin the 2 pieces tog at centre back and front. Sew all round.
c. Thread fine elastic through top ss edge to fit waist closely. Turn to RS and fit to figure, turning stocking seams towards inside.
d. Sew 3 tiny gold beads to each side of the breeches just above the stockings to indicate the side fastenings.

Waistcoat

Outlines of waistcoat sections are given in diagram 3.
For the right front, with green and gold metallic yarn (gd), and size 2¾mm needles, cast on 22 sts and k 2 rows.
Row 3: join in pale green, (gn), and p to last 3 sts, carrying gd to end on WS, p3 gd.
Row 4: k3 gd, (1 gn, 3 gd) 4 times, 1 gn, 2 gd.
Row 5: (p1 gd, 3 gn) 4 times, 1 gd, 2 gn, 3 gd.
Row 6: k3 gd, 19 gn.
Row 7: p19 gn, 3 gd.
Row 8: k3 gd, (1 gn, 3 gd) 4 times, with gn k2 tog, k1. 21 sts.
Row 9: (p3 gn, 1 gd) 4 times, 2 gn, 3 gd.
Row 10: k3 gd, 18 gn.
Row 11: p18 gn, 3 gd.
Row 12: k3 gd, (1 gn, 3 gd) 4 times, with gr k2 tog. 20 sts.
Row 13: p2 gn, (1 gd, 3 gn) 3 times, 1 gd, 2 gn, 3 gd.
Row 14: k3 gd, 17 gn.
Row 15: p17 gn, 3 gd.
Row 16: k3 gd, (1 gn, 3 gd) 3 times, 1 gn, with gd k2, k2 tog. 19 sts.
Row 17: p1 gn, (1 gd, 3 gn) 3 times, 1 gd, 2 gn, 3 gd.
Row 18: k3 gd, 16 gn.
Row 19: p16 gn, 3 gd.
Row 20: k3 gd, (1 gn, 3 gd) 3 times, 1 gn, with gd k2 tog, k1. 18 sts.

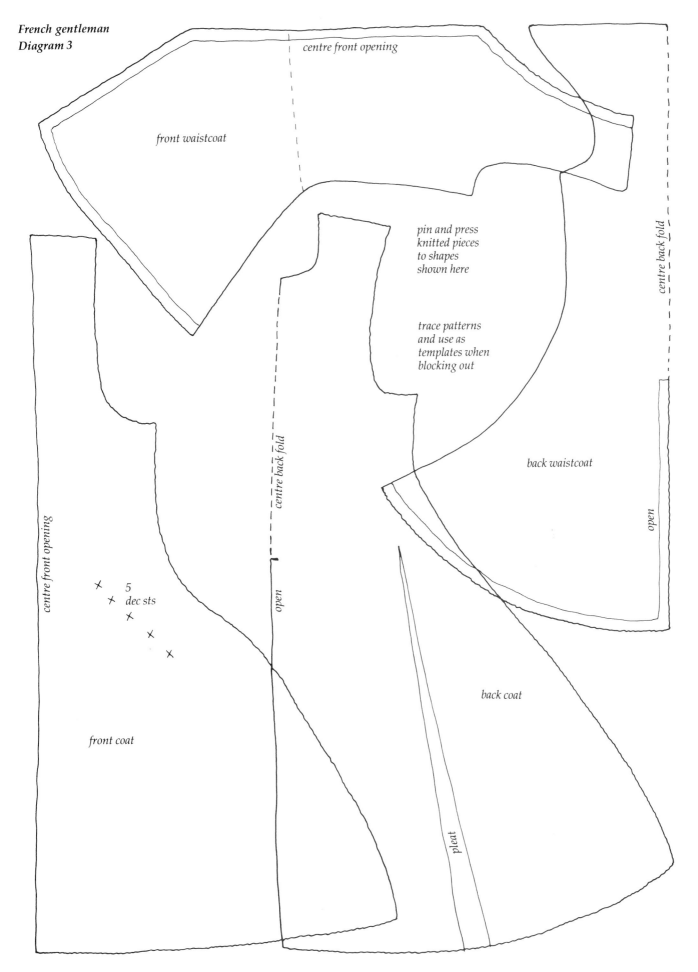

French gentleman
Diagram 3

centre front opening

front waistcoat

pin and press
knitted pieces
to shapes
shown here

trace patterns
and use as
templates when
blocking out

centre back fold

centre front opening

centre back fold

open

back waistcoat

open

5
dec sts

back coat

front coat

pleat

Row 21: (p1 gd, 3 gn) 3 times, 1 gd, 2 gn, 3 gd.
Row 22: With gd, sl 1, k1, psso, k2, k12 gn, leave last 2 sts on LH needle and turn.
Row 23: p12 gn, 3 gd.
Row 24: With gd, sl 1, k1, psso, k2, k3 gn, 3 gd, 1 gn, 3 gd, leave 3 sts on LH needle and turn.
Row 25: p1 gn, 1 gd, 3 gn, 1 gd, 4 gn, 3 gd.
Row 26: With gd, sl 1, k1, psso, k2, k8 gn, leave 4 sts on LH needle and turn.
Row 27: p8 gn, 3 gd.
Row 28: With gd, sl 1, k1, psso, k2, k1 gn, 3 gd, 2 gn, leave 5 sts on LH needle and turn.
Row 29: p3 gn, 1 gd, 2 gn, 3 gd.
Row 30: across all sts, k3 gd, 9 gn, in gn k2 tog.
Row 31: p10 gn, 3 gd.
Cont in colour-patt without shaping for 17 more rows.
Row 49: (WS) cast off 2 sts p-wise, patt to end of row.
Now discontinue gold spot patt but keep gold edge of 3 sts.
Row 50: With gd, sl 1, k1, psso, k2, k7 gn.
Row 51: p7 gn, 3 gd.
Row 52: With gd, sl 1, k1, psso, k2, k6 gn.
Row 53: p6 gn, 3 gd.
Row 54: with gd, sl 1, k1, psso, k2, k5 gn.
Row 55: p5 gn, 3 gd.
Row 56: with gd, sl 1, k1, psso, k2, k4 gn.
Row 57: p4 gn, 3 gd.
Cont on these 7 sts without shaping for 7 more rows.
Cast off p-wise, keeping colours correct.
For the left front, with gd, cast on 22 sts and k 2 rows.

Row 3: p3 gd, join in gn and p to end of row.
Row 4: join in a new length of gd, (this avoids having to carry the gd across the plain rows to the border), k2 gd, (k1 gn, 3 gd) 4 times, 1 gn, 3 gd.
Row 5: p3 gd, 2 gn, (1 gd, 3 gn) 4 times, 1 gd.
Row 6: k19 gn, 3 gd.
Row 7: p3 gd, 19 gn.
Row 8: with gn, k1, sl 1, psso, (3 gd, 1 gn) 4 times, 3 gd. 21 sts.
Row 9: p3 gd, 2 gn, (1 gd, 3 gn) 4 times.
Row 10: k18 gn, 3 gd.
Row 11: p3 gd, 18 gn.
Row 12: with gn, k2 tog, (3 gd, 1 gn) 4 times, 3 gd. 20 sts.
Row 13: p3 gd, 2 gn, 1 gd, (3 gn, 1 gd) 3 times, 2 gn.
Row 14: k17 gn, 3 gd.
Row 15: p3 gd, 17 gn.
Row 16: with gd, k2 tog, k2, (1 gn, 3 gd) 3 times, 1 gn, 3 gd. 19 sts.
Row 17: p3 gd, 2 gn, 1 gd, (3 gn, 1 gd) 3 times, 1 gn.
Row 18: k16 gn, 3 gd.
Row 19: p3 gd, 16 gn.
Row 20: with gn, k1, sl 1, k1, psso, k1, (3 gd, 1 gn) 3 times, 3 gd. 18 sts.
Row 21: p3 gd, 2 gn, 1 gd, (3 gn, 1 gd) twice, 2 gn, leave last 2 sts on LH needle and turn.
Row 22: k12 gn, with gold k1, k2 tog, k1.
Row 23: p3 gd, 11 gn, leave 3 sts on LH needle and turn.
Row 24: (k3 gd, 1 gn) twice, 2 gn, with gd k1, k2 tog, k1.
Row 25: p3 gd, 4 gn, 1 gd, 3 gn, 1 gd, leave 4 sts on LH needle and turn.
Row 26: k8 gn, with gd k1, k2 tog, k1.
Row 27: p3 gd, 7 gn, leave 5 sts on LH needle and turn.
Row 28: k2 gn, 3 gd, 1 gn, with gd k1, k2 tog, k1.
Row 29: across all sts, p3 gd, 2 gn, (1 gd, 3 gn) twice, 1 gd.
Row 30: with gn k2 tog, k9, k3 gd.
Cont in colour patt without shaping for 17 more rows.
Row 48: (RS) cast off 2 sts, patt to end of row.
Row 49: p in patt to end of row.
Now discontinue gold spot patt but keep gd edge of 3 sts.
Row 50: k7 gn, with gd k1, k2 tog, k1.
Row 51: p3 gd, 7 gn.
Row 52: k6 gn, with gd k1, k2 tog, k1.
Row 53: p3 gd, 6 gn.
Row 54: k5 gn, with gd k1, k2 tog, k1.
Row 55: p3 gd, 5 gn.
Row 56: k4 gn, with gd k1, k2 tog, k1.
Row 57: p3 gd, 4 gn.
Cont on these 7 sts without shaping for 7 more rows.
Cast off p-wise keeping colours correct.

Waistcoat back

The back skirt of the waistcoat splits down the centre to allow for riding, so our version is made in 2 pieces

The French gentleman wears a full-skirted coat, buttoned waistcoat, and tight-fitting breeches.

which are then joined at the waist. No spot pattern is worked on the back.

Begin with the LH side. With gold metallic yarn, cast on 26 sts and k 2 rows.

Row 3: join in pale green, noting that only sts in gold will be named as such, as all other sts are in pale green, purl across all sts, carrying gd on WS to last 3 sts, p3 gd.

Row 4: k3 gd, (k4, p2) 3 times, k5.

Row 5: k1, p4, (k2, p4) 3 times, p3 gd.

Row 6: k3 gd, (k4, p2 tog) 3 times, k5. 23 sts.

Row 7: k1, p4, (k1, p4) 3 times, p3 gd.

Row 8: k3 gd, (k1, p4) 3 times, k2, k2 tog, k1. 22 sts.

Row 9: k1, p3, (k1, p4) 3 times, p3 gd.

Cont in patt without shaping for 2 more rows.

Row 12: k3 gd, (k1, sl 1, k1, psso, k1, p1) twice, k1, k2 tog, k1, p1, k1, k2 tog, k1. 18 sts.

Row 13: k1, p2, (k1, p3) 3 times, p3 gd.

Cont in patt without shaping for 4 more rows.

Row 18: k3 gd, (k1, sl 1, k1, psso, p1) twice, k1, k2 tog, p1, k1, k2 tog. 14 sts.

Row 19: k1, p1, (k1, p2) 3 times, p3 gd.

Cont in patt without shaping for 2 more rows.

Row 22: k3 gd, (k2, p1) 3 times, leave 2 sts on LH needle, turn.

Row 23: p in patt back to beg of row.

Row 24: k in patt to last 4 sts, leave these on LH needle, turn.

Row 25: as row 23.

Rows 26 and 27: work in patt across all sts.

Row 28: k3 gd, cut gold yarn, weaving ends in on WS, (k2 tog, k1) 3 times, k2 tog. 10 sts.

Row 29: k1, p9.

Cut green yarn and leave these sts on needle.

Now work RH side, casting on 26 sts to the *free* needle. Work the first 2 rows as the same as the LH side.

Row 3: p3, join in pale green yarn and p to end of row.

Row 4: k5, (p2, k4) 3 times, k3 gd.

Row 5: p3 gd, (p4, k2) 3 times, p4, k1.

Row 6: k5, (p2 tog, k4) 3 times, k3 gd. 23 sts.

Row 7: p3 gd, (p4, k1) 3 times, p4, k1.

Row 8: k1, k2 tog, k2, (p1, k4) 3 times, k3 gd. 22 sts.

Row 9: p3 gd, (p4, k1) 3 times, p3, k1.

Cont in patt without shaping for 2 more rows.

Row 12: (k1, sl 1, k1, psso, k1, p1) twice, k1, k2 tog, k1, p1, k1, k2 tog, k1, k3 gd. 18 sts.

Row 13: p3 gd, (p3, k1) 3 times, p2, k1.

Cont in patt without shaping for 4 more rows.

Row 18: (k1, sl 1, k1, psso, p1) twice, k1, k2 tog, p1, k1, k2 tog, k3 gd. 14 sts.

Row 19: p3 gd, (p2, k1) 3 times, p1, k1.

Cont in patt without shaping for 3 more rows.

Row 23: (WS) p3 gd, (p2, k1) 3 times, leave 2 sts on LH needle, turn.

Row 24: k in patt back to beg of row.

Row 25: p in patt to last 4 sts, leave these on LH needle, turn.

Row 26: as row 24.

Row 27: p in patt across all sts.

Row 28: k2 tog, (k1, k2 tog) 3 times, k3 gd.

Row 29: cut gd, weaving end in on WS, p9, k1.

Row 30: push both sets of sts tog on LH needle and k20, weaving loose end in on WS.

Row 31: (p2 tog, p4) 3 times, p2 tog.

Cont without shaping on these 16 sts in ss for 16 more rows.

Cast off 2 sts at beg of next 2 rows.

Cont without shaping for 6 more rows.

Row 56: inc in first st, k9, inc, k1.

Work 3 rows straight.

Row 60: inc in first st, k11, inc, k1.

Rows 61 and 63: purl.

Row 62: inc in first st, k13, inc, k1.

Row 64: inc in first st, k15, inc, k1.

Cast off.

Pocket flaps

Make 2.

With pale green yarn and size 2¼mm needles, cast on 2 sts and knit one row. Now inc into both sts to make 4, then knit one more row.

Cont to inc into first and last sts of next and every alt row until there are 10 sts. Knit 2 more rows, then cast-off.

With gold yarn, embroider buttonhole st, see page 137, along the 2 angled edges, leaving the straight edge free to be sewn to the waistcoat as shown. Sew a gold bead or button on each flap before attaching them to the waistcoat.

a. Pin all pieces out according to the shapes on diagram 3, and press gently.

b. With RS tog, pin shoulders, leaving a space of one-third for the neck opening. Sew shoulders together.

c. Lay the waistcoat out flat, and using size 2¼mm needles and gold yarn, pick up 28 sts along armhole edge from RS. Knit one row, then cast off. Work the other side to match.

d. Pin the sides tog from WS and sew up, then gently press skirt seams open.

e. With gold yarn, make a few sts across the top of the back opening to hold the 2 edges firm at this weak point. Finish off with 2 small gold beads at each side.

f. Sew 8 tiny gold buttons or beads down the front edge of the waistcoat, and to close the garment, use five press-studs, leaving the lower edges open as shown.

Coat fronts

Front left-hand side, see illustrations of front and back of figure. **With chosen yarn, fine glitter thread and size 2¾mm needles, cast on 30 sts and work in ss for 8 rows.**

Row 9: k1, sl 1, k1, psso, k to end of row.

Cont without shaping for 3 rows.

Rep last 4 rows three more times until 26 sts rem.

Row 25: as row 9.

Row 26: purl.
Rep rows 25 and 26 until 22 sts rem.
Row 33: k1, sl 1, k1, psso, k4, sl 1, k1, psso, k to end.
Row 34: purl.
Rep rows 33 and 34 four more times. 12 sts.
Cont without shaping for 14 more rows.
Row 57: cast off 4 sts, k8.
Row 58: p8.
Row 59: k1, sl 1, k1, psso, k to end.
Cont on these 7 sts for 15 more rows.
Cast off.
Front right hand side. Work from ** to ** as given for left hand side.
Row 9: k to last 3 sts, k2 tog, k1.
Cont without shaping for 3 rows.
Rep last 4 rows three more times until 26 sts rem.
Row 25: as row 9.
Row 26: purl.
Rep rows 25 and 26 until 22 sts rem.
Row 33: (RS) k to last 9 sts, k2 tog, k4, k2 tog, k1.
Row 34: purl.
Rep rows 33 and 34 four more times. 12 sts.
Rows 35 to 42: cont without shaping for 13 more rows.
Row 56: cast off 4 sts p-wise, p8.
Row 57: k8.
Row 58: p1, sl 1, p1, psso, p to end.
Cont on these 7 sts for 16 more rows.
Cast off.

Coat Back

Cast on 36 sts for the left hand side.
Row 1: k16, p4, k16.
Row 2: p16, k4, p16.
Rep rows 1 and 2 three more times.
Row 9: work in patt to last 3 sts, k2 tog, k1.
Cont in patt without shaping for 3 more rows.
Rep last 4 rows 3 more times. 32 sts.
Row 25: k16, p1, p2 tog, p1, k9, k2 tog, k1.
Row 26: p11, k3, p16.
Row 27: k16, p3, k to last 3 sts, k2 tog, k1.
Row 28: cont in patt to end of row.
Rep last 2 rows twice more. 27 sts.
Row 33: k16, p1, p2 tog, k5, k2 tog, k1.
Row 34: p7, k2, p16.
Row 35: k16, p2 tog, k4, k2 tog, k1.
Rows 36, 38 and 40: as row 28.
Row 37: k8, sl 1, k1, psso, k4, k2 tog, p1, k3, k2 tog, k1.
Row 39: k7, sl 1, k1, psso, k3, k2 tog, p1, k2 tog, k1.
Row 41: k6, sl 1, k1, psso, k2, k2 tog, p1, k1, k2 tog, k1.
14 sts.
Row 42: as row 28, cut yarn.
Leave these sts on the needle and make the back right hand side by casting 36 sts on to the *same needle*.
Row 1: k16, p4, k16.
Row 2: p16, k4, p16.
Rep rows 1 and 2 three more times.
Row 9: k1, sl 1, k1, psso, cont in patt to end.
Cont in patt without shaping for 3 more rows.
Rep last 4 rows three more times. 32 sts.

Row 25: k1, sl 1, k1, psso, k9, p1, p2 tog, p1, k16.
Row 26: p16, k3, p11.
Row 27: k1, sl 1, k1, psso, k8, p3, k16.
Rows 28, 30 and 32: cont in patt to end.
Row 29: k1, sl 1, k1, psso, k7, p3, k16.
Row 31: k1, sl 1, k1, psso, k6, p3, k16.
Row 33: k1, sl 1, k1, psso, k5, p2 tog, p1, k16.
Row 34: p16, k2, p7.
Row 35: k1, sl 1, k1, psso, k4, p2 tog, k16.
Rows 36, 38 and 40: cont in patt to end.
Row 37: k1, sl 1, k1, psso, k3, p1, k2 tog, k4, k2 tog, k8.
Row 39: k1, sl 1, k1, psso, k2, p1, k2 tog, k3, k2 tog, k7.
Row 41: k1, sl 1, k1, psso, k1, p1, k2 tog, k2, k2 tog, k6.
14 sts.
Row 42: as row 36.
Now push both sets of sts tog on LH needle, (RS facing), and cont without shaping for 2 rows, 28 sts.
Row 45: k12, sl 1, k1, psso, k2 tog, k12.
Row 46: p26.
Row 47: k11, sl 1, k1, psso, k2 tog, k11.
Row 48: p24.
Cont without shaping for 8 more rows.
Rows 57 and 58: cast off 3 sts at beg of rows and work to end.
Cont without shaping for 14 more rows.
Row 73: k7, leave next 4 sts on a safety-pin, turn and work 3 more rows on these 7 sts.
Cast off, cut yarn and rejoin to rem 7 sts.
Work these in the same way.

Sleeves

Cast on 28 sts and work in ss for 16 rows without shaping.
Rows 17 and 18: cast off 4 sts at beg of rows and work to end.
Row 19: k1, sl 1, k1, psso, k to last 3 sts, k2 tog, k1.
Cont without shaping for 3 more rows.
Rep last 4 rows once more, then rep row 19. 14 sts.
Row 28: purl.
Row 29: as row 19.
Cont without shaping for 3 more rows.
Row 33: k1, sl 1, k1, psso, (k1, k2 tog) 3 times.
Cast off purling the first 2 and last 2 sts tog as you go.

Cuffs

Cast on 6 sts and k 4 rows, see diagram 4 below.
Row 5: inc in first st, k to end.

French gentleman
Diagram 4

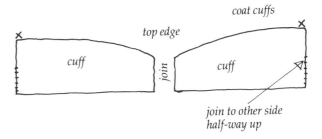

Rows 6, 7 and 8: knit.

Rep the last 4 rows twice more. 9 sts.

Cont straight for 20 more rows.

Row 37: k7, turn, leaving 2 sts on LH needle.

Row 38: k7.

Row 39: k5, turn, leaving 4 sts on LH needle.

Row 40: k5.

Cast off *very loosely* and make 3 more pieces the same.

a. Pin the 3 main body pieces out to shape, see diagram 3, and press gently.

b. Place shoulders tog and sew from WS.

c. Lay pieces out flat, shoulder to shoulder, and pick up sts beg on RS of right front hem. Using chosen yarn for edgings, pick up 45 sts from hem to shoulder seam, 4 sts from side of back neck, 4 sts from pin at back, 4 sts from other side of back neck and 45 sts down front edge of LH side. 102 sts.

d. K 2 rows then cast off.

e. Place side edges of coat tog and pin from hem to underarm, then sew.

f. To edge centre back opening in same way, see illustration of back, lay coat out flat with RS upper most, and pick up 28 sts from top of opening down to hem. Knit one row, then cast off. Now do same at other side in opposite direction. Neaten point of 'V' with 1 or 2 sts and darn ends in.

g. To make an edge along bottom of coat sections, use the same yarn and pick up 30 sts from front edge to side seam, then 35 sts from side seam to back opening. 65 sts.

    Knit one row as folls: k34, inc in 35th st, k to end.

    Cast off and neaten corners, then darn ends in.

    Work other side to match.

    Press all edges gently to regain correct tension.

h. Pocket flaps. With main colour, cast on 12 sts and k one row.

    Row 2: k2, p8, k2.

    Rep these 2 rows twice more.

    Row 7: k1, sl 1, k1, psso, k6, k2 tog, k1.

    Row 8: k2, p6, k2.

    Row 9: k1, sl 1, k1, psso, k4, k2 tog, k1.

    Cast off p-wise.

    After darning ends in, use contrast yarn to embroider an edge of buttonhole st, see page 137, round the wider side and 2 short edges, leaving the cast off edge free to be sewn to the coat, as shown, at a slight angle.

    Make another piece in the same way.

i. To finish the sleeves, first attach the cuff as folls:

arrange the cuff pieces in pairs, narrowest ends tog as shown in diagram 4, and join.

Now make a contrast edging along the top by picking up 40 sts from x to x on diagram.

Row 1: k18, (k2 tog) twice, k18.

Cast off loosely, (k2 tog) twice on centre 4 sts.

Join the other 2 sides tog only half-way up, then work buttonhole sts close together down the 2 free edges, using same contrast colour as top edge.

j. Run a gathering st along bottom edge of cuff and fit over sleeve, matching seams, narrow seams to inside of arm, and the bottom edge. Pin in place, ease gathers and sew.

k. Stitch gold beads or buttons on points of cuff, as shown in illustration of front, hold edges tog.

l. Pin both sleeves into coat and sew in.

m. Sew 7, or more, tiny gold beads or buttons down RH front edge, one on each of the pocket flaps and one on each side of back opening at waistline.

Shoes

Make 2 the same. With contrasting or matching yarn, and size 2¼mm needles, cast on 28 sts and work 5 rows in ss.

Row 6: cast off 12 sts p-wise, p4, cast off 12 sts p-wise.

Row 7: rejoin yarn to centre 4 sts, k4.

Work 6 more rows in ss on these 4 sts.

Next row: (WS) inc in first st, k2, inc in last st.

K 2 more rows, then cast off.

To make the sole, cast on 4 sts, k 22 rows, then cast off.

a. Fold shoe pieces in half with RS tog, and sew back heels. Turn to RS.

b. Pin tops of shoes to side pieces, leaving g st flap free. Sew tog.

c. Attach soles to uppers and sew on, using tails.

d. Sew a tiny buckle to the top of each shoe.

e. Fit the shoes to the feet, placing a tiny piece of padding into each heel. A stitch or 2 may be needed to keep the shoes in place.

Hair bow

With black yarn and fine glitter thread and size 2¼mm needles, cast on 12 sts.

K 4 rows then change to single rib for 14 more rows.

K 4 more rows, then cast off.

Take a length of the same yarn and wrap this round the exact centre of the piece to form a bow shape. Tie the ends tightly and sew the bow to the top of the queue (the tail of the wig), at the back of the head.

Nineteenth century

The expansion of trade and industry in Great Britain during the eighteenth and nineteenth centuries, the development of technology and the consequent rise in wealth of successful venturers, all had an important effect upon society. This was especially noticeable in women's dress, reflecting their attitudes towards their roles, both domestic and social. Whilst poor families remained just as poor as ever, their rich employers had no hesitation in highlighting their own wealth and importance.

The men's dress, sober and conservative, plainly reflected the importance of serious and successful businessmen, heads of thriving households, responsible for wives, children and servants. The quietly dignified clothes and well-cut styles left no doubt in the minds of their contemporaries of the affluence conveyed through such good taste.

Wives had an equally specific role to play in public relations, where they mirrored the well-being of the family and where there were enough servants to do everything, even the smallest chores. Their clothes were meant to reflect the fact that they were social assets to wealthy husbands, the tiny waists and pale complexions implied feminine frailty and the huge skirts were totally impractical for anything but the slowest and most graceful of movements. The frills and extraordinary amount of surface decoration conveyed an air of well-bred languor, which was cultivated from the cradle to the grave with great seriousness.

This clearly shows the stocking stitch triangle which has been inset between the two front edges of the ridged skirt. The bodice and skirt are separate.

Victorian lady *c.* 1845

At the time of our Victorian model, clothes were still being made by hand by skilled dressmakers, who obtained the latest fashion journals from Paris, containing hand-coloured plates to show to their clients. As fabrics were still quite costly, dresses were often remodelled after the first season of wear, and more than one bodice would be made to team with the same skirt, to do duty for both day and evening. This idea can quite easily be used on a knitted version.

As only the top part of the body needed outdoor protection, jackets, cloaks and shawls were much in fashion and hats and bonnets were always worn. Umbrellas, parasols and fans were also used to protect the face from the elements. Dress skirts were at first supported by as many as five layers of petticoats, until the introduction of bone frames, which made things considerably lighter although not so easy to manipulate. The American, Amelia Bloomer, tried to rebel against these self-inflicted obstructions by introducing baggy trousers for women but, except for the underparts of bathing suits and for cycling, these were not well received, being thought outrageously unlady-like – even indecent. No lady would let it be known that she even had legs!

Our figure belongs to the period of the crinoline, before the advent of the wire or bone frame, so she wears many petticoats instead. Make as many as you wish to hold the large skirt in place. The bell-shaped open sleeves shown the ruffles of the chemise worn under the bodice. The separate jacket buttons down the front and the skirt is fastened by a draw-string for easy removal. A full, long-sleeved underskirt (chemise), and long drawers complete her underwear. Tiny brown and patent leather-toed bootees are worn over white stockings, worked all in one piece.

The Paisley shawl was an essential part of the costume, either square or triangular, but our version is a long scarf. Knitted lace or crochet shawls were also equally popular at this time. Other details might include a lace cap, worn indoors as well as out, lacy mittens and a cameo brooch. The simple design of the garments worn by this model indicate that she is not necessarily wealthy, but of genteel birth.

Materials

Hair: oddment of dark brown 4 ply. Padding.
Long drawers: 15gm (¾oz) white 4 ply.
Waist-length underskirt: 25gm (1oz) white 4 ply.
Long-sleeved underskirt (chemise): 50gm (2oz) white 4 ply.
Day-dress: 50gm (2oz) grey 4 ply. 4 tiny grey pearl buttons.
Boots: oddments of white, pale brown, dark grey and sparkling black 4 ply. This includes the stockings.
Paisley scarf: 40gm (1½oz) cream or neutral 3 or 4 ply.

10gm (½oz) multicoloured 3 or 4 ply.

Needles: sizes 2¼, 2¾, 3, 3¼ and 4mm.

Note: embroider the face in colours to match the hair; two large brown eyes and finely arched eyebrows. On this model an attempt was made to give more prominence to the cheeks by knitting tiny, pale pink triangles and applying these with padding underneath. This is entirely optional but does create an interesting contour to the features. Keep the mouth pale pink, as ladies made little use of lipstick at this time.

Hair

With dark brown yarn and size 2¼mm needles, cast on 6 sts, see diagram 1.

Row 1: knit.

Row 2 and all alt rows: purl.

Row 3: inc, k to last st, inc.

Rep row 3 again on 7th, 11th and 13th rows. 14 sts. All other rows are worked straight.

Row 14: purl.

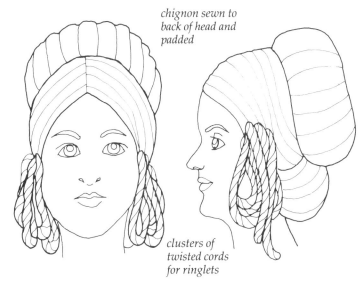

chignon sewn to back of head and padded

clusters of twisted cords for ringlets

dress bodice

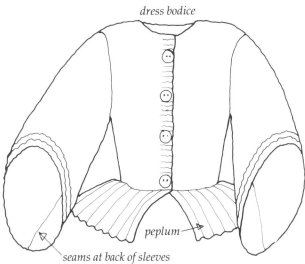

peplum

seams at back of sleeves

Victorian lady
Diagram 1

Row 15: (k2 tog) 7 times.

Row 16: p7.

Row 17: (k2 tog) 3 times, k1.

Row 18: p4.

Cast off and make another piece in the same way.

a. With RS tog, place these 2 pieces tog and sew across cast on edges, then cont down one side to bottom edge.

  Open cast off edges out flat.

b. From this straight edge, pick up 14 sts.

  Change to size 4mm needles and work 12 rows in single rib. Cast off.

c. Turn the cast off edge underneath and lightly stitch this to the pick-up edge. Do not sew up the sides.

d. Place this cap on the head with a tiny piece of padding inside the crown. Pin in place. Pull the sides well forward on to the face, shaping to a 'V' at the forehead. Do not stitch the lower edge, only the part framing the face.

e. Pull the lower back edge upwards on to the back of the head and stitch it in this position. Pull the free edges tog underneath and stitch in place.

f. Make the chignon as folls: with size 4mm needles, cast on 30 sts and work in single rib for 10 rows. Cast off and sew up the 2 short edges to form a tube. Run a gathering thread round both edges, place a narrow strip of padding inside and draw up tightly to form a doughnut shape. Secure sts and sew edges tog to hold padding in.

g. Stitch this piece to back of head using very secure sts.

h. Make bunches of ringlets from a fine twisted cord of the same yarn, or a crocheted cord. Bunch the cords up and tie in the centre, as shown in diagram 1, then stitch them to the sides of the head to hang level with the base of the neck.

Long-sleeved underskirt

The bodice has a back opening and a collar. Make the bodice first. With white yarn and size 2¼mm needles, cast on 30 sts using the loose cast on method.

Row 1: knit.

Row 2: k3, p24, k3.

Rep these 2 rows 8 more times.

Row 19: k6, cast off 3, k12, cast off 3, k6.

Now work on these 3 sets of sts separately as folls:

Row 20: k3, p3.

Keeping an edge of g st, work in ss for 14 more rows. Cut yarn and rejoin to centre 12 sts. Work 15 rows in ss.

Cut yarn and rejoin to last 6 sts. Work as other side for 15 rows.

Now work across all sts as folls:

Rows 35 and 36: (k1, p1) to end of row.

Row 37: inc once into every st.

Rows 38, 39 and 40: single rib.

Row 41: (k2 tog, yfwd) to last 2 sts, k2 tog.

Cast off loosely.

Sleeves

Make 2 the same. Cast on 20 sts and work 16 rows in ss.

Row 17: (k2 tog, k7) twice, k2 tog.

Work 15 more rows in ss.

Row 33: purl (rev ss).

Cast off k-wise.

Make 4 lace ruffles as folls: with size 4mm needles, cast on 36 sts and work one row in single rib.

Row 2: (yfwd, k2 tog) to end of row.

Row 3: knit.

Row 4: change to size 2¼mm needles and k2 tog to end of row.

Row 5: k18, then cast off.

a. Sew the 2 short edges of the ruffles tog then stitch the cast off edge of the ruffle to the lower edge of the sleeve just above the rev ss row. Stitch the second ruffle about 1cm (½in) above this.

b. Set sleeve into bodice, see diagram 1, with the opening at back.

Skirt section

With white yarn and size 3¼mm needles, pick up 30 sts from the loose cast on edge of the bodice.

Row 2: inc into every st to make 60 sts.

Work in ss for 8 rows.

Row 11: (k1, inc) to last st, k1. 89 sts.

Work 50 more rows in ss then cast off and make a border frill using border pattern No. 3, see page 139, or any alternative.

Sew this border to the edge of the skirt section.

a. Press gently and sew back edges tog, leaving a space of 8cm (3in) open at the top. Press seam open.

b. To fasten back opening, choose any of the foll methods; lace up from waist to neck with a cord threaded through edge, use press-studs or use tiny buttons and loops. Thread cords round waist and neck and tie in small bows.

Waist-length underskirt

With white yarn and size 3¼mm needles, cast on 134 sts and work border pattern No. 2.

Cont in ss for 18cm (7in) measured from top of border. (Approx 60 rows).

Next row: (yfwd, k2 tog) to end of row.

Cast off.

a. Press gently and sew side edges tog.

b. Make a cord for waist, or use fine elastic. Thread through waistline holes and tie at back.

Long drawers

Begin at the lower edge. With white yarn and size 4mm needles, cast on 32 sts and work in single rib for 6 rows.

Row 7: *k2 tog, p2*, to end of row. 24 sts.

Row 8: purl.

Rows 9 and 10: work in picot patt, see page 140, p the 2nd row.

Change to size 2¾mm needles and work in ss for 50 rows.

Work 2 rows of picot patt, purling the 2nd row, then cast off.

Make another piece in the same way.

Press each piece lightly under a damp cloth.

a. Measure down from the top ss edges 5.5cm (2¼in) and sew these edges tog for body back and front seams.

b. Divide the legs, pin with RS tog and sew up from frilled bottom edge to close the legs.

c. Make a cord for the waist and thread through holes. Make shorter cords for ankles and thread these through also.

Grey day-dress

This is made in two pieces, see illustration of the front of the figure, a bodice with peplum, and a skirt which gathers at the top to tie at the back with a draw-string. The bodice has a front button fastening.

For the bodice, with grey yarn and size 2¼mm needles, cast on 40 sts.

Row 1: knit.

Row 2: k4, p32, k4.

Row 3: k2, yfwd, k2 tog, k to end of row.

Cont in ss with g st borders, working a buttonhole as row 3 on 11th row. Work 7 more rows after this.

Row 19: k2, yfwd, k2 tog, k6, cast off 2, k16, cast off 2, k10.

Work on these 3 sets of sts as folls:

Next row: k4, p6.

Work 11 more rows of ss with g st edge.

Next row: (WS) cast off 4 and p to end of row.

Work 4 more rows on these 6 sts, then cast off.

Rejoin yarn to centre 16 sts and work in ss for 11 more rows.

Cast off and rejoin yarn to last 10 sts.

Next row: p6, k4.

Cont in ss with g st edge for 10 more rows, making a buttonhole as before on 7th row.

Next row: cast off 4 and k to end of row.

Work 4 more rows of ss, then cast off p-wise.

Fold with RS tog and stitch shoulder edges to each edge of back section, leaving 6 sts in centre for back neck.

Peplum

Using same needles and with RS facing, pick up 39 sts from bottom edge of bodice.

Row 2: k4, p31, k4.

Row 3: k4, (k1, inc) 15 times, k5. 54 sts.

Rows 4 and 5: (k1, p1) 27 times.

Row 6: change to size 3¼mm needles and rep row 4.

Work 2 more rows in rib then change to size 4mm needles.

Work 2 more rows in rib then cast off in rib.

The Victorian lady's grey day-dress is made in two pieces, a jacket with peplum, and a full skirt which gathers at the top. The white ruffles of the chemise can be seen below the bell-shaped open sleeves of the jacket. Notice also, the shape of the skirt, which is supported by several layers of petticoat.

Sleeves

With size 2¼mm needles, cast on 26 sts.
Row 1: knit.
Row 2: k2, p to last 2 sts, k2.
Rep these 2 rows three more times.
Row 9: k7, inc, k10, inc, k7.
Row 10 and alt rows: as row 2.
Row 11: k8, inc, k10, inc, k8.
Cont to inc in this way, twice on every k row with 10 sts in centre, until there are 36 sts.
Next row: purl.
Next row: k16, turn and p back to end of row, keeping g st edges throughout.
Next row: k14, turn and p back.
Cont in this way, knitting 2 less sts each time until only 2 sts have been knitted.
Next row: (WS) k2.
Next row: k across all 36 sts.
Next row: k2, p14, turn and k back.
Then cont in same way as before until only 2 sts at the edge have been knitted, then k across all 36 sts, (rev ss).
Knit 4 more rows g st then cast off.

a. Sew sleeves into bodice armholes with sleeve seam at back so that the deeper part of the cuff lies at the bottom.
b. Darn all ends in and sew 4 tiny pearl buttons to front edge.

Skirt

This is a straight piece of ridged ss with a triangular piece inset at the front, see the illustration of the front of the figure. The top edge is gathered with a draw-string cord and tied underneath the peplum at the back. The bodice peplum fits over the gathers of the skirt.
With size 3¼mm needles, cast on 52 sts and work from side edge to side edge. Work in patt as folls:
Rows 1, 3 and 4: knit.
Row 2: purl.
Cont in this patt until the piece measures 38cm (15in) long. Cast off.
For the centre panel cast on 24 sts and k 4 rows.
Keeping a g st edge of 3 sts at each side, dec on 5th and every foll 8th row until 8 sts rem, as folls:
Next row: k3, k1, sl 1, psso, k to last 5 sts, k2 tog, k3. On foll 8th row, k2, (k2 tog) twice, k2.
Next row: k2, p2, k2.
Next row: knit.
Rep these 2 rows four more times, then the first row once more. Cast off.

a. From the WS, sew this triangular piece between the 2 edges of the front skirt section and press gently

Here, the Victorian lady wears a fashionable Paisley scarf, worked in a mixture of neutral and multicoloured yarns.

under a damp cloth. Make a twisted or crocheted cord and thread this through the top edge of the skirt. Gather and fit on to figure and tie at back with gathers evenly spaced.
b. Fit the bodice over the skirt and arrange the peplum over the gathers.

Boots

Begin at the top with the short stockings. With white yarn and size 2¼mm needles, cast on 14 sts and work in ss for 6 rows.
Change to brown yarn and work 6 rows.
Cut 2 lengths of dark grey yarn about 1m (1yd) long and join in on next row.
Row 13: k2 grey, 10 brown, 2 grey.
Row 14: p2 grey, 10 brown, 2 grey.
Rows 15 and 16: keeping to ss, work 3 grey, 8 brown, 3 grey.
Rows 17 and 18: 4 grey, 6 brown, 4 grey.

Row 19: 5 grey, 4 brown, 5 grey.
Row 20: 6 grey, 2 brown, 6 grey.
Rows 21 and 22: 14 grey. Cut brown.
Work 2 more straight rows in grey, then 2 more in black sparkling yarn to resemble patent-leather toe-caps.
Next row: (k2 tog) 7 times.
Next row: purl.
Cast off.

a. Changing colours where necessary, sew up the side edges, and embroider 4 buttons down the outside edge of each bootee.

Paisley scarf

Paisley shawls were highly prized by fashionable ladies during much of the 19th century and were then made in the towns of Paisley, in Scotland, and Norwich in England, many of them to a characteristic Indian design based on stylized fir-cones. Whilst shawls were square and often entirely covered with pattern, scarves were longer and narrower with a border of pattern at each end.

In this knitted version, the yarn used to simulate the brightly coloured pattern is a multicoloured 3 ply on a neutral background, though 4 ply yarn will do just as well. The usual background colour for Paisley shawls and scarves was cream, but other colours are known, especially black. The scarf measures 50.5 × 17cm (20 × 6¾in).

With neutral yarn and size 3mm needles, cast on 50 sts and knit 2 rows. Join in coloured yarn and knit 2 rows.

Working from the chart pattern, see diagram 2, begin at row 1 and continue to the top, keeping the 2 edge sts in g st.

Now work 136 more rows without pattern, but keeping the 2 coloured edge sts in g st throughout. Use 2 separate lengths of yarn for these to avoid stranding across the whole row.

To work the border at the other end, the chart should be turned upside-down, working from row 24 down to row 1, finishing with 2 bands of solid colour in g st.

Note: *remember*, when working the chart upside-down, the RS rows will now be the *even* numbers, beginning with row 20.

Read the rows from the end at which the number appears.

It may help to cover the rows already worked with a piece of white paper (a postcard is ideal), and move this up one row at a time.

To make the fringe, cut lengths of background coloured yarn measuring about 10cm (4in) long. Take pairs of these cut lengths, double them over and pull the looped end through the g st edges. Open out the loop and pass the cut ends through this, then pull up tightly to the knitted edge.

a. Darn all ends in and trim.
b. Pin out to an exact rectangle and press gently from WS. Do not press the fringe.
c. The shawl or scarf was usually worn draped softly around the upper arms and back rather than the neck area. It was worn both indoors and out, over the day-dress.

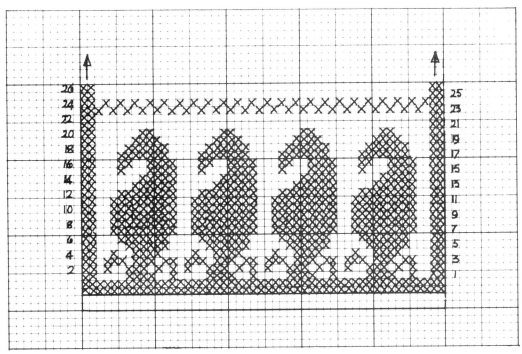

Victorian lady
Diagram 2 *Chart for scarf*

Victorian gentleman

This Victorian gentleman belongs roughly to the same period as the lady, around 1845, although even for a gentleman, details varied in many respects from the ones shown here. Cravats were worn in a variety of ways, some small and tight under the wing-collars, some coloured floppy ones, like this model, and some all black.

Waistcoats varied too, and our gentleman is wearing an up-to-the-minute floral one of bright colours, as opposed to plain grey, checks or stripes. If you choose to use a random-dyed, multicoloured yarn for the waistcoat, remember that the colours tend to stack up on rows with very few stitches.

The trousers and shirt are made in one continuous piece to avoid bulk around the waist; this is possible even if different colours are chosen for the two garments, as the join will be hidden by a waistcoat.

Front and back views show the position of the pockets. The waistcoat covers the join between the all-in-one pants and shirt. The large floppy cravat is tied beneath the high winged-collar, and straps hold the straight pants down tightly over the shoes.

Materials

Hair, moustache and beard: oddment of light brown 4 ply. Padding.

Trousers and shirt (all in one): 25gm (1oz) cream 4 ply. An oddment of the cravat colour is knitted into the shirt collar.

Waistcoat: 10gm (½oz) multicoloured 4 ply. 7 or 8 tiny gold beads for buttons.

Coat: 30gm (1¼oz) dark blue 4 ply. Alternate colours may be brown, green, grey, black, deep plum or burgundy. 6 tiny matching buttons.

Cravat: oddment of any contrasting coloured 4 ply.

Shoes: oddment of black 4 ply. Black card for soles.

Top hat: 10gm (½oz) black or dark grey 4 ply. A small piece of black card for the top, and a piece of thin postcard for the crown of the hat. Glue.

Needles: sizes 2 and 2¼mm.

Note: make the basic body using a medium-tan skin colour. The hair can be any colour you choose; beard and moustache are optional. Embroider the face using the hair-colour for heavy squarish eyebrows, set fairly well down over the eyes. The eyes should be well defined, but it is not really necessary to outline the mouth as this will be hidden by the moustache.

Hair

Make two pieces the same. With light brown yarn and size 2mm needles, cast on 12 sts and work in g st throughout, see diagram 3.

Rows 1 and 3: knit.

Rows 2 and 4: k, inc in first and last sts.

Cont to knit straight for 10 more rows.

Now inc one st at beg of next and every alt row, (i.e., on one edge only) until there are 20 sts.

Cont straight for 5 more rows.

Next row: (k2 tog) 10 times.

K 2 more rows on these 10 sts, then cast off.

Beard

Cast on 3 sts and k 6 rows.

Row 7: inc, k1, inc. 5 sts.

Row 8: cast on 4 sts, k to last st, inc.

Rows 9 and 10: k10.

Row 11: (k2 tog) 5 times.

Row 12: k5.

Cast off and make another piece in same way.

a. Diagram 3 shows how the 2 hair pieces are joined along the shaped edges, then gathered along the cast off edges for the forehead piece. Padding is placed between the hair and the top and back of the head to fill out the shape. The hair is then pulled well down at the back and pinned in place until the beard has been attached.

b. Join the 2 beard pieces tog and fit to the chin.

c. Arrange the hair at the sides over the top of the beard edge. Sew in place all round.

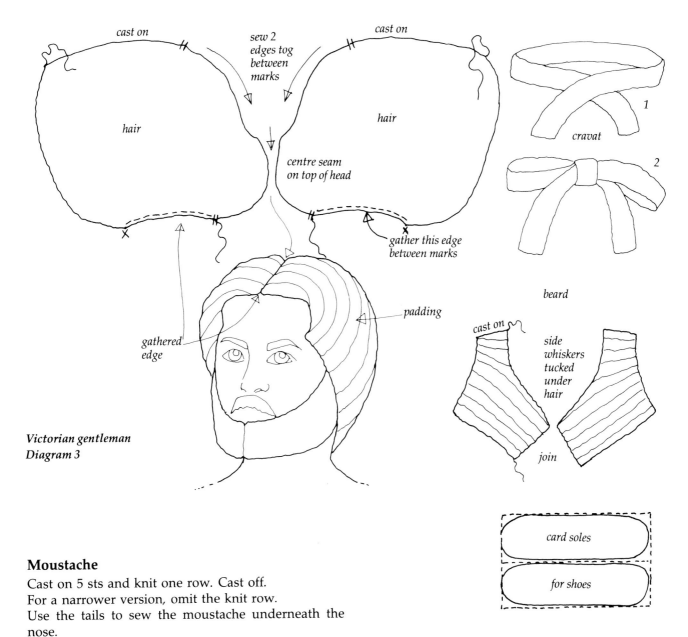

cast on

sew 2 edges tog between marks

cast on

hair

centre seam on top of head

hair

cravat

1

2

gather this edge between marks

gathered edge

padding

beard

cast on

side whiskers tucked under hair

join

Victorian gentleman Diagram 3

card soles

for shoes

Moustache

Cast on 5 sts and knit one row. Cast off.
For a narrower version, omit the knit row.
Use the tails to sew the moustache underneath the nose.

Trousers and shirt

These two garments are made all in one piece. Begin at the bottom of the trousers. With trouser-coloured yarn and size 2¼mm needles, cast on 16 sts and work 10 rows of ss.
Row 11: inc one st at each end of the row. 18 sts.
Cont straight for 9 more rows.
Row 21: as row 11.
Cont straight for 9 more rows.
Cont to inc as before on every 10th row until there are 24 sts.
Work straight without shaping for 31 more rows.
Shape the body as folls:
Row 73: cast off 3, k to end of row.
Row 74: cast off 3, p to end of row. 18 sts.
Work straight for 18 more rows, then cut yarn and leave these sts on a spare needle.
Make another piece in the same way.
When both pieces are complete, knit across all 36 sts.

Purl one row.
Now sew these 2 pieces tog while still on the needle, from the beg of the cast off edges, round the curve up to the last 2 rows. If you are making the trousers and shirt in different colours, this is the place to cut the yarn and join in the new one.
Continue making the shirt as folls:
Next row: (k2 tog, k4) 6 times. 30 sts.
Work in ss for 7 more rows.
Next row: (k4, inc) 6 times. 36 sts.
Work in ss for 13 more rows.
Divide for the armholes:
Next row: k7, cast off 4, k14, cast off 4, k7.
On each set of sts separately, work in ss for 11 rows.
Do not cast off but keep each set of sts on the same needle, (or a spare one), until all 3 sets are completed.
Next row: knit across all 3 sets of sts. 28 sts.
Next row: (p2, p2 tog) 7 times.

Change to cravat colour (do not cut shirt colour), and work 2 rows.

With shirt colour, knit 1 row and weave cravat colour in on WS. Cut cravat yarn.

Next row: (collar) p10, cast off one st, p10.

Work separately on these 2 sets of 10 sts for 2 rows each.

Cast off p-wise.

Darn all ends in except those needed for sewing up.

Sleeves

Cast on 24 sts and work 8 rows in ss.

Row 9: (k2 tog, k2) 6 times.

Work 23 more rows in ss.

Row 33: (k2 tog, k6) twice, k2 tog.

Work 13 more rows, then cast off.

a. To make up the trousers and shirt, begin with the sleeves and sew these up, from the WS, from wrist to armhole.
b. With WS tog, sew sleeves into armholes.
c. Fold the leg pieces with WS tog, and stitch down each leg from top 4 cast off sts to ankles. Turn to RS.
d. Slip the figure into the suit and pin up back opening.
e. Sew back opening. If necessary, keep collar upright by slip stitching it to hair and beard.

Waistcoat

Knitted throughout in ms for extra firmness and made entirely in one piece.

With multicoloured yarn and size 2¼mm needles, cast on 39 sts and work in ms for 14 rows.

Row 15: keeping patt correct, dec one st at each end of row.

Row 16: work in ms to end of row.

Rows 17 to 22: rep rows 15 and 16. 31 sts.

Divide for armholes.

Row 23: ms 5, cast off 4, ms 13, cast off 4, ms 5.

Work on these 3 sets of sts separately as folls: ms on first set of 5 sts for 20 rows.

Cast off, cut yarn and rejoin to centre set.

Ms on centre set for 18 rows.

Cast off, cut yarn and rejoin to third set.

Ms on these 5 sts for 20 rows, as other side.

Cast off and darn unwanted ends in.

a. From WS, join shoulder edges, allowing a space of at least 5 sts at the back neck. Turn to RS and fit to figure.
b. Join centre opening with invisible seam and sew tiny gold buttons along the join.
c. Gently pull down lower edge of waistcoat as far as the centre join of the trousers and hold in place with a few invisible sts.

Cravat

Using the same yarn as the cravat neckband (knitted into the shirt collar), and size 2mm needles, cast on 50 sts and then cast them off again. Make the centre piece on 8 sts in the same way. See diagram 3 for the tying instructions.

Coat

Begin with the back section, see illustration showing the front and back of the figure.

With dark blue (or alternative), yarn and size 2¼mm needles, cast on 44 sts and k 2 rows.

Row 3: purl.

Row 4: k10, p2, k8, p4, k8, p2, k10.

Row 5: p10, k2, p8, k4, p8, k2, p10.

Rep rows 4 and 5 four more times.

Row 14: k2 tog, k8, p2, k8, p2 tog, (p2, k8) twice, k2 tog. 41 sts.

Row 15: p9, k2, p8, k3, p8, k2, p9.

Cont in this patt for 6 more rows.

Row 22: k2 tog, k7, p2, k2 tog tbl, k6, p2 tog, p1, k6, k2 tog, p2, k7, k2 tog. 36 sts.

Row 23: p8, k2, (p7, k2) twice, p8.

Cont in this patt for 6 more rows.

Row 30: k2 tog, k6, (p2 tog, k7) twice, p2 tog, k6, k2 tog. 31 sts.

Row 31: (p7, k1) 3 times, p7.

Work 2 more rows in this patt.

Row 34: k2, (k2 tog, k1) 9 times, k2. 22 sts.

Rows 35 to 53: work in ss for 19 rows.

Rows 54 and 55: cast off 3 sts, work to end of row.

Cont straight for 6 more rows.

Row 62: inc in first and last sts. 18 sts.

Work 3 more rows without shaping, then rep last 4 rows again. 20 sts.

Row 70: k6, cast off 8, k6.

Now work on the first 6 sts for 2 rows.

Next row: cast off 3 p-wise, p to end.

Next row: k3.

Next row: p2 tog, p1, pass first st over 2nd, cut yarn. Rejoin yarn to rem 6 sts and p6.

Next row: cast off 3, k to end.

Next row: p3.

Next row: k2 tog, k1, pass first st over 2nd, cut yarn.

Left front

Cast on 10 sts and k 2 rows.

Row 3: k1, p1, k1, p7.

Row 4: k6, (p1, k1) twice.

Rep last 2 rows until 53 rows have been worked.

Row 54 (armhole): cast off 3, work to end.

Rows 55 to 71: work straight on 7 sts.

Row 72: work to last 2 sts, k2 tog.

Row 73: p2 tog, p4.

Work 2 more rows in ss then cast off.

Right front

Cast on 10 sts and k 2 rows.

Row 3: p7, k1, p1, k1.

Row 4: (k1, p1) twice, k6.

Rep last 2 rows until 52 rows have been worked.

Row 53 (armhole): cast off 3 p-wise, work to end.
Rows 54 to 71: work straight on 7 sts.
Row 72: k2 tog, k1, p1, k3.
Row 73: p4, k2 tog.
Work 2 more rows in ss then cast off.

Sleeves

Make 2 the same. Cast on 30 sts and shape the shoulder by part-row knitting, as folls:
Row 1: k25, turn.
Row 2: p20, turn.
Row 3: k15, turn.
Row 4: p10, turn.
Row 5: k to end of row.
Row 6: p30.
Rep these 6 rows once more.
Cont straight in ss for 4 more rows.
Row 17: k2 tog, k to last 2 sts, k2 tog.
Cont straight for 2 more rows.
Rep last 4 rows until 20 sts rem.
Next row: (WS) k1, p1, to end of row.
Work 7 more rows in ms then cast off in patt.

Collar

Cast on 41 sts and work in ms for 4 rows. Change to ss and work 6 rows.
Row 11: k37, turn.
Row 12: p33, turn.
Row 13: k29, turn.
Row 14: p25, turn.
Row 15: k21, turn.
Row 16: p17, turn.
Row 17: k13, turn.
Row 18: p9, turn.
Row 19: k to end of row.
Row 20: p41.
Cast off, leaving last st on needle.
Turn the knitting end-ways, with RS facing, and pick up 4 sts from the end of the collar, stopping short of the ms rows.
Row 1: (k1, p1) twice.
Row 2: (p1, k1) twice.
Row 3: **cast on 5 sts, then (k1, p1) 4 times, p1.
Rows 4, 6, 8 and 10: work in ms to last 2 sts, k2 tog.
Row 5: ms 8, keeping patt intact.
Row 7: ms 7.
Row 9: ms 6.
Cont to dec in the same way on alt rows until only 2 sts rem. Pass first st over 2nd to cast off, and leave longish ends for sewing up.**.
With RS facing, pick up 4 sts (as before), from other end of collar, working from centre towards inside edge.
Row 1: (k1, p1) twice.
Row 2: (p1, k1) twice.
Now follow instructions as for other side from ** to **.
a. With RS tog, sew the 2 edges of back section to right and left fronts, matching lower borders. Do not sew shoulders.

The Victorian gentleman is smartly dressed in a top hat, long coat and floral waistcoat.

b. Lay back and side pieces out flat and pin out carefully, keeping 2 front edges quite straight, not curved. Press *very gently* under damp cloth and unpin when cool.
c. Sew two shoulder edges.
d. From WS, sew up sleeve pieces, matching ms cuffs.

123

e. With RS tog, set sleeves into bodice of coat, matching underarm seams to side seams, and sew in. Turn to RS and press gently if necessary.

f. Fold collar in half and mark centre with pin. Place this marker at the centre back neck of the coat, with RS of collar on *inside* of coat (i.e., RS to WS), and pin in place.

g. Now pin the rest of the collar along the neck edge of the coat as far down as the pointed ends, so that when the collar is rolled back, the RS will be uppermost, and the seam underneath. Check that both points of the lapels are level.

h. Beginning at one pointed end of the lapel, sew along collar (WS of collar to RS of coat), towards the back neck. At the centre back point, fasten off and begin again at the other point. Fasten off.

i Roll the collar over to the outside of the coat, flatten the lapels and press very gently under a damp cloth using the point of the iron.
Fit the coat on to the figure and pull the collar well up on to the back of the neck.

j. Sew 3 or 4 tiny buttons down the edge of the right front just above the waistline.

Pockets

Make 2 the same. With size 2mm needles, cast on 10 sts and work 2 rows in ss.
Row 3: inc in first and last sts.
Row 4: (k1, p1) 6 times.
Row 5: (p1, k1) 6 times, then cast off in ms.

a. Sew pockets on to sides of coat, across side seams with the top edges just level with bottom edge of waistcoat. Try on the figure for correct position before sewing.

b. Sew top edges only, leaving flaps open. Pockets on the model are angled very slightly upwards, towards the front of the jacket.

c. Sew 2 more buttons close tog at back of coat (in the centre) on the same level as the pockets.

Shoes

Make two the same, see diagram 3. With black yarn and size 2¼mm needles, cast on 20 sts.
Rows 1, 3 and 4: knit.
Row 2: purl.
Cast off.

a. The cast off edge is the top. Fold each piece in half with RS tog and sew up 2 short side edges. Darn ends in.

b. The folded end is the toe. Sew along the top about half-way and leave the base open.

c. Cut the card soles as shown in the diagram and paint, or use a pencil to colour the white edges black. Fit the shoe on to the foot, (no socks needed), leaving the base open. Glue the black card sole on to the edges of the knitted shoe all round. It is easier to do this while the shoe is on the figure. A tiny piece of padding may be inserted down into the heel of the shoe.

d. When the shoe sole is quite dry, make a crochet chain using a size 2mm hook and trouser-coloured yarn. About 10 chains should be enough. This is for the trouser-strap which passes under the shoe. Attach one end of the chain to the base of the centre trouser seam, pass it under the foot and attach the other end into the outer edge of the trouser border. This should be pulled quite tightly so that the trouser edge fits well down on to the shoe.

Hat

With black or grey yarn and size 2¼mm needles, cast on 40 sts and work in ss for 18 rows.
Row 19: (RS) purl.
Row 20: (p2 tog) 20 times.
Row 21: k20.
Row 22: p20.
Row 23: (k2 tog) 10 times.
Row 24: p10.
Row 25: (k2 tog) 5 times.

a. Gather the last 5 sts on to a wool needle and draw up tightly. Sew across the top and down the sides, matching the ridged row-ends at the top.

b. Cut a piece of black card to a circle measuring 3.5cm (1½in) in diameter. Glue this disc inside the top of the hat, firmly pulling the ridge of knitting on to the extreme edges of the card. Hold firmly until dry.

c. Cut an oblong of bendy card measuring 12.5 × 4cm (5 × 1½in). Roll this up into a tube and, without glueing, insert it into the top of the hat. Allow it to spring open and note the amount of overlap on the card. Hold it in this position, remove it from the hat, then glue or staple the edges together.

d. Lightly glue the outer part of the card tube and insert it again into the hat with the join matching the back join of the knitting. Press in place until dry, allowing a tiny edge of knitting to remain free where the brim will be attached.

e. To make the brim, cast on 60 sts and k 2 rows.
Row 3: (k2 tog, k1) 20 times, then cast off.
Sew the 2 short edges tog to link the circle.

f. Slip this circle over the top of the crown and slide it down to the bottom, matching both seams at the back. From the under-side, sew the brim to the crown. Pull the brim into a slight peak at the front and back and curl the sides upwards.

g. The hat should be fitted well down on to the forehead of the figure.

Lady in swimming costume, 1885

Following the introduction of 'bloomers' by Mrs Amelia Bloomer, an American, in the 1890s, they were gradually accepted as being the most suitable type of garment to wear for sporting activities. A few years earlier than this, however, this young lady of 1885 is about to enter the bathing-hut on wheels which will take her into the sea, where she can remove her dress in privacy well away from the shore.

The costume shown here is slightly modified from a more complex model and consists of only two main pieces. The bloomers and short-sleeved shirt are knitted all in one piece and sewn up the back. The overdress is sleeveless but has a fully gathered skirt tied by a draw-string, and a large cape collar. A large mob-cap covers her hair and she protects her feet from the pebbles with rope sandals, tied criss-cross to the knees.

The all-in-one pants and top are covered by an overdress with cape collar. The overdress is removed when the lady enters the water unseen by those on the shore.

Materials

Hair: 10gm (½oz) dark brown 4 ply. Padding.
Costume: 50gm (2oz) orange 4 ply, 20gm (¾oz) white 4 ply and press-studs or small buttons. Fine white elastic.
Mob-cap: 10g (½oz) each of orange and white 4 ply. Padding.
Shoes: oddment of white 4 ply.
Needles: sizes 2 and 2¼mm and one spare.
Optional, size 2mm crochet hook for cords.

Hair

With dark brown yarn and size 2mm needles, cast on 30 sts and work in ss for 24 rows, see diagram 4.
Row 25: (k2 tog) 15 times.

a. Gather the last row on to a wool needle and run this twice though the sts. Draw up tightly for the top of the head then sew along the 2 adjoining edges for 2cm (½in). Finish off securely.
b. Gather the cast on edge but do not secure until later.
c. Pad inside this shape for the back of the head and fit it in place. Pin all round the head, see diagram 4.
d. To make the roll at the nape of the neck, cast on 30 sts and work in ss for 8 rows. Cast off.
    With WS tog, sew up the long edges to make a sausage shape. Fold this over into 3 parts, zigzag fashion, flatten it slightly and pin close to the head at the nape of the neck, see diagram 4. Sew in place.
e. The forehead curls are made of either a crochet chain or a twisted or plaited cord measuring about 28cm (11in) when unstretched. This is then stitched down in a continuous length to form a tumble of curls over the front part of the crown and forehead.

Bloomers

With orange yarn and size 2¾mm needles, cast on 40 sts and work 2 rows in double rib.
Rows 3 and 4: change to white and work 2 rows, then cut white.
Rows 5 and 6: pick up orange and rib as before.
Row 7: (k2, inc, k1) 10 times.
Row 8: p50.
Cont in ss for 34 more rows. Cast off 10 sts at beg of next 2 rows.
Row 45: k2 tog, k to last 2 sts, k2 tog.
Row 46: purl.
Rep rows 45 and 46 three more times. 22 sts.
Rows 53 to 56: work in ss without shaping.
Row 57: (yfwd, k2 tog) 11 times for the waistline holes.
Row 58: p22.
Cut orange yarn and leave these sts on spare needle. Now work the other leg in the same way.
Place both sets of sts on same needle with RS facing, and p in rev ss across all 44 sts. Cut orange yarn.
The vest now continues from this point on the bloomers. Join in white yarn and p one row.
At this point, lay the knitting flat with WS uppermost,

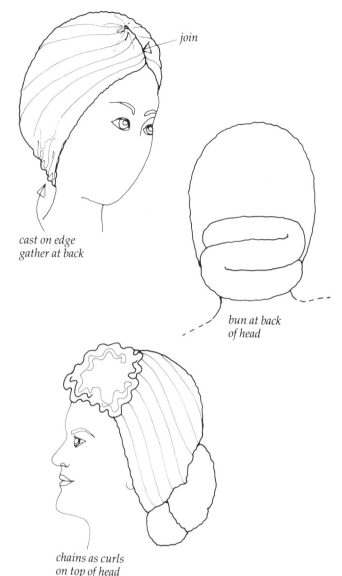

*cast on edge
gather at back*

*bun at back
of head*

*chains as curls
on top of head*

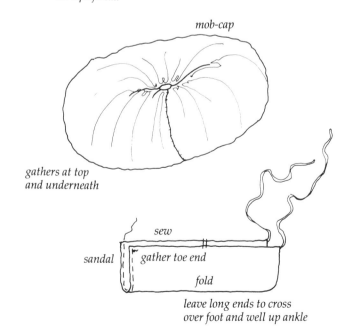

mob-cap

*gathers at top
and underneath*

sew

sandal   *gather toe end*

fold

*leave long ends to cross
over foot and well up ankle*

***Lady in swimming costume
Diagram 4***

126

The young lady's shirt and bloomers are knitted in a mixture of orange and white 4 ply yarns.

and sew up the 2 edges lying in the centre of the needle for the front centre seam, from the cast off 10 sts as far as the rev ss row. Work 10 rows in ss. Do not cut white yarn but join in orange.

Rows 12 and 13: (counting from first white row), work in ss.

Rows 14 and 15: with white yarn, work in ss, cut yarn. Divide for armholes:

Row 16: with orange, k9, cast off 4, k18, cast off 4, k9. Work on these 3 sets of sts separately.

Row 17: p9.

Rows 18 and 19: join in white and work in ss.

Rows 20 and 21: in orange, work in ss, cut orange.

Rows 22 to 26: in white, work in ss.

Row 27: cast off 4, p to end.

Rows 28 and 29: work 5 sts in ss.
Cast off.

Join orange yarn to centre sts and p18.
Join in white and work 2 rows, then 2 rows of orange, cut yarn.

Next row: in white, k5, cast off 8, k5.
Work 7 more rows on each side separately, then cast off.
Join orange yarn to last set of sts and complete as other side, working 6 rows of white before casting off for shoulder shaping.

Sleeves

With white yarn, cast on 20 sts and work 4 rows in single rib. Now work 4 rows of ss.
Cast off.

a. With RS tog, fold the sleeve pieces across and sew up edges. With RS tog, fold leg pieces across and sew centre back from cast off 10 sts to waistline.
b. Fold in other direction with sides of legs tog, matching centre seams, and pin. Beg at lower edge of one leg, sew all the way up towards centre seams, then down other leg.
c. With RS tog, sew shoulders, then fit sleeves into armholes with seams underneath. Turn garment to RS and fit on to the figure.
d. The back bodice opening may either be sewn up or made to fasten with buttons and loops, or press-studs.
e. Make a crochet cord for the waist measuring 30cm (12in) and thread this through the holes to tie at front. Elastic may be used instead. Allow vest to blouse over the waistline.
f. Thread orange yarn through top of ribbed borders at lower edge of trouser legs, draw up and tie. Elastic may be used for this also.

Overdress

With orange yarn and size 2¾mm needles cast on 100 sts and k 3 rows, see the illustration showing the front of the figure.

Row 4: join in white, knit.

Row 5: k4, p92, k4.

Rows 6 and 7: with orange, keeping g st edges correct, work in ss.

Rows 8 and 9: with white, keeping g st edges correct, work in ss.
Rep these last 4 rows once more, then cont in orange alone for 28 more rows of ss.

Row 42: (k2 tog) 50 times.

Row 43: k2, p46, k2.

Row 44: (yfwd, k2 tog) 25 times.

Row 45: as row 43.

Row 46: k2, (k2 tog, k6) 6 times.

Row 47: k2, p40, k2.

Rows 48 and 49: work straight in ss.

Row 50: k2 tog, k to last 2 sts, k2 tog.

Row 51: k1, p to last st, k1.
Rep rows 50 and 51 twice more. 38 sts.

Row 56: k2 tog, k4, cast off 4, k18, cast off 4, k4, k2 tog.

Cont in ss on these 3 sets of sts for 11 more rows. Cast off each set in turn.

a. With RS tog, fold each shoulder piece over on to the back neckline and sew the 4 sts at each side, leaving a space of 10 sts in the centre.

Collar

With RS facing, and beg at 5th row above holes at waistline, pick up sts as folls: 15 sts up right front, 10 sts across back neck, and 15 sts down left front as far as 5th row above holes. 40 sts.

Row 1: p40.
Row 2: (k3, inc) 10 times.
Row 3: WS facing, k50.
Row 4: p50.
Row 5: k2 tog, k46, k2 tog.
Row 6: p48.
Row 7: k2 tog, (k6, inc) 6 times, k2, k2 tog.
Row 8: p52.
Row 9: k2 tog, k48, k2 tog.
Row 10: p50.
Row 11: k2 tog, (k3, inc) 11 times, k2, k2 tog. 59 sts.
Row 12: p59.
Row 13: cast off 4, k to last 2 sts, k2 tog.
Row 14: cast off 4 p-wise, p to last 2 sts, p2 tog.
Row 15: cast off 6, k to last 2 sts, k2 tog.
Row 16: cast off 6 p-wise, p to last 2 sts, p2 tog.
Cast off rem 35 sts.
With RS of collar facing, use orange yarn, beg on LHS to pick up 72 sts all the way round the edge of the collar, (i.e., from the last pick-up sts at beg of collar).
Row 1: (WS) knit, cut orange yarn.
Row 2: join in white, knit.
Cast off k-wise in white.

a. Press the garment gently, then fold the collar back over the shoulder line as shown. Make a cord and thread this through the waist holes. Fit on to the figure and tie at the front.

Mob-cap

With orange yarn and size 2¼mm needles, cast on 20 sts and work in ss, 2 rows orange, 2 rows white alternately for 71 rows, see diagram 4. End with a white row.
Cast off p-wise in white.

a. With RS tog, lay the cast on and off edges tog and sew up to form a tube.
b. Gather one edge of the tube to form a cap and finish off securely, then use double yarn to gather the other edge to fit around the head.
c. To keep the rounded shape of the hat, use a narrow length of padding all round the inside and squeeze the cap to flatten it. Place the mob-cap on the head, well down at the back as shown, and tie with a bow behind.

Shoes

Make two the same, see diagram 4.

With white yarn and size 2mm needles, leave a long end and cast on 16 sts. Knit 18 rows.
Cast off, leaving another long end.

a. Fold as shown in the diagram. Run a gathering thread through one end and draw up to form the toe.
b. Cont to sew the top edges to half-way, leaving the rest open.
c. Close up the back edge for the heel.
d. Thread the two long ends along the top edges to half-way across the opening and use these as ties, to criss-cross round the legs. Tie the ends just underneath the lower edges of the bloomers.

Boy in sailor suit, 1890s

Sailor suits were very popular, for both boys and girls, all through the Edwardian era and beyond. Details changed here and there; some were three-piece outfits of jacket, waistcoat and knee-breeches, others had a jumper-type top, as shown on our model. French navy was the usual colour, or white with navy trimmings. Girls wore knee-length skirts to match, with or without pleats, and high boots over white knee-length socks.

In the version shown here, the navy top buttons down the back to make dressing easier. The shirt underneath has mid-length sleeves and is continuous with the knee-breeches. This has no fastenings but is sewn up at the back. The hat is a straw sailor-hat, with a decorative 'ribbon' hanging at the back. This hat was also worn by girls, although sometimes a matching 'Tam o'Shanter', a type of large floppy beret, was worn instead.

Photographs taken at this time, especially by the seaside, show many versions of this type of dress.

Materials

Hair: oddment of brown tweedy 3 or 4 ply. Padding.
Shirt: 10g (½oz) white 4 ply. 10g (½oz) pale blue 4 ply.
Suit: 25g (1oz) light navy 4 ply with 4 tiny matching buttons.
Hat: 10gm (½oz) straw-coloured 4 ply.
Socks: oddment of any bright coloured, or white, 4 ply.
Boots: Oddment of black or dark brown 4 ply.
Needles: sizes 2, 2¼, 2¾mm and one spare.

Hair

With brown tweedy yarn and size 2¼ mm needles, cast on 20 sts and work 18 rows in g st.
Row 19: cast on 8 sts and k to end of row.
Row 20: k 28.
Row 21: (k2, k2 tog) 7 times.
Row 22: k21.

The tunic top, buttons down the back for easy removal but the all-in-one vest and breeches are sewn up. Boots and socks are also knitted all in one.

This view of the boy's sailor suit shows the large collar and button details of his jacket.

Row 23: (k2 tog) 10 times, k1.
Row 24: k11.

a. Gather up the last 11 sts on to a wool needle and draw up tightly to form the top or the head. Sew down towards the fringe to close the 2 edges.
b. Gather the back edge. Fit the hair on to the head and pin the front piece on to the forehead.
Pad the space at the back of the head underneath the hair, arrange the gathers and sew in place all round.

Knee-breeches

With light navy yarn and size 2¾mm needles, cast on 18 sts and k 2 rows.
Row 3: purl.
Cont straight for 18 more rows of ss.
Row 22: cast off 3, k to end.

Row 23: cast off 3 p-wise, p to end.
Cont straight for 8 more rows. Leave these sts on a spare needle and cut yarn.
Work another leg in the same way.
Place both sets of sts on same needle with RS facing and k24.
Cut blue yarn and join in white.
The shirt now continues from this point on the breeches.
Work 2 rows in ss.
Join in pale blue and work 2 rows in ss.
Keeping the colour-pattern of white and blue stripes, cont without shaping for 10 more rows, (i.e., 4 white and 3 blue stripes).
Now divide for armholes.
Row 15: with blue yarn, k5, cast off one st, k12, cast off one st, k5.

129

Work on these 3 sets of sts separately for 9 more rows, ending with a blue stripe.

Rows 25 and 26: in white, knit.
Cast off.

Sleeves

With white yarn, lay the body piece out flat with RS uppermost and pick up 18 sts from armhole to armhole, beg at front neck and ending at back neck.

Row 1: in white, purl.
Cont to work as before in white and blue stripes for 15 more rows, ending with a blue stripe.

Last 2 rows: knit both in white.
Cast off and work other sleeve to match.

a. Fold the piece in half lengthways with RS tog, and sew centre front seam from cast off 3 sts towards waistline.
b. Sew centre back seam in same way.
c. Fold piece across in other direction and pin leg edges tog, matching centre front and back seams. Sew up one leg and down the other.
d. With RS tog, fold sleeves and sew along edges, matching stripes from cast off edge to neck. Turn to RS.
e. Slip garment on to figure and pin edges of back opening from RS. Sew this back opening up neatly from RS, leaving an open 'V' of 3 stripes at the neck edge.

Tunic top

With light navy and size 2¾mm needles, cast on 36 sts and k 2 rows, see illustration showing front of the figure.

Row 3: purl.
Cont in ss for 16 more rows.
Row 20: k5, cast off 4, k7, k2 tog.
Leave rem sts on spare needle and turn to WS.
Row 21: p8.
Next row: k to last 2 sts, k2 tog.
Next row: purl.
Rep last 2 rows twice more, 5 sts, then work 6 more rows on these 5 sts and cast off.
Rejoin yarn to second 5 sts left on needle and work 13 rows.
Cast off.
From the spare needle, remove 5 sts and work 14 rows, then cast off.
On the rem 13 sts, k2 tog tbl, k11.
Next row: cast off 4 p-wise, p8.
Cont to dec as before on neck edge on alt rows until 5 sts rem, the cont straight for 7 more rows.
Cast off.

a. Join both shoulders then, with RS facing, pick up 20 sts along one back edge from hem to neck. This is for the back buttonhole band.
   Next row: k4, (yfwd, k2 tog, k2) 4 times.
   Next row: k20.

Cast off and pick up 20 sts from other side, k 2 rows, then cast off.

Sleeves

Make 2 the same. Cast on 14 sts.
Rows 1, 2 and 4: knit.
Rows 3, 5, 6 and 7: purl.
Row 8: inc in first st, k to last st, inc.
Work 3 more rows in ss.
Rep last 4 rows until there are 24 sts.
Work 3 rows straight.
Next row: (part-row knitting to shape shoulder) k20, turn.
Next row: p16, turn.
Next row: k12, turn.
Next row: p8, turn.

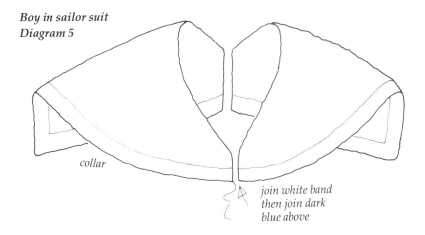

Boy in sailor suit
Diagram 5

collar

join white band
then join dark
blue above

Next row: k16.
Next row: p24 and cast off.

a. Sew sleeve seam.
b. Turn cuff to inside and slip st in position.
c. Set sleeve into armhole from WS.

Collar

Work in g st throughout, see diagram 5.
For the RHS, with white yarn, cast on 12 sts and k 1 row.
Row 2: (RS) k2 white, join in navy, k10 twisting 2 colours tog on WS.
Row 3: K10 navy, 2 white.
Rep last 2 rows 4 more times.
Row 12: keeping white border throughout, k to last 2 sts, k2 tog.
Row 13:** k11.
Cont to dec at neck edge on alt rows until 6 sts rem. then work 3 rows between each dec row until only 2 navy and 2 white sts rem.
Work 6 more rows on these 4 sts.
Next row: (WS) (k2 tog) twice.
Next row: k2 white, pass first st over 2nd to cast off. Darn both ends in on WS. **
For the LHS, with white yarn, cast on 12 sts and k one row.
Row 2: (RS) join in navy yarn, k10, weaving in white yarn along back as far as last 2 sts, k2 white.
Row 3: k2 white, k10 navy.
Rep last 2 rows of pattern 4 more times.
Row 12: keeping white border throughout, k2 tog, k to end.
Work from ** to **, as given for RHS.

a. Join collar at front, see diagram 5, and pin in place on neck edge of tunic with RS tog. Sew all round and turn to RS.
b. Make a navy and white cord about 25cm (10in) long for the bow at the front. Tie this and stitch in place as shown.
c. Sew 4 tiny buttons down the RS of jacket border, slip tunic on to figure and fasten up. This piece may first need pressing along the lower edge.

Hat

With straw-coloured yarn and size 2¼mm needles, begin with the brim. Cast on 60 sts and k 3 rows.
Row 4: (k1, k2 tog) 20 times.
Row 5: k40.
Row 6: (k2, k2 tog) 10 times.
Row 7: k30, then cast off.
Sew the side edges tog to form a circle.
For the crown, cast on 30 sts and k 6 rows.
Row 8: (k2 tog) 15 times.
Row 9: k15.
Row 10: (k2 tog) 7 times, k1.

a. Gather the last sts on to a wool needle, take the needle through the sts a second time and draw up tightly. Sew the edges tog, sit the crown inside the brim matching the 2 joins at the back.
b. From the inside, stitch the 2 pieces tog all round.
c. Make a navy cord of about 25cm (10in) long and tie this round the base of the crown to form a knot with hanging ends. Slip st this band in place.
   The hat is placed well back on the head with the brim turned up. If necessary, it can be stiffened, see the instructions on page 138.

Boots and Socks

All in one piece. Make 2 the same.
With black yarn and size 2mm needles, cast on 28 sts and work 6 rows in ss.
Row 7: cast off 8 sts, k12, cast off 8.
Row 8: rejoin yarn to centre sts and p12.
Rows 10 to 15: work in ss, then cut yarn.
Row 16: join in sock coloured yarn and work 6 more rows in ss, then cast off.

a. Wrap the sock around the leg with the edges at centre front. Pin in place and then sew down from top towards boot.
b. From the top of the toe, sew up the top of the boot towards the sock.
c. Run a gathering thread round the end of the toe and draw up. Secure tightly to form the rounded toe, then sew across the sole of the boot towards the heel. Finish off securely.

Gibson Girl, or golfing lady *c.*1900

In the early years of 1900 American artist, Charles Dana Gibson, portrayed a distinctive female shape which accentuated a tiny belted waistline, forward sloping bosom and backward sloping hipline. 'Gibson Girls'as these figures came to be known, dressed in a tailored skirt with a high-collared, tie-necked blouse of white linen. This style, although quite short-lived, became the rage in both America and Britain, especially with sporting young ladies who found it practical and flattering.

Although strictly against the rules of fashion, our Gibson Girl wears no combinations, chemise or corset! The bulk of the second front-fastening garment beneath her high-necked blouse would have spoiled the shape, so she wears instead a sturdy and warming red flannel petticoat over her knee-length drawers. To reduce the bulk even further, the skirt, belt and blouse are made all in one piece. The green golfing skirt is made in four panels joined at the waist. The cream blouse, with leg o' mutton sleeves, fastens down the front with tiny buttons. Her hat is a tiny pillbox worn over the fashionable coiffure of 1900.

Materials

Hair: 25gm (1oz) orange 4 ply. Padding.
Drawers: 25gm (1oz) white 4 ply.
Petticoat: 25gm (1oz) dull red 4 ply. Fine elastic.
Boots and stockings (all in one): oddments of brown and white 4 ply and some tiny brown beads for buttons.
Blouse: 20gm (¾oz) cream or white 4 ply. 18 tiny white pearl buttons.
Skirt: 25gm (1oz) mid-green 4 ply.
Hat: oddment left over from skirt.
Belt and mittens: oddment of brown 4 ply, as boots.

Needles: sizes 2¼, 2¾, 3¼mm and one spare.
Note: ears are required for this model.
If your model, like this one, is red-haired, embroider the face as though for this colouring, with green, grey or brown eyes, with fine brown eyebrows and a pale red mouth.

Hair

With orange yarn and size 2¾mm needles, cast on 56 sts loosely, leaving a longish tail for gathering and sewing, see diagram 6.

Gibson Girl
Diagram 6

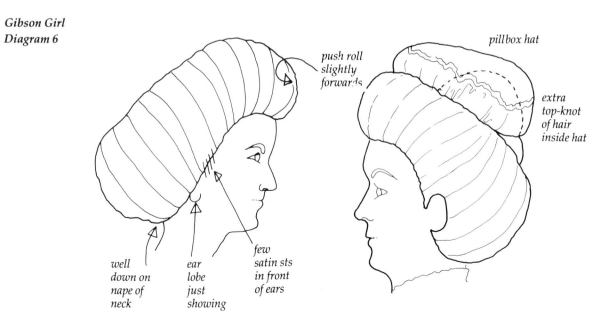

push roll slightly forwards

pillbox hat

extra top-knot of hair inside hat

well down on nape of neck

ear lobe just showing

few satin sts in front of ears

Work 10 rows in single rib.

Row 11: (k2 tog) 28 times.

Gather these sts on to a wool needle, cut yarn leaving an end hanging.

a. Use a separate length of yarn to sew up the 2 side edges to form a tube.
b. Run the cast on tail through the cast on edge and draw up just enough to fit snugly round the head as shown in the diagram. Pin in place and sew.
c. Place padding inside roll, more at the back than the front. Push front hair roll forwards on to forehead.
d. Gather cast off edge at top of head, leaving a hole. Secure thread.
e. Make the top-knot as folls: cast on 18 sts and work 6 rows in single rib. Gather sts on to wool needle, taking the thread twice through sts. Pull tightly and fasten off. Sew up sides to form a dome.
f. Pad this piece gently and place over hole at back of head. Match both seams at back, pin and sew on.
g. Complete the hair-style by making 2 or 3 satin sts in front of the ears, using the hair-coloured yarn, see diagram 6.

Drawers

The instructions for these knee-length drawers are exactly the same as for the Victorian Lady of 1845, see page 116, except that only 40 rows are worked on each side instead of 50 rows.

They tie just below the knee and over the top of her stockings.

Red flannel petticoat

With dull red yarn and size 3¼mm needles, cast on 120 sts.

Rows 1 and 2: (k2, p2) to end of row.

Rows 3 and 4: (p2, k2) to end of row.

Rows 5 and 6: purl.

Row 7: knit.

Rows 8 and 9: purl.

Row 10: (k1, p1) to end of row.

Rows 11 and 12: purl.

Row 13: (RS) (k2 tog, k28) 4 times.

Cont in ss, dec 4 sts on every 5th rows as folls:

Row 18: (p2 tog, p27) 4 times.

Row 23: (k2 tog, k26) 4 times.

Row 28: (p2 tog, p25) 4 times.

Row 33: (k2 tog, k24) 4 times.

Row 38: (p2 tog, p23) 4 times.

Row 43: (k2 tog, k22) 4 times.

Row 48: (p2 tog, p21) 4 times.

Row 53: (k2 tog, k20) 4 times.

Row 58: (p2 tog, p19) 4 times.

Row 59: (k2 tog) 40 times.

Work 3 rows in single rib.

Row 63: change to size 2¾mm needles and work 1 more row.

Cast off in rib.

The smooth line of the four-panel skirt shows off the tiny belted waist, and the trim white blouse with its high neckline was a hallmark of good taste during the early 1900s.

a. Pin out flat and press very gently.
b. From WS, sew 2 side edges tog.
c. Thread fine elastic through waistline and adjust to fit.

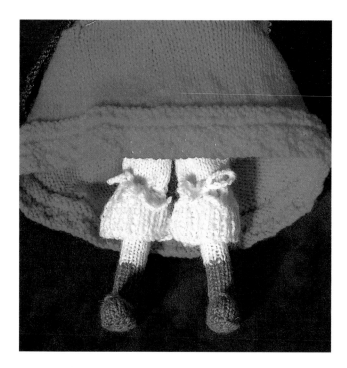

This detail reveals a bright red petticoat, knee-length drawers and sturdy brown boots.

Boots and stockings

Made all in one piece. Make two the same.

With brown yarn and size 2¾mm needles, cast on 24 sts and work 4 rows in ss.

Row 5: k5, cast off 14, k5.

Now push these 2 sets of sts tog, noting that the cast off sts form the top of the boot, and p10.

Work 10 rows of ss on these 10 sts, then change to white yarn and work 2 more rows.

Next row: inc in first and last sts to make 12.

Cont in ss for 9 more rows.

Next row: k5, inc, k6.

Cont for 9 more rows, then cast off.

a. With WS tog, sew up white stocking.
b. Sew back of boot from heel to top.
c. From RS, close gap on top of foot using a lacing-type st and pulling the toe in slightly to eliminate the point at this end.
d. *Either* cut a card sole as for the Victorian man, see page 121, or make a knitted one as folls: cast on 4 sts and k 17 rows. Cast off and sew this piece to the under-side of the boot while it is on the foot.
e. Either embroider knots down the outside of the boots to represent buttons, or sew on tiny metallic beads.

Skirt and blouse

Made all in one piece with a knitted-in belt, see the illustration showing the front of the figure.

Begin at the lower edge of the skirt panels, and make 4 pieces.

With green yarn and size 2¼mm needles, cast on 30 sts and work in ss throughout, with a g st hem.

Rows 1, 2, 4 and 6: knit.
Rows 3, 5 and 7: purl.
Row 8: k2, k2 tog tbl, k22, k2 tog, k2.

Work 9 more rows on these 28 sts, then dec in this way on the next and on every foll 10th row until 18 sts rem. Leave sts on spare needle.

Make 3 more pieces in the same way.

Slide all 4 panels on to the needle with WS facing, and p72 sts.

Next row: (k2 tog) 36 times.

Now sew the side edges from hem towards the needle to make one piece of fabric.

Next row: change to size 2¾mm needles and p36. Cut green yarn.

With brown belt colour, knit 4 rows, then cut yarn. Change to cream or white yarn for blouse and knit 1 row.

Row 2: (of blouse) (p2, inc in next st) 12 times. 48 sts.

Row 3: k3, (p1, k1) 3 times, p1, k4, (p1, k1) 3 times, p1, k6, (p1, k1) 3 times, p1, k4, (p1, k1) 3 times, p1, k3.

Row 4: p3, (k1, p1) 3 times, k1, p4, (k1, p1) 3 times, k1, p6, (k1, p1) 3 times, k1, p4, (k1, p1) 3 times, k1, p3.

Rep these 2 rows three more times.

Divide for armholes:

Row 11: k3, rib 7, cast off 4, rib 7, k6, rib 7, cast off 4, rib 7, k3.

Now work on these 3 sets of sts separately as folls:

Row 12: keeping ss and rib st patt as before, work 13 more rows on first 10 sts.

Next row: (RS) at armhole edge, cast off 5 sts in rib, patt to end of row.

Leave these 5 sts on a safety-pin and rejoin yarn to centre set of 20 sts. Work 11 rows in patt.

Cast of first and last 5 sts on next row, break yarn and leave centre 10 sts on same pin as others.

Rejoin yarn to last 10 sts and complete 13 rows before casting off 5 sts at shoulder, leaving last 5 sts on needle.

Slide all neck sts on to one needle in order as folls: first LHS 5 sts, then back 10 sts, the RHS 5 sts. 20 sts.

RS should now be facing ready for next row.

Push shoulder edges on to WS and sew these tog as far as needle.

For the 20 neck sts, work 2 rows in single rib, then cast off in rib.

Front bands, using size 2¼mm needles, begin at RH front edge with RS facing and pick up 24 sts from waist to neck.

Next row: (k2, yfwd, k2 tog) 5 times, k4.

Knit 1 more row, then cast off.

On LH front edge, begin at the neck and pick up 24 sts. Knit 2 rows, then cast off. Darn all ends in.

Sleeves

Using size 2¾mm needles, cast on 48 sts.

Row 1: k46, turn.
Row 2: p44, turn.
Row 3: k42, turn.
Row 4: p40.

Cont to leave 2 extra sts on every row until 18 sts are unworked at each end, then cont on the same p sts to end of row.

Now work 6 complete rows in ss.

Row 9: (counting from side edges), k2 tog, (k3, k2 tog tbl) 4 times, k2 tog tbl, k2 tog, (k2 tog, k3) 4 times, k2 tog. 36 sts.

Row 10: p36.

Row 11: (k2 tog) 18 times.

Work straight on these 18 sts for 7 more rows.

Row 19: (k2 tog, k6) twice, k2 tog.

Work 2 more rows on the rem 15 sts, then cast off p-wise.

Make another sleeve in the same way.

a. With RS tog, sew side edges of sleeves from cuff to top, then cont with a gathering thread all round top edge.

b. Draw up top edge, pushing most of fullness towards the top, and fit this into armhole. Pin in place.

c. Sew in securely, turn to RS and run a gathering thread around the elbow at the dec row. Draw in slightly to fit snugly to the arm, then fasten off.

d. Pin skirt section out flat and press very gently. Sew up rem front seam as far as the belt and press this.

e. Turn to WS and sew the belt at front opening.

f. Sew tog overlapping front bands at the lower edge with the buttonhole band on outside. Sew 6 tiny pearl buttons down button-band in line with holes.

g. With belt yarn, run a gathering thread through centre groove of the belt and use this to draw up the garment on to the waistline. It ties at the back in a tiny bow.

h. Sew 6 of the same tiny buttons down each outside edge of the lower sleeve from gathering thread to cuff.

Hat

With yarn used for the skirt and size 2¼mm needles, cast on 58 sts.

Rows 1, 3 and 4: knit.

Row 2: purl.

Row 5: (k2 tog) 29 times.

Row 6: p14, p2 tog, p13.

Rows 7 and 8: knit.

Row 9: (k2 tog) 14 times.

Row 10: k14.

Row 11: (k2 tog) 7 times.

a. Gather the last 7 sts on to a wool needle and draw up securely to form the centre of the top of the hat. Sew up the side edges to form a circle.

b. Run a gathering thread through the cast on edge and draw up slightly for the under-side. Secure the thread.

c. Pull the shape out a little to form a flat pillbox and sew this to the head as shown.

Mittens

With same yarn as belt and boots, and size 2mm needles, cast on 12 sts and work in ss for 8 rows. Gather the last sts on to a wool needle and sew up the sides. Stitch the mitts on to the wrists of the model.

The leg o'mutton sleeve of the Gibson Girl narrows down to the forearm and is finished with six tiny pearl buttons.

Knitting know-how

Tension

Tension is not discussed in the instructions, for various reasons, but basically because so many different oddments of yarn were used in the making of these models, that it would have taken as much time working out the tension squares as in making the clothes. Also, on the many occasions when one garment was made several times over in different yarns, it did not seem to matter in the slightest about the difference in tension. The garments are so small that everything is likely to fit, provided you use the suggested needle size and yarn (even though types vary quite a bit) and follow the instructions carefully.

Obviously, if you already know that you tend to knit loosely, or tightly, you will have to keep a careful check as you go along. Check the garments, piece by piece, to make sure that everything is as it should be whilst not forgetting that, when pressed, the individual sections will 'grow' a little.

Casting on and off methods

1. On such small items, the casting on may alter the size of a garment. The method used throughout is the one where the RH needle is inserted *between* the last 2 sts on the LH needle, to make a new stitch.
2. Occasionally, it is recommended that the loose cast on method is used to make a loopy edge, and this is where the RH needle enters the last stitch on the LH needle, to make a new one.
3. Always leave a long 'tail' when casting on and off, as these can be used later for sewing up.
4. Instructions which require stitches to be cast off in the middle, or part-way along a row, tend to be ambiguous, as knitters know that to cast off a stitch, you first have to knit two of them. The instructions, therefore, tell you what the *end result* should be, so that if the row reads, 'k4, cast off 4, k2, cast off 4, k4', this describes what remains on the needle at the end of the row.
5. Casting off is done in the usual manner by knitting 2 sts and slipping the first of these over the second and proceeding in this way to the last stitch. This stitch provides a loop for the cut end to be passed through and pulled up.
6. Cast off knit-wise or purl-wise instructions should be adhered to, as in some cases they follow the stocking stitch formula and, in others, they may form a decorative edge. They will also indicate the right and wrong sides of the fabric.

The stitches

1. Most of the garments are made in combinations of stocking stitch, garter stitch and ribbing. In cases where the instructions say, 'continue in ss', this means beginning with a knit row unless otherwise specifically stated.
2. Reverse stocking stitch is simply where the reverse, or purl side of stocking stitch is used as the right side, usually when a different texture is required. This may change more than once in a garment piece.
3. Increases and decreases. Always make an increase by knitting into the front and back of the same stitch and *never*, in these instructions, by picking up the strand lying between two stitches.
   Decreases are made in two ways, and generally, though not invariably, the decrease at the beginning of a row is the k1, sl 1, k1, psso method, slanting towards the left. At the end of the row it is likely to be k2 tog, slanting to the right. Which one you actually work will not make any difference to the shape of the garment, only to its appearance.
4. Count the stitches on the needle at regular intervals and check with the number given in brackets at the end of some of the rows.

Picking up stitches from a side edge

This is a time and labour-saving method which is highly recommended. Always remember the following points:

1. Pick up from the right side, (RS), of the knitted piece so that the ridge will fall on to the wrong side.
2. Use the same sized needle as used on the knitting, or a smaller one for the pick-up row only.
3. If you have difficulty, use a crochet hook and transfer the stitches on to a needle.
4. Use pins placed at measured intervals to space the pick-up stitches evenly along the edge of the knitting.
5. Some of the instructions may number the pick-up row as 'Row 1' and subsequent rows as 2, 3 and 4, so that the purl row always falls, as usual in stocking stitch, on the even row. At other times, the instructions may begin with the first full row of knitting, (a purl row), as Row 1, but only where the number of following rows is not so great as to lead to confusion.
6. If you really dislike the idea of picking up stitches,

don't worry, as in most cases the extra piece can be made separately and sewn on afterwards.

Fastenings

In England, buttons were known as early as 1327 and, in the American Colonies, button making began c.1706. For your purposes, the problem will be to find buttons small enough to relate to the size of the figures. Another problem is the bulk created when one edge of knitting overlaps another and then has buttons on top of this, so adding to the bulk. However, the instructions call for buttons here and there, although alternatives are press-studs, preferably the transparent kind, and sewing up. This last method, however, would be unpopular if the figures are to be dressed and undressed. The choice must be yours.

Zip fasteners are definitely not suitable as they were not manufactured until the 1920s and anyway, they are too bulky. Draw-strings are useful as fastenings for waist and wrist, also the neck. Tiny patches of fabric fastening are another alternative, although not aesthetically sound for the same reasons as zip fasteners. Lace-up neck openings are possible and the Renaissance man has one, but these need to be re-threaded when dressing and undressing. Elastic, whilst not historically accurate, is useful for gathered areas where draw-strings might also be used, but be sure that this is of the fine round type and of a colour to blend in with that of the garment.

Sewing up

1. Attaching the 'skin' is dealt with on page 14, but for clothes, the important thing is to make and assemble them in the same order as given in the instructions. Outer garments have to be fitted over the top of the undergarments and this can alter the size considerably. Also, because some of the smaller items are made from the oddments of yarn used for larger ones it is best to be certain of the latter before deciding on the colour of the accessories.

2. Note that many of the making up instructions, always labelled a, b, c, and so on, may contain extra bits of knitting for borders or collars, so have your needles and yarn ready at hand. Use the long cast on and cast off ends to sew with, wherever possible.

3. There are two choices of stitch for sewing up, see diagram 1. The over-cast method is generally adequate for these small items, but keep stitches

Knitting know-how
Diagram 1
Sewing and embroidery sts

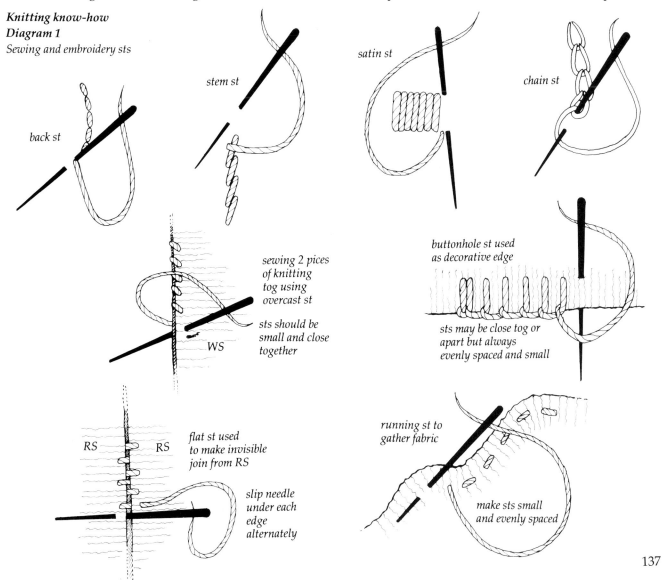

back st

stem st

satin st

chain st

sewing 2 pices of knitting tog using overcast st

sts should be small and close together

WS

buttonhole st used as decorative edge

sts may be close tog or apart but always evenly spaced and small

RS   RS

flat st used to make invisible join from RS

slip needle under each edge alternately

running st to gather fabric

make sts small and evenly spaced

137

close together, and only stitch into the extreme edges and always use the same yarn as the one used for the knitting, changing colours where necessary.

The flat stitch method is particularly useful where the garment is actually on the figure, while being sewn up from the RS. It is almost invisible.

The backstitch method of sewing up is not recommended here for these tiny pieces, as it takes up too much of the fabric and this may affect the final fit.

4. Boots, shoes and stockings are sometimes made in one piece, or sometimes separately; some have card soles, some knitted soles and some are just joined underneath the foot. Check to see whether the figure has stockings knitted in as part of the skin. If the legs do not show at all, then the legs can be made with built-in stockings of the colour of your choice, instead of the skin-colour. With separate shoes, it may be easier to sew the soles of the shoes on to the uppers while the shoe is on the foot; just take care not to sew this on to the foot itself!

5. Sleeves should be set in according to diagram 2, unless the 'flat-out' method is used, when this will be stipulated in the instructions. If, for some reason, either the armhole or the sleeve-head requires reduction, simply run a gathering stitch round and gently draw up the edge until it fits.

To set a sleeve head in an armhole, see diagram 2, turn the bodice to the WS. Keep the sleeve RS out and place the top of the sleeve into the armhole as shown, with seams together. Now pin in place and ease any fullness at the top with a gathering thread,

Knitting know-how
Diagram 2
Setting in sleeve

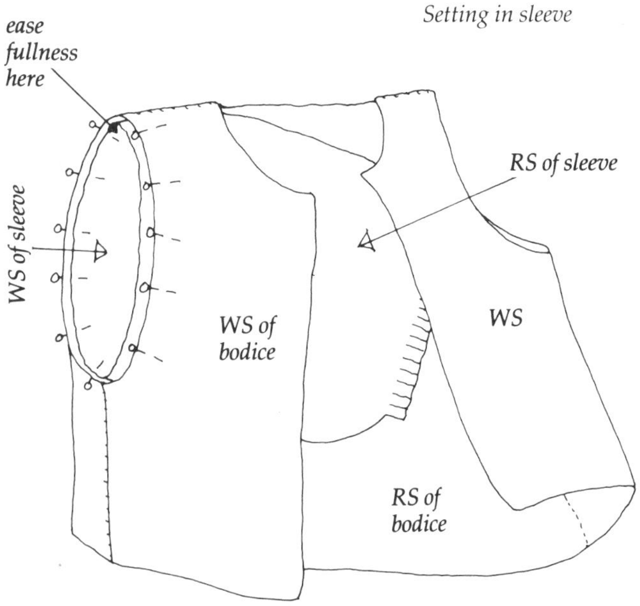

ease fullness here

WS of sleeve

RS of sleeve

WS of bodice

WS

RS of bodice

see diagram 1. Sew into place with an overcast stitch in a matching yarn.

Pressing

The skins need no pressing before they are fitted on to the figures but all the other costume pieces benefit from a gentle pressure, under a damp cloth, before being sewn up. A man's cotton handkerchief is ideal for this. This pressing not only determines the finished shape of the costume, but also adds considerably to its final dimensions and combats the tendency of stocking stitch to roll up at the edges. Do not press ribbing or garter stitch.

After darning in unwanted ends, pin each piece out on to an ironing-board. Place pins at right angles to the edges, close together. On symmetrical pieces, check that all sides are the same. Lay a damp cotton cloth over the entire piece and hold a hot iron over the top, but do not allow the full weight of the iron to rest on the fabric. Touch the cloth very gently here and there, to steam the fibres into position. Remove the heat and the cloth and allow the knitting to recover for a few minutes before unpinning. Keep pieces flat until required.

Stiffening

Some pieces, particularly hats, may benefit from being stiffened in a solution of sugar. To do this, first assemble the piece, then immerse it completely in a solution of hot water and as much sugar as can be dissolved in it. Just keep spooning sugar into the water a little at a time, until it will not dissolve any more when thoroughly stirred. Wet the knitted piece completely in this solution, lift it out and drain it on a pad of absorbent paper. Do not pour the liquid away until you are sure you have the result you require. Ease the knitting into shape, padding any part which threatens to collapse and leave to dry. It should be quite rigid.

Picot holes

A draw-string, or elastic, is threaded through picot holes at the appropriate places, but in case you forget to make any, it can also be threaded through the knitting. Picot holes are made as follows; on a RS row, wrap the yarn round the needle to make an extra stitch, then k2 tog. Continue to work yfwd, k2 tog, to the end of the row. On the next row, purl across all stitches, including the yfwds of the previous row. You should have exactly the same number of stitches as before.

Cords and elastic

Many of the undergarments are secured by draw-strings round the waist and wrists, this being the way in which most were fastened before the invention of elastic. Fine, round elastic is quite acceptable, if you prefer to use it. To make cords, however, either work crochet chains, twisted or plaited cords, or even use a narrow ribbon.

All versions should be very fine and to the same scale as the garment, as too large a knot or bow will cause an ugly lump under the outer garment. Other bought cords are equally acceptable.

Border patterns

Patterns 1, 2, 4 and 5 are worked from the lower edge and the width can be adjusted. The multiples of stitches are given and these are shown from * to * in each row. As an example, for pattern 1 cast on 20, 38, 56 stitches and so on, and repeat the pattern the required number of times.

Patterns 3 and 6 are knitted sideways and can be made to any length.

PATTERN 1
This old pattern is also called 'fan and feather stitch'.
Cast on multiples of 18 sts, plus 2 extra.
Row 1: (RS) k1, *(k2 tog) 3 times, (yfwd, k1) 6 times, (k2 tog) 3 times*, k1.
Rows 2 and 3: k to end.
Row 4: p to end.
Rep these 4 rows until border is required depth, then cont in ss if necessary.

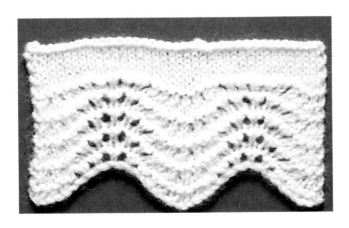

PATTERN 2
Cast on multiples of 11 sts, plus 2 extra.
Row 1: (RS) k1, *k2 tog, k3, yfwd, k1, yfwd, k3, sl 1, k1, psso*, k1.
Row 2 and every alt row: p to end.
Rows 3 and 5: as row 1.
Row 7: k1, *k2 tog, k2, yfwd, k3, yfwd, k2, sl 1, k1, psso*, k1.

Row 9: k1, *k2 tog, k1, yfwd, k5, yfwd, k1, sl 1, k1, psso*, k1.
Row 11: k1, *(k2 tog, yfwd, k1) twice, yfwd, sl 1, k1, psso, k1, yfwd, sl 1, k1, psso*, k1.
Row 13: *p2, k9, rep from * to last 2 sts, p2.
Row 14: *k2, p9, rep from * to last 2 sts, k2.
Rep rows 13 and 14 three times more, making 8 rows in all, the work row 13 again.
Next row: (WS) k to end.
Knit 2 more rows thus completing the border with a band of rev ss.

PATTERN 3
Worked sideways over 9 sts. Work the required length, then sew it to the edge of the garment.
Row 1 and every alt row: (RS) k to end.
Row 2: k3, k2 tog, yfwd, k2 tog, (yfwd, k1) twice. 10 sts.
Row 4: k2, (k2 tog, yfwd) twice, k3, yfwd, k1. 11 sts.
Row 6: k1, (k2 tog, yfwd) twice, k5, yfwd, k1. 12 sts.
Row 8: k3, (yfwd, k2 tog) twice, k1, k2 tog, yfwd, k2 tog. 11 sts.
Row 10: k4, yfwd, k2 tog, yfwd, sl 1, k2 tog, psso, yfwd, k2 tog. 10 sts.
Row 12: k5, yfwd, sl 1, k2 tog, psso, yfwd, k2 tog. 9 sts.
These 12 rows form the pattern. Rep as given for the instructions for the garment, or until long enough to go round the hem.

PATTERN 4

This is a simple version of pattern 2. Cast on multiples of 11 sts, plus 1 extra.

Row 1: *k1, yfwd, k3, sl 1, k1, psso, k2 tog, k3, yfwd*, k1.

Row 2: p to end.

Rep these 2 rows until the border is the required depth, then k one row to finish off with rev ss. Cont in ss if required.

PATTERN 5

Cast on multiples of 7 sts, plus 2 extra.

Row 1: (RS) k to end.

Rows 2 and 4: p to end.

Row 3: k2 *yfwd and round needle, p1, p3 tog, p1, keep yfwd, k2*.

Rep rows 1 to 4 three times more, then k two rows. Cont in ss for the required depth.

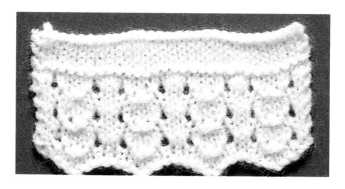

PATTERN 6

Worked sideways over 5 sts. Work the required length, then sew to the edge of the garment.

Row 1: k to end.

Row 2: k1, yfwd, k2 tog, k1, inc in last st. 6 sts.

Rows 3 and 5: k to end.

Row 4: k1, yfwd, k2 tog, k2, inc in last st. 7 sts.

Row 6: k1, yfwd, k2 tog, k3, inc in last st. 8 sts.

Row 7: cast off 3 sts, k to end. 5 sts.

Begin again at row 2 and rep as many times as required to go round the edge of the garment.

Picot patterns

The basic pattern consists of only 2 rows over an even number of stitches.

Row 1: (yfwd, k2 tog) rep to end of row.

Row 2: p to end.

The bottom sample shows this used above ten rows of double rib, so that a ribbon can be threaded through for an ankle or wrist fastening.

The centre sample shows how the two picot rows have been placed between two rev ss ridges, as folls:

WS: k to end, to make the lower ridge.

RS: (yfwd, k2 tog) to end of row.

WS: p to end.

RS: p to end, to make the upper ridge.

Then cont in ss.

This creates a decorative insertion pattern but it can also be used for gathering a waistline on an outer garment.

The top edge shows the picot holes followed immediately by the cast off row. This is used on the tops of underskirts and other places where the garment does not show.

Special effects

Knitting is a very malleable craft and simple patterns can often produce the most striking effects.

DIAPER PATTERN

Used on Queen Elizabeth's gown, see pages 60–66. This is an attractive and simple stitch worked with two yarns and a slip stitch method. The effect is that of an intricate textured brocade, or embossed embroidered fabric, but two rows only of one yarn are followed by two rows of the second. Couldn't be simpler - perfect for a beginner!

It also has the advantage that it can be used on both sides, but choose yarns which do not contrast too greatly in tone or colour, as a spotty effect may otherwise be produced and on a small scale this may be difficult to handle. The sample shows both sides of this pattern.

Bottom: white background, yellow contrast. Right side.

Centre: white background, gold contrast. Wrong side, as seen on Queen Elizabeth's gown.

Top: multicoloured background, gold contrast. Right side, as seen on the High Priest's short tunic.

Two colours, using A as the background and B as the contrast. With A, cast on multiples of 6 sts plus 5 extra sts.

Row 1: with B, k4, *yfwd, sl 3 p-wise, yb, k3*, to last st, kl.

Row 2: with B, p4, *yb, sl 3 p-wise, yfwd, p3*, to last st, pl.

Row 3: with A, k to end.

Row 4: with A, p to end.

Row 5: with B, kl, *yfwd, sl 3 p-wise, yb, k3*, to last 4 sts, yfwd, sl 3 p-wise, yb, kl.

Row 6: with B, pl, *yb, sl 3 p-wise, yfwd, p3*, to last 4 sts, yb, sl 3 p-wise, yfwd, pl.

Row 7: as row 3.

Row 8: as row 4.

These 8 rows form the pattern. Repeat as necessary.

OPEN-DIAMOND PATTERN

Used on the Italian Renaissance lady's overgown, see pages 36–42. Cast on multiples of 10 sts.

Note: to make one st at beg of row 1, wrap yarn right round needle, instead of usual yfwd method used at all other times in the pattern.

Row 1: *make one st, sl l, kl, psso, k5, k2 tog, yfwd, kl*.

Row 2 and all alt rows: kl, p8, kl.

Row 3: *kl, yfwd, sl l, kl, psso, k3, k2 tog, yfwd, k2*.

Row 5: *k2, yfwd, sl l, kl, psso, kl, k2 tog, yfwd, k3*.

Row 7: *k3, yfwd, sl l, k2 tog, psso, yfwd, k4*.

Row 9: *k2, k2 tog, yfwd, kl, yfwd, sl l, kl, psso, k3*.

Row 11: *kl, k2 tog, yfwd, k3, yfwd, sl l, kl, psso, k2*.

Row 13: *k2 tog, yfwd, k5, yfwd, sl l, kl, psso, kl*.

Row 15: *yfwd, k7, yfwd, sl l, k2 tog, psso*, to last 2 sts, yfwd, sl l, kl, psso.

At the end of every row 15 there will be multiples of 10 sts plus one st, so at the end of row 16, k2 tog to revert to the original number.

These 16 rows form the pattern.

Bibliography

Ashelford, Jane *Dress in the Age of Elizabeth* Batsford, London, 1988

Ashelford, Jane *The Sixteenth Century (Visual History of Costume Series)* Batsford, London, and Drama Books Publishers, New York, 1983

Buck, Anne *Victorian Costume* Ruth Bean Publishers, Bedford, 1984

Cumming, Valerie *The Seventeenth Century (Visual History of Costume Series)* Batsford, London, and Drama Books Publishers, New York, 1984

Foster, Vanda *The Nineteenth Century (Visual History of Costume Series)* Batsford, London, and Drama Books Publishers, New York, 1984

Nunn, Joan *Fashion in Costume* The Herbert Press Ltd., London, 1984

Ribeiro, Aileen *The Eighteenth Century (Visual History of Costume Series)* Batsford, London, and Drama Books Publishers, New York, 1983

Rose, Clare *Children's Clothes* Batsford, London, 1989

Selbie, Robert *The Anatomy of Costume* Crescent Books, New York, 1977

Wilcox, R. Turner *Dictionary of Costume* Batsford, London, 1969

Worrell *Children's Costume in America 1607–1910* Scribners, New York

Yarwood, Doreen *European Costume* Batsford, London, 1975

Yarwood, Doreen *The Encyclopaedia of World Costume* Batsford, London, 1978

Index

OTHER KNITTING TITLES FROM SEARCH PRESS

Have You Any Wool?
The Creative Use of Yarn
Jan Messent

A wealth of original and fun ideas are illustrated in this book as Jan Messent shows how oddments of yarn can be used to create a variety of unusual woolly toys and objects. Basic knitting and crochet stitches and shapes are magically transformed into fairytale characters, landscapes, fruit and vegetables, animals and tapestries. Children will delight in the bewitching princess and the pea and the simple card wrapping techniques, while adults will find inspiration in this rich new world of texture and colour.

Wool 'n Magic
Jan Messent

Wool 'n Magic gives a completely new slant on knitting, crochet and embroidery. You can use your skills to make unique garments and items, combining all three techniques and discover a world of texture, fabric and colour to delight your imagination. Within these pages you will also find ideas and designs for picture knitting, a patchwork town and landscapes, colour experiments using nature as a source and many more fascinating projects.

Knit the Christmas Story
Jan Messent

This Nativity scene can be made from the simplest materials by beginners and more experienced knitters. The three-dimensional figures stand about eight inches (20cm) tall and are made from simple rectangles of knitting shaped over heavy card pieces with standing bases. The familiar and well-loved figures are all there, with angels, shepherds, sheep, ox and ass, and the three kings worshipping round the crib with Mary and Joseph.

Knit an Enchanted Castle
Jan Messent

Enter a world of enchantment and create an enchanted castle where witches, wizards, unicorns, dragons and knights on horseback live. Inside the castle lives the handsome prince who one day hopes to find a beautiful princess. Well, that's the beginning of the story. With a little imagination, oddments of yarn and some knitting needles, you can create your own fairytale.

Knitted Gardens
Jan Messent

This latest book from Jan Messent will appeal to both knitters and garden-lovers alike. It contains delightfully innovative ideas for both simple and more exotic garden designs for bedspreads, shawls, wall-hangings and rugs. There are also three-dimensional gardens such as the, Victorian kitchen garden, and a variety of wildlife, plants, tubs, tools, trees and clothed soft figures. There is plenty of basic 'know-how' and useful hints on the correct choice of yarns and stitches, and how to plan and control group projects.

Traditional Island Knitting
Pam Dawson

Containing twenty-six designs and full knitting instructions for a variety of sweaters from the Channel Islands, Aran Isles, Shetlands, Fair Isle, Iceland and the Falklands. There are also fascinating titbits on the history and folklore of the garments and a 'helping hands' section for all the basic stitches.

Aran Island Knitting
Pam Dawson

This is taken from the Aran knitting chapter in *Traditional Island Knitting* and features stitch patterns which highlight authentic Aran designs. There are also several patterns, with row-by-row instructions, for traditional and more modern garments.

How to make Ceramic Character Dolls and their accessories
Sylvia Becker

If you have always longed to own an original doll, then *Ceramic Character Dolls* shows you how you can achieve this. This delightful book contains informative text, diagrams and full-colour photographs and shows every stage of making your own doll. Discover how to make the head, arms and legs from either modelling clay or porcelain, how to model and paint details and how to make the fabric body. There is also a range of clothing patterns, useful information and guidance on designing dolls, and an inspirational gallery of beautiful models.

The Knitted Farmyard
Hannelore Wernhard

The Knitted Farmyard gives instructions for knitting and crocheting a complete three-dimensional farmyard, with fields, trees, cows, hens, pigs, the farmer and his family. All the figures are made from oddments of knitting yarns.

If you are interested in the above books or any other of the art and craft titles published by Search Press please send for a free colour catalogue to:
Search Press Ltd., Dept. B, Wellwood, North Farm Road, Tunbridge Wells, Kent TN2 3DR.